The 48 hour
AUTHOR

How to write & publish your book in 48hrs.

By: Bo Bryant & Thax Turner

http://www.The48HourAuthor.com

DEDICATION

To the doers! If you are reading this book, it is likely that you
are a doer. The world runs on doers. There will always be
more reasons why something can't be done, but those that
excel are the ones who realize that while everyone else is out
there making excuses, the "doer" puts their head down and
defies the odds. Most people stop at the start… "It's too
hard", "I don't have time", "It won't work", etc. (Trust us, that
list of excuses could fill up an entire book by itself.)

Nike got it right nearly 30 years ago when they said…

"JUST DO IT!"

CONTENTS

ACKNOWLEDGMENTS

We would like to acknowledge failure. For teaching us the best lessons we could ever hope to learn.

We would also like to acknowledge perseverance, for allowing us to fail again and again until we finally won.

We would like to acknowledge experience, the offspring of failure and perseverance, for giving us something to write about.

We also acknowledge passion, pain, learning, teaching and collaboration. For these are the tools in life that allow us to build our castles and our armies!

CHAPTER 1
INTRODUCING
"THE 48 HOUR AUTHOR"

"You can recognize a pioneer by the arrows in his back."
— Beverly Rubik.

Learn on our backs so that you don't have to take the arrows, taking the trail is much easier than blazing it.
— Thax & Bo

We know that you have a book inside of you! If you have always dreamed of being a writer, you can live out your dreams of writing your own book and getting it published. We are going to show you how you can become an author and do it in less than 48 hours.

Before we dive any deeper, let's break down the concept of the 48 hour author.

As authors of multiple, best selling books, we are experts in the writing and publishing process. Particularly so when it comes to professional, non-fiction books.

When we wrote our first book it certainly took more us than 48 hours.   What we learned after that first book, however, is that it didn't have to. Throughout the process of writing, publishing and selling over a half a dozen titles, we became pretty efficient and effective at doing it.

Along the way we would often joke with each other about how simple this process was. We would find ourselves saying, "Thank goodness other people don't know what we know or we would have a ton of competition". Somewhere along the way, that concept shifted radically. I think it was from all of the people we met while promoting books and from the feedback we got from our family and friends. They would often make comments about how cool it was that we wrote all of these books and, invariably, most people would say something to the effect that they themselves have always wanted to write a book. We also started to pick up on jokes around the dinner table with family and friends when people would say in jest, regarding some random topic; "Trust me, I could write a book on the subject".

We would often look at each other and smile. And then we thought, why wouldn't we share this gift with the world? We love teaching, coaching and training. Why not tell people what we know? Why not share just how easy it is? Additionally, we also thought people might really enjoy all of the amazing benefits we had experienced from becoming authors and best sellers. So we decided to take a break from our regular pursuits and move forward with this idea of giving the people what they had been asking for... **Our secret blueprint on how to write, publish and sell a book in 48 hours.**

Our first book took less than one week to write. The success from the first book was so much better than we expected that it came natural to write our second book.

Our second book was done in 4 days. The 3rd book was done in 3 days. But those weren't 24 hour days. We wrote our books when we had free time. The writing was fast and furious because we had a burning desire to get this information out of our heads and onto paper. It also helped that we retained a lot of content that we had amassed from different training seminars, lectures and speaking engagements about the subjects we wrote our books on.

Today we use a very effective and impactful outline (which we will share in Chapter 4) that allows us to write a 100 - 120 page book and get it proof read, edited, published and in circulation in less than 48 hours of total time invested on our part. (In fact, we are timing our efforts for this book and we forecast that we will be able to have this one finished in 24 hours. We'll report on the outcome in the very end and let you know how we did.)

What's more, we typically do it for as little as a couple hundred bucks. This is exactly what **"The 48 Hour Author"** is going to teach you to do.

In addition to teaching you our secret and highly coveted process we are also going to give you access to all of our little tricks, tips, hacks and even the expert resources we use (which cost next to nothing) to help you bring your book to fruition.

We will also show you the step by step process to self-publishing so that your book can go from concept to creation. And yes, if you follow our process and use our resources, you will be able to have a published, professional book in less than 48 hours of total time invested.

Just remember, we sell shovels, not gold... you have to do the work and when you do, we will help you cross the finish line!

What is self-publishing? Self-publishing is the way

that many writers today are choosing to get their books out to the public. Self-publishing today is not the same as it was years ago when you had to spend thousands of dollars to publish your book. Today, you can self-publish a book for next to nothing. All you need is a little education, instruction and a good self-publishing service online.

The case for self-publishing: We have met a few people who have looked down their noses at self-publishing. They have bought into a stigma attached to self-publishing, a fear that it is less than reputable or has less of a shine. Those people have told us they would prefer to get their books published in a traditional way. To them we say good luck. To those on the fence, here are a few things to consider.

Why are you writing your book?

This is a big question and one that requires some honesty. See if you can identify with any of these questions.

- **Do you want to become a millionaire book author on the New York Times best seller list?**

- **Are you doing it for fame and/or celebrity?**

- **Do you want to leave a legacy behind?**

- **Do you want to establish credibility or authority?**

- **Do you have a burning desire to unleash a story or perspective that has to get on the page?**

If your answer to any one of these questions is yes, then we implore you to explain how that could only be accomplished through a traditional publishing route?

While the sequence, order or expectation of how to accomplish any of these things may not happen like they do in the movies or how you may have imagined, that does not preclude them happening at all by choosing to self-publish.

As serial entrepreneurs, we have made a business of creating building and selling companies for years. Many of our initial concepts were boot-strapped, underdog concepts that were put together with nothing more than elbow grease and duct tape, but by the time we sold these businesses they were big, profitable and shiny.

Self-publishing is no different. It is an elegant way to create, package and brand your book from the ground up. While this may not be the conventional route to becoming rich and famous, much like the businesses we have created, it is a boot strapping way of getting your first goal accomplished. Writing your book!

We would also posit that even if you are still not sold on the idea of self-publishing that you might consider this question.

If you were going to submit your manuscript to a publisher, which scenario do you think would have more impact?

SCENARIO 1

Write and print a manuscript of around 100 pages on 8 ½" x 11" paper, put it in a nice binder with a cover and send it to the publisher, like thousands of people do every day.

...or

SCENARIO 2

Self-publish your manuscript in a fully formatted book, complete with professional art work, layout and an actual ISBN number, complete with a listing and sample preview on Amazon. And then imagine you were to also include a copy of the first month's sales and profits from the book along with reader feedback and reviews.

Regardless of which scenario you choose, this book has

value for any aspiring author, so let's begin.

OUR STORY....

We'd like to share our reason and initial motivation for writing our books. We will also share our experiences and outcomes that came after our first publishing. We do this in hopes that you can relate, or better yet, that this story may serve as a bit of added motivation and/or possible approach while outlining potential outcomes for you to consider when writing yours.

As sales leaders, coaches and motivators we stood in a pretty crowded field. While we were both acknowledged as experts in our fields there was still a lot of noise. Outside of our circle of influence we were relatively unknown, both to our competition and maybe even a little more to a border audience. The first book we worked on together was marketing book called "Whisper Marketing". The book was jam-packed full of marketing and branding strategy for small business and was based on subjects we'd been teaching on for years. The book's content and ideas are a combination of materials, thoughts and insights we have been researching, practicing in businesses and even presenting to large audiences for years. Because we knew this content backwards and forwards the idea of writing a book, while always one of interest really came to fruition when we met with a friend that had written a number of books and was crushing it with his consulting business. He helped walk us through the book writing process and got us headed in the right direction. As we mentioned earlier in this chapter, the process was unbelievably easy.

After the first book came out and we got our proofed copies we couldn't believe how beautiful the book looked and felt. Others around us couldn't believe what we had accomplished. Almost overnight people started introducing us as "my friend the author". The recognition spilled over into introductions to new clients and business associates and the momentum did nothing but grow and garner us a higher level of prestige. Our social circles grew from a regional to all over the US. We started experiencing sales globally after that, which led to some new relationships from China to the U.K.

Our first book and each subsequent book has really helped to "level us up" in our field and catapulted us into a whole new level of awareness and status.

After the first we book we had built an "audience" or a "following" which helped us in having even greater successes with our second book, "On The Menu" and our third book "The Rain Makers". Our 4th book allowed us to reach out of the professional world and write a passion project based on business/life balance called the "Modern Day Spartan" where we were finally able to tell our personal and professional story and help motivate people to join us in a business evolution. Our 5th book "Profit Pro Plus" came naturally as a compliment to a software start up company we had developed which served as an educational insights book directly related to the software company.

By this time, writing books had become "old hat". In our free time we decided to continue along the path we took from our first two books and write on the subject matter of expertise we had taught and lived for years. That led to our 6th book called "Branding Authority".

To put all of this in perspective, we began writing our first book on December 11, 2013.

This book will be the 7th book in less than 2 years.

We are not super human, we didn't have to work every waking hour of the day, we have been gainfully employed (over employed in fact) the entire time and we were still able to spend our weekends and vacation time with our lovely families.

Certainly we've had to become better at managing our time while taking on these projects but there was an unforeseen benefit from writing our books that aided us in that effort. Rhetoric! It is not a dirty word, it is a fact of life and one that we embrace. The work, or professional, rhetoric that we speak every day and have spoken for a number of years is specific and unique to us. The benefits of writing our books was that capturing our ideas (and yes, our rhetoric) became a time saver. Now, instead of having to introduce a smaller audience or group to our ideas and concepts it was all encapsulated in our books. People could now learn from and about us without us even being present. If any part of this story appeals to you or sounds like something you could use to separate yourself from the pack, we encourage you read on and then get started immediately!

CHAPTER 2
GETTING STARTED
"The Process"

"The secret of getting ahead is getting started."
— Mark Twain

While we are experts in the Non-fiction genre of writing, this book does not exclude fiction writers.

Most people equate writing a book with writing a novel, which is a fictional story. This is not the case when it comes to writing, especially writing today. The market for non-fiction books is out-pacing the fiction market, more now than ever before. Cookbooks, how-to books, motivational books, industry insights and biographies are all examples of non-fiction books that sell very well and are often self-published. In order to get a non-fiction book published by the mainstream press, you need to either have a well known name or a very unique idea. You also need to be extremely lucky as there is heavy competition in the mainstream press for authors, especially unknown authors.

Fiction books tell a story; they have a conflict and a resolution. Non-fiction books do not follow along the same lines. There is no conflict in writing a cookbook for example, but there are conflicts in the category of business or expertise, especially when writing against legacy thinking or from a disruptive point of view. There is a calling for all types of non-fiction books and this can be an easy way to publish your first book.

If you are writing a non-fiction book, you need to do heavy research and be very well versed in the topic of which you are writing. You should also have an angle to your book that makes it unique when compared to others in a similar genre. Motivational books are a good example as they're flooding the market right now. What can you do to make your book different?

One example of a different type of motivational book is the Laws Of Attraction series. This took an old idea, put a new spin on it and created a series of very successful motivational books.

Biographies do not always have to be about famous people. You can write a biography about anyone who has led an extraordinary life or influenced many people. Cleverly crafted biographies about ordinary people who prove to be inspirational to others are very popular today. You need to have permission of the person about whom you are writing or permission from their estate in order to write a good biography. There have been unauthorized biographies that have made a sensation, but still required the person to do a lot of research on the subject, although they are not given the same amount of respect as biographies that are done with the consent of the person around whom the book is centered. You also risk running into a lawsuit, such as with the case of Kitty Kelley who wrote a slew of unauthorized biographies about famous people and found herself being sued by the late Frank Sinatra.

Cookbooks are very popular, especially when it comes to self-published books. Your cookbook needs to have something different though, a unique angle, in order to sell. Why would anyone buy your book of French recipes when they can get the same from Julia Child's cookbooks? One way to make yours unique is to add a bit of the French countryside and perhaps some fiction in with the recipes. This will prove to be entertaining to the reader as well as informative.

As outlined in the previous chapter, if you are going to write a novel, then you have to prepare. Your novel should be of a genre that you like and most of all, something that you would buy yourself if it were available in the bookstore. You can put a lot of creative passion into your novel and turn it into something that will stand out. Many people self-publish their novels because the competition is so great and to get a novel by an unknown author published in the mainstream press is becoming increasingly difficult.

Lastly, we also like interview books. These are subject matter books where you don't have to create anything more than a provocative or insightful question guide and a good summary. You move through multiple people and perspectives from within your industry, conduct your interviews, and with the interviewee's permission and an insightful summary, you can have a great book.

When you self-publish, you do not need an agent to help you get your book to the publisher. Working with an agent is a good idea if you are trying to publish in this way, but the Catch 22 is that some mainstream press companies will only work with an agent. And most agents will only want to work with a person who has had a previous novel published. Needless to say, this makes it very difficult for someone to break into the mainstream press with their book.

Even if you did manage to get a book published by a publisher, you would still have to market the book on your own. If you self-publish, you can do the same type of marketing. Because so many people today buy books online, self-publishing is quickly becoming the publishing form of choice for authors writing both fiction and non-fiction.

TIP: Whether you write fiction or non-fiction is up to you. If you have a lot of creative energy and can make up plots and characters in your head, fiction writing may be for you. If you consider yourself an expert in a certain field, non-fiction writing is for you. You can use self-publishing for both non-fiction and fiction books.

We think it is important to impress upon the reader that the first step is to write the book. While there are multiple phases and elements involved in the publishing and sales process, it is important to follow the steps and break the process into segments. This is why it is said that most people "stop at the start". They talk themselves out of following their dream or accomplishing something big because they get defeated by something along the way. Often this defeat kicks in just from allowing ourselves to get overwhelmed by the entirety of the process.

Like anything multifaceted or complex, if you don't metaphorically "eat the elephant", one bite at a time, it doesn't get eaten. And what you are meant to consume ends up consuming you.

Consider this the motivational part of the journey. We will be here to coach you and root you on, to give you motivation and inspiration along the way.

Our first suggestion is to tackle one project at a time and we will show you how, step by step all along the way. In the following chapters we will look at each segment in depth. With that, lets break down the 5 elements of this process.

1. **Writing your book.**

2. **Reread & Rewrite**

3. **Editing your book.**

4. **Publishing your book**

5. **Marketing/Promoting/Selling your book.**

The first thing that you need to do is know your genre or subject matter. The one rule of writing is that you should write what you know. If you have a specific genre that you read, work in, or study as an area of expertise, chances are that this is what you will want to write about. Take a look at your interests and the type of books that you read before you decide on your genre or subject matter. Your book should never be just about making money - it should be about something for which you have a passion. There are many different genres and areas of subject matter available in both fiction and non-fiction. The majority of our expertise comes from Non-fiction and thus, that will be our point of reference along the way. However, the processes, tactics, tips and tricks that we use to write Non-fiction have a lot of carryover regardless of the type of book you want to write. That being said, before you start your book, have a plan of what it will be about and the genre it will fit into.

You need to have a specific genre or subject matter when you are writing a book so that you will be able to market it properly. Some books will cross genre lines - such as business and marketing or art and science. Some books will fit neatly into a specific genre or subject matter. It should be clear what the book is about to the reader so that they will be interested enough in what you have written to buy the book. Most readers have types of books that they like to read and tend to stick with one or two genres or subject matter areas.

Additionally, here is a list of the genres, by category, that the industry uses to classify books. These categories are created by the **Book Industry Study Group** or **BISG and their** categories are referred to as the **Book Industry Subject and Category** or **BISAC**. Each BISAC comes with a unique 10 digit identification code to define the listing of a published work for database catalog purposes. Think of it as the publishing industry's Dewy Decimal System (which it is soon likely to replace).

In the marketing chapter we will even teach you some tricks on how you can select a specific category and subcategory to help ensure a greater likelihood of achieving a **"number one best selling author"** status.

(See recent BISAC Categories & subcategories in the appendix)

- **ANTIQUES & COLLECTIBLES**
- **ARCHITECTURE**
- **ART**
- **BIBLES**
- **BIOGRAPHY & AUTOBIOGRAPHY**
- **BODY, MIND & SPIRIT**
- **BUSINESS & ECONOMICS**
- **COMICS & GRAPHIC NOVELS**
- **COMPUTERS**
- **COOKING**
- **CRAFTS & HOBBIES**
- **DESIGN**
- **DRAMA**
- **EDUCATION**
- **FAMILY & RELATIONSHIPS**
- **FICTION**
- **FOREIGN LANGUAGE STUDY**
- **GAMES**
- **GARDENING**
- **HEALTH & FITNESS**
- **HISTORY**
- **HOUSE & HOME**
- **HUMOR**
- **JUVENILE FICTION**
- **JUVENILE NON-FICTION**

- **LANGUAGE ARTS & DISCIPLINES**
- **LAW**
- **LITERARY COLLECTIONS**
- **LITERARY CRITICISM**
- **MATHEMATICS**
- **MEDICAL**
- **MUSIC**
- **NATURE**
- **PERFORMING ARTS**
- **PETS**
- **PHILOSOPHY**
- **PHOTOGRAPHY**
- **POETRY**
- **POLITICAL SCIENCE**
- **PSYCHOLOGY**
- **REFERENCE**
- **RELIGION**
- **SCIENCE**
- **SELF-HELP**
- **SOCIAL SCIENCE**
- **SPORTS & RECREATION**
- **STUDY AIDS**
- **TECHNOLOGY & ENGINEERING**
- **TRANSPORTATION**
- **TRAVEL**
- **TRUE CRIME**

The reason we listed these categories, beyond just giving you a feel for which genre your book will fall under, is to also give you a little reverse engineering element to apply to your book. If you write your book without the end in mind (or the category it will end up in) your perspective or tone could be missing from your narrative.

Additionally, we have listed the subcategories in the appendix and it is worth reviewing those subcategories so that you can have an even greater understanding of your own narrative. If you write your book with your category and subcategory in mind, the message will come across more clearly to your reader and deliver along the lines of their expectations, based on the category and subcategory definition that your book falls into.

Keeping that in mind, you also need to make your book stand out in a way that will set it apart from other books of the same genre or in a genre that is less popular, which will pretty much guaranteed.

For example: If you are writing an Italian Cookbook, how do you make it stand out from the other Italian cookbooks that are already on the market? It can certainly be harder to create or provide a unique perspective. But if you were to write an Italian Cookbook with some history of the food and how these recipes came to be, how they evolved, how they were later interpreted or even brought to the United States (for example). You could classify that book under History and Food. This category and subcategory are less saturated and more likely to give you better visibility.

Once you find your genre and know what you are writing about, you should start to think of marketing your book. A good place to start when it comes to the marketing of your book is its title. The title will help make it something that readers will choose when they see it in bookstores or online. This will set it apart from other books of its kind and entice readers to buy it. Many authors are finding that they can make a career out of self-publishing their books and marketing them to the right audience. We will cover marketing in greater depth in the final chapters of this book.

After you have figured out what you are going to write about and what will make your book stand out among others, you can then start to outline your book. You should write down a synopsis of the book and the point that you are trying to make. Good books carry a message, make sure that your book has a message that your readers can take away from the book at the end.

While you may like free-form writing, which is writing without doing any sort of outline, you should still have an idea of the topics/transitions and the ending of the book in your head. When you are writing fiction, characters tend to come to life as you write. Your ending may change as you rewrite so it is important to be flexible. The way that you write depends on the type of person that you are. If you prefer to have everything ironed out for your book, then you should do an outline that will tell you where you are going. This is like having a roadmap on a car trip.

TIP: Once you have your synopsis and a concise way of being able to explain what your book is about, consider using a "naming committee" to help you come up with a catchy title. A naming committee doesn't have to be anything more than getting some creative coworkers, friends and/or family members, whose thoughts and opinions you respect, and start working on marketable titles that will grab the viewer's attention.

The other advantage of writing out your topics/transitions is that when you get stuck, you can jump around to another topic/transition. You can rework ideas as you move on in your book.

Everyone has a different style when it comes to writing books. There are some people who do not want to use a roadmap on a trip, they just want to go. If this sounds like you, then just start writing and the ideas will start flowing through you. Over-thinking and over-planning the book can bog you down and keep you from writing. Too little thought can keep your book from reaching a conclusion. It takes a lot of creativity as well as some structure in order to write a successful book that people will want to read. We ask you to consider our outline or adopt one that you feel comfortable with but if you get stuck on the outline then just start writing!

TIP: You should read books in the genre or on the subject of interest in order to get the feel for this type of writing. As an aspiring author you shouldn't just read the book but you should also review the book's layout, chapters and flow to get some inspiration, ideas and a concept for your our outline. Reading is a good way to improve your writing skills as well. Before you start writing your book, read the genre and subjects from authors that you like and model the elements that you like in your book.

CHAPTER 3

RESEARCH YOUR BOOK

"If we knew what it was we were doing, it would not be called research, would it?"
— Albert Einstein

In order to write your book, you are going to have to do some research. Even if you are writing an autobiography or a fiction novel, you still have to go back and research incidents that happened and most likely look up dates, names and possibly even resources. You want to do research to make your book as authentic and well written as possible. Nothing is worse than writing a book where you get facts, dates, names and other information wrong.

Research different types of books that have been successful in the genre that you have chosen for your book. When you are performing research, you can use your local library as well as the internet. If you are writing fiction, you will need to research even more. For example, if you are writing a murder mystery, you need to know police procedures as well as how murderers are caught. You can discover this information through your research, start by taking a look at the books at the local library. Some authors go as far as to take a class in something that they want to learn about at a community college so that they can be better prepared for their book.

You do not want to get bogged down with research, however. Many writers enjoy research so much that they neglect to write their book. This is not what you want to do. You want to research your book so that you have the right information, but not write a thesis. Too much research can stunt the creative flow of your book. You can research as you are writing or you can do what we do and leave a **highlighted notation** in your book and do the research when doing your reread and rewrite by going back to it.

The internet makes it easier to do research now more than ever. You can get most of the information that you need to research your book if you go online.

It is a good idea to research the subject matter or characters (even if they are fictional) in your book. Discover some information about the personality traits of people. A good writer is very much in tune with psychology and the way that people think, react and process information. In fact, if you want to get in touch with the characters that you create, you can do so by learning a bit of psychology. This doesn't just apply to fiction writing. Character perspective is needed even for non-fiction books. The ideas, experiences and information you are going to express and share will come from your perspective and thus you become the character. In order to engage the reader, the character needs to explain their thinking, relate by telling stories, using humor, interjecting personality and rationalizations. These are all critical elements used to hook your audience.

Writers are often advised to take creative classes so that they can get in touch with the way that people think and react to certain situations. By learning how others think, you will be able to bring more to the book than your own perception of how to react in a certain situation or how to convey your point with better impact. This will help you with dialog as well.

Realistic dialog is very important when writing a book. If you understand how and why people react in a certain way and speak in certain terms, you can give your characters more depth.

You can take a writing course to learn how you can write a good book or even join a writing group or online forum. The more input that you get from other writers and the more information that you share, the better your book will be.

There are conferences, workshops and seminars that you can attend for writers, you can make all of these part of your writing research. In addition to researching your book, you should also research the components that make up a good book.

A good book has the following:

NON-FICTION

- A Unique Perspective
- Insights
- New Ideas
- Instruction
- Story Telling

One of the most successful practices and by far the most complimented element of our writing style is that we write in our "authentic voice". Here's what we mean. When we write, we do so in a way that sounds exactly how we speak in a group setting or face to face. This is charming to people because it makes them feel more comfortable with you. We want that because we are fully immersed in the public spotlight doing seminars, key note speeches, meet & greets, etc.

When we do meet people, they often comment, "Wow, you sound exactly like you do in your book."

Our friends have even told us, "Man, when I was reading your book, it was like you were sitting right here with me having a beer." We take those as the greatest compliments of all.

If you are character writing, the character needs a unique voice as well. Whatever the point of view or writing style, making the narrator's voice real and relevant will take your readers on a journey that they will want to return to.

While fiction is not our genre we are still well versed on the elements needed to create a good piece of fictional writing as well.

FICTION

- Three dimensional, believable characters
- A conflict

- A climax
- A resolution to the conflict

You need to have some sort of conflict in the book that is presented right from the start. The conflict must be resolved by the ending of the book. This does not mean that your book has to have a happy ending, but you cannot leave anything hanging out there that remains unresolved. You also want to craft your book so that it reaches a climax, which builds up throughout the book.

Another thing that you need to determine is which point of view you want to use to write the book. You can choose first person narrative, which is an easier style to write but is limited to the thoughts and actions of the main character or narrator of the story. You can write first person observant, which tells the story from the point of view of another character who is observing the action. You can choose third person and still write from the point of view of the main protagonist. When you are writing from the third person, you can also delve into the point of view of other characters in the book. Of all styles of writing, third person omniscient, which sees into the heads of all the characters, is the most difficult to write. Take a look at books that you like to read and see which writing style will best fit your book. The point of view that you write from can make or break your book. For example, the Sherlock Holmes books by Sir Arthur Conan Doyle were a flop at first, until he changed the point of view coming from Dr. Watson, which was first person observant.[2]

In addition to point of view, you also need to decide if you are writing in the past or present tense. Most books are written in the past tense, although you may want to take a look at "Presumed Innocent" by Scott Turow to see an example of first person narrative in the present tense. Writing in the present tense is more difficult, but lends more action to the book.

Do your research by studying other books and your own writing style to see which point of view and tense you wish to use in your book. First person narrative, which is also called prose writing, is the easiest, but has limitations. Third person omniscient is the most difficult, but opens up the thoughts and feelings of other characters in the book. This type of research should be done before you start your book, but can be changed if you find that it is not working for you and how you want to tell a story.

CHAPTER 4

COMPLETING THE FIRST DRAFT

"Great things are done by a series of small things brought together."
— *Vincent Van Gogh*

Once you have decided on the book that you want to write, you should start on your first draft. This may change by the time the book is completed, although chances are that you will keep some of the information that you have in your first draft in the final book.

Everyone writes in a different way. There are those who rewrite as they are going along and those who complete the first draft before attempting any rewriting. It is best to write the first draft and get it all on paper, or computer, before you start any rewriting. This can allow you to see the direction that your book has taken and how it looks. We have found that when you rewrite in the midst of writing the book, going back and forth, ideas can get lost, confusing and/or out of order. You should not get discouraged if your first draft is less than magnificent - this is only your first draft.

Many writers who write fiction like to get that first draft finished before they start any research into the book that needs to be finished. Having the first draft competed does not mean that you have completed your book, but that you have completed a rough draft of a book. The average book is about 80,000 words, although a rough draft of a book may be less.

In some cases, writers will sketch out a first draft that is mostly narrative. It contains only sparse dialogue, to be put in later when re-writing. If you are writing a fiction book, this is a good way to get the book down on paper, see if the plot makes sense, and make sure that you present a conflict and resolution to the conflict.

There are two types of conflict that can be contained in your book. These are either internal conflicts or external conflicts. These conflicts are important in both fiction and non-fiction. In non-fiction writing these ideas can convey that ah-hah! Moment or illustrate how an unconventional idea that has proven successful is pushing against legacy thinking. Internal conflicts are those that take place in the minds of the characters of the book. They can be due to their perception of the world or their perception about another individual.

External conflicts are those that are caused by outside influences. Misunderstandings or third parties getting in the way are examples of external conflicts that arise in fiction books.

A good way to figure out the conflict in the book is to present the reader with a question that will be answered at the end of the book. This type of conflict is often used in murder mysteries. The reader does not know who committed the murder until the climax of the book, after which the conflict has been resolved. A good book presents not only external conflicts, but internal conflicts as well. It may also present a series of conflicts in the book that come together to be resolved by the time the book ends. It is important to create conflict in a fiction book that will keep the reader reading and wanting to see a resolution in the end.

A good book also makes a point. There can be symbolism in the book as well as a subtle message that the book is trying to get across to the reader. While not all books contain these variables, they are found in some of the great novels.

Another factor you want to add into your fiction book is foreshadowing. This should be presented throughout the book, but especially in the beginning. This gets the reader hooked early on so that they want to keep reading to see what happens next in the book. They will be anxious to get to the end of the book to discover the reason for the foreshadowing. Foreshadowing implies that something will happen to change the world of the characters early in the book. This intrigues the reader and makes them want to continue reading.

The first paragraph of your book is probably the most important part of the book. This is the paragraph that will either hook or bore the reader. One problem that many authors have when it comes to writing a book that is interesting is a slow start. This fails to pull the reader in and keep them interested in reading the book. Including foreshadowing in the first paragraph is a good idea. Another thing that you can do to make your book more interesting to the reader is to start in the middle. Instead of starting the book from the beginning, you can start in the middle of the story and then take the reader back, through the use of dialog and narrative, to the beginning of the story to fill them in on history.

The climax of the book is also important in a fiction book. The plot should slowly build up to the climax. You may have several anti-climaxes in the book as well as other conflicts that are resolved. The main conflict in the book must be resolved by the end of the book.

Do not make the mistake of introducing characters at the end of the book who factor heavily into the resolution of the plot. For example, if you are writing a murder mystery, you need to have the murderer factor into the book early on. Some writers will make it look as if someone is obviously guilty but the culprit is someone who the reader does not suspect. You want to keep your reader hungry for more as they get to the end of the book.

While the first paragraph, climax and conflict resolution are integral parts of the book, do not fill your book with fluff. Each character in the book should factor somewhat into the plot. Each sentence in the book should move the plot forward. This does not often happen in the first draft of the book but will happen as you continue with re-writes. Remember that any book, even a non-fiction book, does not appear on paper the way that it comes out of your head. You have to be prepared for re-writing.

TIP: We write non-fiction books. Our point of view is that of the "Subject Matter Experts". Here is the exact step by step process that we use to get our books out in less than 48 hours of total time invested.

1. Identify the subject.

2. Find a subject category and subcategory within the BISAC listing to help identify your narrative.

3. Make a list of every topic you know about the subject.

4. Download the book size and preformatted template.

5. Start writing, typing, voice recording or dictating what you know on each topic. Don't think, just go.

6. Start by writing an introduction chapter explaining your perspective and outline what the reader will take away from the book.

7. Continue on writing as much as you can on each topic. When you run out of steam, move to another topic.

8. Lay out your order of topics in a way that makes sense to follow.

9. Review your book: Reread, rewrite and cleanup.

10. Share with friends and family (if interested) for initial feedback and initiate a "Naming Committee".

11. Make edits and adjustments based on the feedback and the time you have had to reflect.

12. Send to editor.

13. Enlist a graphic artist for your book cover art work.

14. Receive Proof from the editor, read your edited version and make final adjustments if needed.

15. Upload in the self-publishing platform of choice

16. Order "Proof Copies" and give to friends and family again for one last review.

17. Make any last changes needed and finalize your publishing.

18. Launch your marketing funnels and campaigns

19. You are now an author… promote, promote, promote!

20. Rinse, wash and repeat.

CHAPTER 5

REREADING & REWRITING

"Half my life is an act of revision."
— John Irving

Ernest Hemingway suggested rewriting a book 30 times before it is ready for publication. His reasoning was that each time the writer goes over the book for rewriting, they have a better understanding into the minds of the characters. The more you get to know your characters, the more you will be able to write convincing dialogue and narrative that will suit them.

This is tremendous insight for writing your masterpiece fictional novel, however, we take a slightly different stance when it comes to a non-fiction work. While rewriting is important there is a critical rule to understand.

Your book will never be complete if you expect it to be completely perfect.

Case and point, after writing our first book we were just a couple of professional guys reaching out to an audience of presumed, like minded guys out there that we believed could benefit from our unique message.

And guess what? We were right!

We had tremendous success with our first publication of the book. However, we went from being professional guys with a perspective, to becoming authors. Once we became authors we entered a different realm of social circles and started reaching a larger, more global audience. We were both enlightened and more aware of things we didn't even know existed and that expanded our perspective. That perspective enhanced our knowledge about our topic and eventually led to expanding our book.

This is something we never could have known without publishing our book. And there was a silver lining... the beauty of self-publishing is the ease of access and the ease of application when it comes to knocking down the first edition of your book and expanding on it to create a second edition. If it weren't for this burning desire to write additional books we would likely be on edition 3 of our first book.

The point is, if your message should ever mature or if you should ever have a need to update your content, you can. In fact, we encourage it. It will make your next project that much better.

Additionally, as the world continues to change, evolve and advance faster than it ever has in our short history so too will the information that you can continue to add to your book. Bottom line, IT WILL NEVER BE PERFECT! So, don't strive for perfection, strive for temporary completion.

Another important thing to remember when you are rewriting is to not be afraid of making major changes or adjustments in your book. If something is not working, doesn't flow properly or just does not feel right, change it. It is important not to get married to your book. While you have a natural passion for the book, you should also be open minded enough to realize if something is not working in your layout or flow, you have to fix it.

The best way to start rewriting is to read through your first draft. You can then note inconsistencies and other problems that occur. You should begin your rewriting from the beginning of the book to the end, especially if you are writing a fiction book that will have character development. Even if you are writing non-fiction, you still want to rewrite your book to tighten it up.

Try not to use a passive voice when you are writing. This is when you put in words like "would have" and "was." Try to use more action words in your book, otherwise it may tend to get sluggish. Also, go over the dialog and make sure that it feels natural. You want to look at dialog as well as consistency when you are rewriting your book.

Do not be surprised if your book has an ending that is not what you initially imagined. Many times, writers grow to like a different momentum or conclusion as they evolve toward the completion of their book. The creative process takes on a mind of its own when an author is writing a book. This often points out inconsistencies in the book and with the ideas. This is the purpose of the rewrite. We found in all of our books that in the beginning, even with the end in mind the tone and/or idea changed and the book became a little disjointed. When the end was complete and we were happy with it, we had to go back and line up the beginning to make it flow more naturally and in a way that made more sense. Don't worry about this happening. It is natural and even expected.

Each time you to rewrite the book, you are making it a

better story. You have a better feel for the ideas in the story with each rewrite and they become more tangible to you as they will to your audience. So much so that you can figure out all kinds of ways of enhancing each chapter to support the beginning and ending in a more dynamic way. Again, be careful, this can be overdone and slow you down.

The more you get to know the ending or conclusion of your book, the more naturally its initial chapters will flow during the rewrite.

Make sure that there are no loose ends in the book and that every sentence drives your plot/idea forward. Get rid of unnecessary dialogue that will slow down the process of your book as well as unnecessary descriptions or long, incomplete thoughts or ideas. The best books are those that continue to move the plot/idea forward and have meaning in every sentence.

Do not mistake rewriting as checking for grammar or spelling. This will be done when you are proofreading your book or sending it out for editing, although you should naturally make any corrections when you see them. Proofreading is very different than rewriting and will be discussed shortly.

One thing that you may want to do to make your rewriting easier is to give yourself a rest between the rewrites. This allows you to look at the book with fresh eyes and get a fresh start reading it. If you have a friend or trusted person to whom you can give the book, you can ask them to critique it. They may be able to see glaring errors in the plot that you might have overlooked. We have done this by sending out a chapter at a time and by sending out a complete rough draft.

Our experience has taught us that the latter is a better approach for one primary reason. A chapter is a moment in time. While sending out a chapter at a time, we thought we were being proactive but as we would later find out, there was way too much criticism or correction that could have been averted if they had just read the whole book at once.

Getting a complete picture offers your reviewer or even your friend or associate an opportunity to say, "I think it would make more sense if you put the middle paragraph from page 30 over on page 19 to complete that thought. It would flow better and make more sense".

We found suggestions like these to be more helpful because the reader had context and that helped us improve our content.

We can't emphasize enough how important it is to have someone else review your work. While you are close to your book, you may also be too close. It is helpful to have that second pair of eyes read the book after you have rewritten it to sufficiency.

Remember, you can rewrite a book too much when it comes to non-fiction. There has to be a point where you say that you are satisfied with the story/idea and what it conveys. After you have completed your book and feel that it is publication worthy, you are ready for a grammar check and then on to editing.

TIP: Take people's perspective with a grain of salt. Be flexible but remain true to your "Authentic Voice". There are some instances when grammatical rules are broken, especially when it comes to your specific dialogue. You want to make sure that you have proper grammar used in your book but you do not want to sound robotic.

CHAPTER 6

PROOFING YOUR BOOK

"Unity is strength... when there is teamwork and collaboration, wonderful things can be achieved."
— *Mattie Stepanek*

We recommend sending your book out for proof reading for two reasons.

1. Another perspective is invaluable .

2. Time is worth money and our time is worth a lot more than the time and cost it would take us to proofread our work as quickly and effectively as a pro.

However, if you do decide to proofread your book on your own, take the book and print it out for proofreading. Then, starting with the last page and moving backward, use a ruler to look at each line in the book. We do this because when we read, our eyes naturally gloss over words that we are familiar with and often do not see that they are misspelled. This is why it is important to take your time and proofread your book from finish to start. By going up one line at a time, you will not be reading, but looking for errors that your eyes would ignore if you simply read the book. This is a tedious process, but this is what we have found to be the best practice. Remember, you are only looking for spelling mistakes and mistakes in punctuation. This is not the editing process.

Again, you can hire a professional proofreader for this purpose. They will go through the book the way that suits them and deliver you a product that has changes. They will put proofreading marks on your paper, of which you should be familiar. They will not make the changes for you, but signal you to make the changes.

It is vital that you proofread your book or have someone else do it for you. If you have a book published by the mainstream press, this service is done for you. If you are self-publishing, however, you do not have this luxury. Although there are many self-publishing companies online that offer proofreading services for a reasonable price to their clients. However, we have found that these services usually charge more than freelancers that you can find online.

One place that you can find proofreaders who will go

over your book for you is Elance.com. This site has a multitude of freelancers offering their services. Be sure to check out their profile as well as reviews from other clients before you ask them to proofread your material. You can put your project on the site for bidding. Be sure that you do not automatically go for the lowest bid that there is and check out the experience and customer satisfaction that signify that the proofreader knows what he or she is doing.

We have used a number of services but we have ultimately settled on an online service called Fiverr.com. We like their format and we have had the best success on this site but that is purely subjective. Find the one that is right for you and research as many as you can.

At Fiverr you can find amazing freelancers, in all kinds of categories, to hire out their respective talents one job at a time. And while there is a vetting process (yeah, we learned the hard way), it is a tremendous service and an amazing and affordable resource.

TIP: When exploring **fiverr.com** for a proofreader, copy editor, graphic artist or any other service,

- Review multiple people/offers in the category.
- Ask them for examples that they can share with you.
- Review their rating by other users and consider the number of gigs they have had.
- Have a very specific and clear expectation for them and communicate it clearly and get confirmation before hiring them for a service.

If you decide to proofread your book yourself, take your time and do it correctly. Do not rush through this process as an array of misspelled words in your book will make it look less than professional to the reader. You want your book to be as professional as possible so that the reader will not get turned off. You can keep it free from typos, punctuation and spelling errors by doing careful proofreading or hiring someone who you can pay to do the job for you.

Even if you have someone else who is not a professional proofreader take a look at your book, you can have a fresh pair of eyes look at the book so that they can see errors where you may not. Remember that you have a very strong connection to your book that others do not. You have most likely read it over and over again. Having someone who has not yet seen the book, take a look for errors, can help you out tremendously. Most professional proofreaders will charge by the page or even by the word count. This may be an investment that you will want to make if you are serious about making sure that your book is error free.

Remember that even books published by the mainstream press have errors. Having one error in the book is not the end of the world. Having a book chockfull of errors, however, can make your book look shoddy and not well put together.

CHAPTER 7
EDITING YOUR BOOK

"We are the products of editing, rather than of authorship."
— *George Wald*

We believe the editing process to be the most critical part of the book. There is a lot of nomenclature and similar sounding concepts along the way to publishing your book. So, just to be clear, copy editing and editing are completely different than proofreading.

Copy editing (in particular) for a book will help you with flow but it also helps tighten up your book. In some cases, the copy editor will eliminate repetitive sentences or words that bog down your book. Copy editing is not like regular editing, which will take a good look at your book to see if it makes sense. A traditional editor will usually make suggestions for broader changes than a copy editor. A copy editor will read your book with a fresh pair of eyes and pick out errors. They will also pay attention to style. They can help you to overcome awkward phrases that you may not notice in your book as well as other grammatical problems. You may say something in a way that you do not mean to when you are writing a book. It may make sense to you, but not to others. A traditional editor may miss this but a copy editor will usually catch it.

We prefer outsourcing it to a freelance site like Fiverr.com or Elance.com for the same reasons that we outsource our proofreading. However there are other options. Most of the self-publishing sites offer editing and copy editing services for an extra charge. The work doesn't turn around as fast and is a little more expensive but it is good work all the same. We will discuss this option in more detail when we get to the publishing portion of the book

You can also choose to edit your own book if you like. In the self-editing process you need to pay attention to style as well as grammar. It pays to have good grammatical skills and have a certain style that you use for your book when you are considering your own editing.

Option three is traditional publishing. If you are fortunate enough to have a company that will publish the book for you, they will typically do the editing for you as well.

> **TIP:** We choose to stick with Fiverr.com for our copy editing needs as well. We have had great success with one copy editor in particular who is a retired English and Creative Writing teacher that now offers her services on Fiverr. She gets a little extra spending money and an obvious joy from reading and helping others. Best of all, the service is more personal and more affordable than other "professional services" we have used.

Writers often have a habit of switching styles when they are writing. Most writers have a creative streak that causes them to write. It can be difficult for them to edit their own work just as it can be difficult for them to proofread their own work. Spending the money for editing is one of the best investments that a writer can make. If you choose to copy edit your own book, more power to you. But we strongly recommend that you at least hire someone to do a general edit of your book, even if it is just a second set of eyes and another perspective. This often costs about $100, but can be the best money that you spend when you are self-publishing and copy editing your own book. An editor typically ensures that the book makes sense and is written in the same style.

CHAPTER 8
SELF-PUBLISHING

"Writing a book makes you an expert in the field. At the very least, when you hand someone a book you wrote, it's more impressive than handing a business card."
— James Altucher

Years ago, if someone wanted to get a book self-published, they had to pay thousands of dollars. A press would publish the book for the individual and give them a certain amount of copies or what is known as a "minimum run". All of the copies, plus the fees that were involved in setting the press and printing, were paid for by the author. Those who did seek to have their books self-published were not thought of as good authors. The name used for self-publishing then was vanity press. It was thought that those who got their books published this way just had the money, not the talent, that was needed to be a writer.

The same is not true now. Because so many people

purchase books online, more so than at the bookstore, self-publishing is seen as much more respectable. And because the mainstream press takes very few authors and is so competitive, it is also seen as a way for a writer to have their voice heard.

There have been stories of those who submitted, just for fun, a first chapter and query letter of a great novel to publishers to see if they actually read them. They were returned with standard rejection letters. Many publishing houses will not take writers who are not represented by agents. This makes it very difficult for someone to get their book published as most agents who deal with these publishers only deal with established authors.

Some decide to publish their books using small press publishers. These publishers will not charge a writer for printing their book, but will also not have the clout to get the book reviewed in the New York Times. The writer has to do all of the marketing for the book and only receives a small portion of the royalties. Needless to say, it makes more sense for a new writer to self-publish their book and market it themselves. They can use modern self-publishers that print to order and do not charge an enormous fee for publishing a book. The books are given ISBN numbers and are listed on places like Amazon, where most people are buying books today. The author can also have their book in a bookstore as long as it has an ISBN. There are many ways for a self-published author to market their book.

Since you will most likely do the marketing anyway when you get your book published, you might as well self-publish your book with a publisher that does print to order or "print on demand" publishing. This way, you get a higher percentage of the profits and the book can be listed online for those who are interested in buying it. Self-publishing is the way that many writers today, even those who have been published by small press, are deciding to publish their book.

Three places that you can go online to self-publish your book are Lulu.com, Booklocker.com and Createspace.com. All of these are well known with self-publishers and print on demand per order. You can get other services from these companies as well, including formatting your book, audio books, cd's and more.

Createspace.com and Lulu.com give you the tools to format your book on your own. You need to submit a PDF to Lulu in order for them to be able to print your book. If you have a PDF converter or Adobe, you can format your own book through this company. They give you a choice of hardcover or soft cover as well as different sizes of the book that are available. If you choose a plain cover with just lettering, you can get the book printed for free on Createspace.com or for less than $200 on Lulu. The books are listed on the Createspace.com and Lulu websites, respectively, and you can also get them listed on Amazon with both sites. This is a good option for those who have little money, limited computer skills, or are not able to format the book on their own. Both sites have upgrade options that you can pay for while Createspace.com will allow you to do the entire thing for free and we will show you how, this is how we do ours.

Booklocker.com does not offer you the choice to format, although for those who do not know how to format a book and are afraid of formatting it in the wrong way and then paying for a book that is virtually unreadable, this is the best option. It is also less money than other self-publishing sites that provide formatting services. This also allows you to get your book listed on Amazon.com as well as the Booklocker.com site.

All of these sites print to order, which means that you do not have to order a bunch of books. They will print a book when a customer orders it and ship it out for you, directly to that customer. You get paid a percentage of the books that you sell, which is a higher percentage than what you would get with a mainstream publisher and much more than you can get with small press publishing. If you take the time to market your book, which you can do, you can end up making a lot more money and getting your book out to even more readers.

Take a look online and find a website that will offer you print to order books. You will get a percentage of the books that you buy for yourself as well. You can purchase the books yourself and get them in bookstores as well as book fairs and exhibits for self-published writers. Most bookstores will take a book as long as there is an ISBN on it. The book publisher will also include a barcode on the book.

There are a lot more options open now than ever before for those who want to self-publish their books. With internet and computer technology, it is much easier for any writer to get their book published through self-publishing. An increasing number of writers are seeking out self-publishing to make money and get their books out to the public who are eager to read them.

BEFORE YOU EVEN START WRITING YOU BOOK...DO THIS FIRST!

This may seem out of sequence but you will need to trust that there is a method to our madness. Before you even begin typing your first page use this little tip to save yourself a lot of time. (Again, we learned this the hard way)

Set up your online publishing account. We like to use Createspace.com. And now that you have a firm grasp on the concept of self-publishing, we'll walk you through the specific steps we use to publish our books on Createspace.com and why we take this step before we even get started writing each book.

Step1.

Create a Createspace.com account. It is free and simple. Just go to http://createspace.com and find the "sign up " option located on the left hand side of the page. Enter your personal information and you will be all ready to go.

Step 2.

Create a new title. Once you log in you will see an option on the left hand side of the page to access your **"Member Dashboard"** or an option to **"Add New Title"**. Select the **"Add New Title"** option. You will have a 4 step process to follow.

    A. Name your project. This is the name of your book. Don't get hung up on this part. You can always go back and change the name at any time.

    B. Choose **"Paperback"** in your media type options.

    C. Then choose your setup process. You will have two options. For your first book we recommend you choose the **"guided"** option which will walk you through the process step by step.

    D. Now select the **"Get Started"** option.

Here is a screenshot of what it looks like.

Start Your New Project

* Required

1 **Tell us the name of your project** *

You can change your title at any time before you submit your project for review.

2 **Choose which type of project you want to start** *

○ Paperback   ○ Audio CD   ○ DVD

                                      ○ Video Download

3 **Choose a setup process** *

| Guided | A step-by-step process with help along the way. | Get Started |
| Expert BETA | A streamlined single-page experience for those familiar with the process. | Get Started |

Step 3.

Now you are ready to get your **ISBN**. Create space
gives you the option to have your ISBN automatically
assigned by them or you can choose to create your
own. We opt for the former but the choice is yours.

TIP: An ISBN, or International Standard Book Number, is a unique [1]13-digit number assigned to every published book. An ISBN identifies a title's edition, publisher, and physical properties such as trim size, page count, and binding type.

ISBNs are used by bookstores, retailers, and libraries identify books by their ISBNs. We print an ISBN barcode in the lower right corner on the back of every book we manufacture.

You have four ISBN options: you can either use a CreateSpace.com -assigned ISBN, a Custom ISBN*, a Custom Universal ISBN*, or you can use your own ISBN. Both custom ISBN options are offered through an agreement with Bowker.

Step 4. (THE BIG STEP)

Pick your book's size and format. This step is the main reason we sign up on a self-publishing site before we even start writing our book. In the 4th step of the Createspace.com process you will be given the option to pick your book's size as well as a preformatted option that you can download to your computer which is already done with the entire book's layout, title page, index, page numbers and headers. Best of all, it is preformatted in the selected size option that you pick for your book. You can download this format straight to your computer and open it with MS Word from either a Mac or a PC.

We do this step first, then we open our preformatted template and finally we begin writing directly in the template. The time, energy and frustration this will save versus having to copy, paste and mess with all of the formatting issues later on is one of the biggest hacks we can give you relative to time and ease of application.

Step 5.

Your Interior. This is where you select some of the aesthetic option you will apply to your book. Create Space gives you the option to design your book's interior in either color or black and white as well as your paper type which can either be white or cream colored paper.

Step 6.

Loading your interior. The big gap in the creatspace.com process will come between steps 5 and 6. Step 6 is where you upload your edited, proofed copy of your book and in order to do that you would have had to write the book, have it proofed and then have it copied. Once you have done all of that you can simply save your MS Word document as a PDF with the "Save As" option and now you are ready to upload your book.

Once you upload your book, Createspace.com will take a 24 hour period to review it for errors. These are only formatting errors which, again, is why "Step 4" is so critical.

TIP: When writing our first book we did not follow this process and after converting a standard 8.5" x 11" MS Word format to the preformatted book type we had a ton of formatting errors with our margins and pictures. The worst part was after writing for 24 hours, we found out that we then had to make the corrections and then resubmit our book again which took another 24 hours. Fortunately, Createspace.com will give you a chance to preview your errors before submitting it for the review process.

Step 7.

Your book cover. While your interior is being reviewed this is a great time to do some work on your book cover. Since you would have followed this process you would have already preformatted your book cover to match the size of your book. Whether you did it yourself or hired it out, you should have your art work formatted to scale so that you can upload it in the cover editor available in this step. Createspace.com has a number of predesigned covers with a simple step by step process that allows you to import your front and back cover images and any information right there on the site. The finished result is a beautiful, professional cover complete with your images, background color selected for the book, your ISBN number and bar code along with a spine (if your book is thick enough). Once done, submit your cover and you are 24 hours away from reviewing your overall finished project.

Step 8.

Reviewing your book. This is the most exciting part of the process. You have two options when it comes to reviewing your book. You can either do a digital review or you can order a physical, tangible printed copy known as a "Proof Copy". The cost to order a proof copy and have it sent to our house has averaged around $3.00 per book. That's it. Just $3.00 to have your masterpiece printed and shipped to you so you can touch it, feel it, read it, take selfies with it, whatever. We think this is such an amazing experience and one that can literally be done anywhere from $0.00 if you do all the editing and book cover on your own to just a few hundred dollars for the art and editing. That's it. The cost to have Createspace.com build this for you is free and the cost to print and ship is dirt cheap.

Step 9.

Approve your final review. After you review the final version of your book and, pending any edits (which would cause you to repeat some of the earlier submission steps), you are now ready to get your book to the world.

TIP: Since the "Proof Copy" is so cheap (and so cool) we tend to order 5 (the max allowed at one time) so that we can read our books, keep one or two as a memento, and also so that we can hand a few physical copies out to some trusted friends to review the hard copy and give us any feedback before we rush to approve the final project.

Step 10.

Setting up your sales channels. This is the exciting part. Createspace.com is owned by Amazon (which might be why we love them the most). Setting up your sales channel is also a very easy stage and one that comes with a step by step process with tips, tricks and hints all along the way. Here you can make your book available in the Createspace.com store, through Kindle and other e-readers as well as through the Amazon.com site. Simply follow the step by step path they provide for you and you will be ready to start telling the world all about your book and all of the different places they can find it. We will cover more information on this in the marketing section. But it is worth noting, there is no direct cost to set up any of these sales channels through Createspace.com. They are all free and easy. You will be asked to set your pricing and of course they will take a margin cut through all of these sites for each book sold but we assure you, based on our research their "cut" is equal to or better than most that we have looked at and their process is certainly easier than any of the other sites that we are aware of.

CHAPTER 9
PRINTING YOUR OWN BOOK

"If you think it's expensive to hire a professional to do the job, wait until you hire an amateur."
— Red Adair

Another way to get your book self-published is to print it yourself. Hard to believe anyone would want to do that, especially after just reading the previous chapter, but we do both have a dog in the fight since we don't get any royalties from Createspace.com or any other Amazon affiliated companies. Our preference for Createspace.com is simply one of personal choice.
That being said, you can choose to print your own book. You can do this at a number of different places, although you'd have to format your book yourself as well as prepare it for the printing press.

Online printers will print up your book. You can get an ISBN number yourself by going to the isbn.org website. You'll need one number for all of your books. You can get them in a barcode to put on your book when self-printing.

It used to be less costly to print your own book but based on the technology, expertise, sheer volume and scale that companies like Createspace.com have, that could be arguable at this point. Another option, if printing on your own, is to use an offline printer as opposed to an online printer. You just have to get everything ready for printing. This includes the cover, which will be made of a thicker paper and can be glossy or matte. The cover is an important part of the book, so it is a good idea to hire a graphic artist to design the cover if you are planning on printing the book yourself.

If you are a graphic artist or you know one, great! If not, we recommend finding a freelance service like Fiverr.com or even EnvatoMarket.com (we use Envato and their entire marketplace all the time). Just keep in mind, before you look to hire someone to do your art work, you should have a very clear idea in mind so that you can explain it clearly in order to get the results you want. Follow the same recommendation when it comes to vetting a graphic artist that we used when hiring a proof reader or a copy editor.

Maybe you want to create your cover with artwork

that you have, artwork that is available online or through some other art outlet. In addition to the freelance sites that will do your entire cover for you, there is also artwork that is already available for sale online. We have used these sites too. Sites like EnvatoMarket.com, GraphicRiver.com, GettyImages.com and so on. If you opt for going in this direction you will need to make sure that any art work you purchase is available for licensing and distribution rights and also ensure that the graphics or art quality is available in a high resolution (or hi-res) format.

In order to get an ISBN, you'll have to set up a publishing company of your own. You can do this easily enough[3] and then apply for the ISBN. It can be costly to pay for these numbers on a singular basis, which is why it often pays to have a self-publishing company print the book and get the ISBN for you. Because they order in bulk, they get them at a lower price. If you are planning on printing up more than one book, you can order a series of 10 ISBN numbers and get a discounted price. Self-publishing companies order these by the hundreds, which is why they can provide a number for customers included in their printing price. As a quick callout, Createspace.com builds theirs into the price of printing and there is no upfront cost whatsoever involved in self-publishing through Createspace.com (just to be clear).

The disadvantage of printing your own book is that you cannot get it listed on online sites such as Amazon. You can distribute it to bookstores and gift stores, however, as long as you have the ISBN. In some cases, such as with certain gift shops, they may take books that are just printed crudely without an ISBN on a consignment basis.

Printing your own book is a lot of work but it works for some people. It simply takes some knowledge on how to format the book as well as designing the cover. You may end up spending money on a graphic artist if you want to get your cover to look professional. The self-publishing site we use doesn't have costs associated with publishing your book and they have a lot of formatting options already built in. More on that in a bit.

You may also come to find that you will have to do your own final editing and proofreading when you are printing up your own book. This can be very time

consuming, which is why many writers prefer to pay
the money to a self-publishing company or a
freelancer. Printing your own book may work if you
have a small literary magazine that you put out. It can
work if you just want to distribute books personally
and sell them. It can also work if you are planning to
just sell your book on your own. You have to
remember, though, that even with an ISBN a book
store may be reluctant to put a book on their shelves
that does not look as if it has been professionally
printed. Decide how you want to sell your book and
where, then decide how you wish to have it printed.

CHAPTER 10
YOUR BOOK IS PRINTED...

NOW WHAT?

*"Without promotion, something terrible happens...
nothing!"*
— P. T. Barnum

After you have your book printed and ready to go,
what do you do? You do the same thing that you
would if your book was published by a mainstream
publishing company - promote it!

There are many ways that you can promote your book
both online and off. One thing that you will want to do
is promote your book by getting some positive reviews
on Amazon. This is fast and free. If you have your
book listed on Amazon, you can get reviews for the
book done by a book reviewing service. You can send
them a disk with the book on it in PDF format and have
people read it and give it a good review. While you do
not get paid for people buying the book, you also do
not have to pay to have them review it. The more

reviews it gets, the more it will rise on Amazon.

You should have a website as a teaser for your book. When you have a website, you can sell books directly from the site or you can send the buyers to Amazon by embedding an amazon or createspace.com link right on your website. You can become an affiliate of Amazon and get paid a commission on all of your sales. You can also have a post office box where people can order your book by mail. You can even direct them to the self-publishing company where they can find the book. You can then market your website by using strategies that are used to market any website but that's another book... and likely one that we will write since we love websites and marketing as much as we love writing books! (Stay tuned)

You can place book reviews on various book review websites online. You can also post a link to the book website on these sites.

If your book is non-fiction, you'll want to write articles and place them in article hubs on the internet. Article hubs will allow you to place free articles online. Do a

Google Keyword Analytics to find the right keywords for your book. You can then write articles with these keywords and place them on various sites with a backlink to your site. You can even copy your reviews or excerpts from your book, put them in article or blog form and post them on free business sites like linkedin.com.

In addition to promoting your book online, through the use of the website and book reviews, you can also join writing groups that are for self-published writers. There are many sites that are made for self-published writers that you can take advantage of and use to promote your book. You should also look into local libraries that often have groups for self-published authors. There are year-round book fairs for self-published authors as well.

You can send your book to different newspapers and local magazines that review books. Bear in mind that papers like the New York Times and magazines like the New Yorker have many books that people want them to review. You have a better chance of getting your book reviewed by magazines that are genre-related to the book that you have written.

Small, independent bookstores will feature your book, especially if they are local bookstores. You should take your book in there, having bought several copies for selling, and have a book signing. This can be advertised through flyers and in the bookstore itself. As the bookstore gets a commission for each book that you sell, they are more than happy to have local authors come in and sign books. This brings business to the store and gets you recognition.

If you have a small local newspaper, you can use them for publicity for your book. Small, hometown newspapers are an ideal way to spread the word about your book.

Take a look at your local parks department to see if they have anything for self-published authors. Many parks departments have book signings for those who self-publish.

You can also take your book to gift shops that will sell it on consignment. This is an ideal way to sell cookbooks that are self-published. Be sure to match the type of marketing that you do to get the word

about your book out there to the venue. Leave no
stone unturned when you are marketing your book.

CHAPTER 11
ONLINE MARKETING TO SELL YOUR BOOK

"The aim of marketing is to know and understand the customer so well the product or service fits him and sells itself."
— *Peter Drucker*

The best way to sell your book is online. Your first venue will usually be the self-publishing company that prints your book. They not only print books but also sell books that are written by their authors. You can depend on many sales from a self-published book from the website. There is an additional cost typically associated with these services but one that we have found to be worth it.

Most of the online print to order sites will list the books on Amazon, which is the largest book seller worldwide. Getting your book listed on Amazon is the same as having it on a shelf in a bookstore. But remember that if no one knows that you have a book out, they will not find it unless they stumble upon it.

Be sure to tell family and friends that you have published a book and encourage them to buy it online rather than from you. Most websites rate books on the sales, so you want to make sure that any sales go through the website or more importantly through Amazon, as they are the top book sellers and the book sales you achieve through Amazon will help you to become a "Best Selling Author".

Here's a little "hack" we use to ensure that we achieve that status. Remember when we talked about the importance of selecting your BISAC Category and Subcategory (full listing is available in the appendix of this book). Well the reason we do that is so that we can look at the number of books on Amazon in our category when deciding our category.   If you can place your book strategically in the right category (one with lower competition than most) you can increase your chances of reaching Number 1 status faster. Additionally there is another way to help you promote your book and help you to achieve this ranking. You can make your book available on kindle through Amazon at a discounted price, either permanently or temporarily and you can do so in away that will guarantee sales. Here is what we do. We make our kindle book available for .99¢ for one day. That day happens to be on our "Launch" day. We promote through every social media site, our website, to our friends, to our family, from stage, videos on Youtube.com and Vimeo.com, Instagram.com and twitter.com, we tell anyone who will listen... that for one day only, they can help us achieve **"Best Selling Author"** status and get an awesome book out of the deal for only .99¢.

We simply provide a link or give them the directions on how to find the book on Amazon and on that day we push it like crazy. We typically rack up a couple hundred sales in just a few hours and while we don't make any money to speak of, we achieve that status and that status launches our exposure and ensures incredible future sales through Amazon.com.

While that might be one of our best and most proven strategies there are many more ways to market your book online. Use social networking sites like Facebook and Twitter to get the word out about your book (be sure to add a link to your website or to Amazon directly to your book's sales page).

You can also place links to the book's page on various forums. You do want to get a website so that you can spread the word about the book. Developing your own website and getting a host is neither difficult nor expensive. You can do so and have them up in matter of minutes. We use GoDaddy.com who provides both domain names and website builders with amazing and simple to use website templates which are practically done for you. You can literally get this done in as little as an hour. That may be another book but trust us, when buying and building the website for this book, that is exactly what we did... in 48 minutes, top to bottom. And the cost of the entire thing; domain name, website and all, only $32.98.

You cannot afford to ignore the power of online marketing when it comes to selling your book. The fact is that today the majority of all book sales are generated online, in fact the vast majority of authors sell their books online. You want to be sure that you do your best to market the book as much as possible on the internet.

Digg.com is another site where you can put comments and information about your book. Digg usually takes articles that can be "dugg" by others. You should have all of your family and friends digg the article up so that others can see it. The more exposure you get online, the better off you are.

Another site that you can use is Propeller. This is the Yahoo equivalent to Digg. Anyone with a Yahoo account can buzz an article up. If you get enough buzzes to your article, it may appear on the Yahoo home page. You can write an article using a pen name about a local writer who has written a book and place it on these sites so that others will boost it up on the engine.   This is one way to get recognition for your book online.

You need to have as much exposure as you possibly can for your online book. Make sure that your book features on Amazon as well as the site where it is printed. Also be sure that you have a website that tells a little bit about the book and gives readers an incentive to buy the book.   You cannot get overexposed when you are promoting your book online.

You will find that you get more from online sales than you will from book store sales. While it is important to get as much exposure as possible for your book, you need to concentrate heavily on online sales. Get as much online exposure as you can for your book.

NETWORKING

How to Build Authority and Brand Awareness Through Networking

Wouldn't it be nice if you could become an authority in your niche overnight and 'leapfrog' the competition? If you could skip the normal route of gradually climbing the ranks and instead go straight to the top as a thought leader?

Well, as it happens, there is at least one way you can do this – and that's to network properly with other thought leaders in your niche.

The Theory

If you can network with other thought leaders in your niche and if you can align yourself with them/work with them, then you will be able to create more opportunities to associate yourself with them in the eyes of your fans.

What this then means is that right away, you will gain some of the trust and authority they have simply through your connection to them.

For instance, if you could get a top digital marketer to say that your book or e-book on making money was great, then you would not only get exposure from them but also the seal of approval that would come with that.

The same goes for having a guest post published on a top blog – again you will benefit because people trust them and will thus be more likely to trust you by extension.

How to Work With Top Bloggers

So that's all great in theory but how do you actually get to the point where those big bloggers are going to be happy to promote you?

There are many popular methods for working with other bloggers in content marketing and these provide a 'framework' of sorts that you can use to structure your own interactions. The guest post is one example – it's generally accepted that many blogs will accept contributors and provide them with a link back if the content is good.

Another option is to do an 'ad swap'. Here you will promote another blogger to your mailing list in exchange for them doing the same for you. That way you both benefit by gaining exposure to an audience the other has built a relationship with.

LinkedIn and networking events provide good opportunities to meet these bloggers and to discuss working with them. An important tip, whatever your strategy, though is to avoid the temptation to go straight for the biggest bloggers in your niche first. A smarter strategy is to start nearer to the bottom and work your way up as you gain exposure for your own brand.

We know that we can't possibly list every strategy for online marketing here in this book. Like we said, that is another book altogether. That being said, check out http://The48HourAuthor.com often for new ideas, tips, tricks, hacks and anything else we might have forgotten or even learned since the publication of this book.

CHAPTER 12
OFFLINE MARKETING TO SELL YOUR BOOK

"In marketing you must choose between boredom, shouting and seduction. Which do you want?"
— *Roy H. Williams*

You will want to get maximum exposure offline as well. We have already talked about groups that you can join, getting your books in bookstores and doing book signings.

One of the best practices we use when it comes to Off line marketing, is simply handing out our books to people in our industry or area of interest. We tend to seek out the "influencers" in these categories and we simply give them a copy of our book. We tell them that we admire them and would value their opinion on our book. While all of that is true, the upside is that these people are usually so flattered that they end up becoming our biggest fans and advocates. They tend to tell everyone they know and that has really helped

The 48 Hour Author

us move to some books in our industry with a real grassroots effort.

Additionally, we love mailing our books to industry leaders, local media or heads of companies and organizations that our books apply to and this does very well for us too.

TIP: Here is a cool money saver when it comes to mailing out books. The USPS has a shipping exception called "Media Rate". This is a low cost alternative to traditional mailing costs and channels. The book might get there a little slower but when you are mailing tons of books, it's a worthwhile consideration.

As stated in an earlier chapter, book signings are the best way for you to get exposure with your book. You can do them in any local bookstore. They will be glad to have you. You can bring your books to the bookstore to sell them.

Most larger bookstores, such as Barnes & Noble and

91

Borders will want you to go through the main office in order to have your book stocked on their shelves. These stores will want to see a copy of your book before they place an order. This can be time consuming for you, but is well worth a try.

You are better off, however, approaching the manager of the bookstore and offering them the books on a consignment basis. They will let you do a book signing and you can bring your own books, but will have to give a commission to the store.

You can use a book distributor to distribute your book to local bookstores and get them on the shelves. This may be easier than going the corporate route. You will have to buy the books from the publishing company in order to get them to the distributor.

The distributor will then work to get the books to the major bookstores. Again, this is a tough sell. Best sellers from major presses have more shelf space in bookstores as well as prominent shelf spaces. Just like in the supermarket, the biggest distributors have the most attractive shelf space. If you think that you will see your book on the center shelf at the major bookstore, think again. If they take your book, it will be in the shelves. This is why you need to promote the book with book signings. You should still do what you need to do in order to get the book in the bookstore.

There are still plenty of local, independent bookstores available. They are much more receptive to local authors and will eagerly take your book on a consignment basis. They will be glad to have you go in there and do a book signing. Take a look at independent bookstores in your area.

Make sure that you join an offline group of self-publishers and take advantage of book fairs that are primarily for self-publishing authors. You can also make up bookmarks for your book and hand them out at these fairs. They should have information about the book as well as where readers can find it.

You'll have to do some legwork to get your book out there to the public, but you need to be sure to do as much as you can to get the book information out there. The more you continue to promote your book, the more interest it will garner.

When you go through the time and work of putting all of your creative talent into a book, you'll want to do whatever you can to make sure that the book is read. Most good writers are not as interested in the money book can generate as they are in the book being read by others.

Working hard to complete and print your book and then having others enjoy your writing is one of the best things a writer can experience.

If you have ever thought about writing a book but aren't sure if you can get a publisher, you should consider self-publishing your book. Instead of trying to get an agent and a publisher to look at your book, only to give you a small percentage of the profit, you can easily self-publish your own book and have others read it.

Go online and take a look at the following sites:
www.createspace.com

www.lulu.com

www.booklocker.com

These are three of the most popular sites online for self-publishing. Take a look at their frequently asked questions and rates to see which is right for you. Then get started writing and making your dream come true!

BONUS

BRANDING MISTAKES

Have no doubt about it. Your book is a brand. And so we would like to offer you this little bonus insight section on the Top Branding Mistakes That Are Making Your Book Suffer.

Creating a consistent brand for an online business is a highly effective way to get more customers and clients, to increase awareness about your organization and to generally propel yourself to new heights. Having a strong brand will create many more opportunities for you and will mean that every aspect of your business helps to strengthen every other aspect.

But creating a brand isn't easy and that's why there are so few sites on the net that have the strong presence and identity that they need. Here are some of the most common mistakes that companies and individuals will make when creating their brand...

Lack of Consistency

This applies both to your visual consistency – in terms of the way your brand looks across various channels and your consistency in terms of the topic, industry and values that you put out.

The point of a consistent brand is that it should represent a certain degree of quality and a certain predictability in terms of what users get. People should know that something with your logo on it will be something that they enjoy.

So if your website is talking about puppy dogs one week

and programming the next, you're going to lose people. Likewise, if you put out a brilliant product one month and the next thing you release is garbage, people won't be able to trust you in the future. Stay consistent and stay true to your vision.

Poor Visuals

Aesthetics are an important aspect of your branding and if you don't have a strong logo and strong visuals through your advertising and web design, then your brand isn't going to be memorable to your customers and users. If your logo is a grainy JPG that looks like something you made in college, then it might be time to hire a professional or at least have a rethink.

Missed Opportunities

Every business card, social media account, invoice and email is a chance to strengthen your brand. Make sure you include your logo everywhere and don't miss an opportunity to show it off.

Lack of Self Awareness

When creating your branding, you are creating the way that people are going to see you. To do this effectively though, you need to be objective and realistic. If you're a one-man-band tinkering in your free time, then don't try and brand yourself as a global corporate enterprise. It will ring false and your brand will fail as a result.

ABOUT THE AUTHORS

Bo Bryant & Thax Turner live in Southern California with their respective wives and children. They have authored over 6 books and counting (at the time of this publication). They have reached "Best Selling Author" status twice and continue to disrupt the market with their simple, fun and insightful approach to writing and teaching techniques to Entrepreneurs and Intrapreneurs alike.

Thax & Bo feature a weekly radio show for Entrepreneurs and thought leaders in business. As certified coaches the duo is always in search for finding simpler solution to the otherwise misunderstood concepts and strategies as they relate to success, business, life, balance, spirituality and family.

Thax and Bo are passionate about education, coaching and consulting and are constantly looking for more effective ways to impact the live of those they meet. Stay tuned for more as they are always working on something! Or, go back and see some of the other projects they have contributed to the world.

For more information about Thax and Bo or about this book head on over to http://The48HourAuthor.com

Appendix

BISAC BOOK LISTING
CATEGORIES AND SUBCATEGORIES

ANTIQUE & COLLECTABLES

ANT000000	ANTIQUES & COLLECTIBLES / General
ANT001000	ANTIQUES & COLLECTIBLES / Americana
ANT002000	ANTIQUES & COLLECTIBLES / Art
ANT003000	ANTIQUES & COLLECTIBLES / Autographs
	ANTIQUES & COLLECTIBLES / Automobiles see Transportation
ANT005000	ANTIQUES & COLLECTIBLES / Books
ANT006000	ANTIQUES & COLLECTIBLES / Bottles
ANT007000	ANTIQUES & COLLECTIBLES / Buttons & Pins
ANT054000	ANTIQUES & COLLECTIBLES / Canadiana
ANT008000	ANTIQUES & COLLECTIBLES / Care & Restoration
	ANTIQUES & COLLECTIBLES / Cars see Transportation
	ANTIQUES & COLLECTIBLES / Ceramics see Pottery & Ceramics
	ANTIQUES & COLLECTIBLES / China see Porcelain & China
ANT010000	ANTIQUES & COLLECTIBLES / Clocks & Watches
ANT011000	ANTIQUES & COLLECTIBLES / Coins, Currency & Medals
ANT012000	ANTIQUES & COLLECTIBLES / Comics
	ANTIQUES & COLLECTIBLES / Costume see Textiles & Costume
	ANTIQUES & COLLECTIBLES / Dance see Performing Arts
	ANTIQUES & COLLECTIBLES / Disneyana see Americana
ANT015000	ANTIQUES & COLLECTIBLES / Dolls
ANT053000	ANTIQUES & COLLECTIBLES / Figurines
ANT016000	ANTIQUES & COLLECTIBLES / Firearms & Weapons
ANT017000	ANTIQUES & COLLECTIBLES / Furniture
ANT018000	ANTIQUES & COLLECTIBLES / Glass & Glassware
	ANTIQUES & COLLECTIBLES / Gold see Silver, Gold & Other Metals
	ANTIQUES & COLLECTIBLES / Hummels see Figurines or Popular Culture
ANT021000	ANTIQUES & COLLECTIBLES / Jewelry
ANT022000	ANTIQUES & COLLECTIBLES / Kitchenware
ANT023000	ANTIQUES & COLLECTIBLES / Magazines & Newspapers
	ANTIQUES & COLLECTIBLES / Medals see Coins, Currency & Medals
ANT024000	ANTIQUES & COLLECTIBLES / Military
	ANTIQUES & COLLECTIBLES / Movies see Performing Arts
	ANTIQUES & COLLECTIBLES / Musical Instruments see Performing Arts
	ANTIQUES & COLLECTIBLES / Nautical see Transportation
	ANTIQUES & COLLECTIBLES / Newspapers see Magazines & Newspapers
ANT028000	ANTIQUES & COLLECTIBLES / Non-Sports Cards
ANT029000	ANTIQUES & COLLECTIBLES / Paper Ephemera
ANT025000	ANTIQUES & COLLECTIBLES / Performing Arts
	ANTIQUES & COLLECTIBLES / Pewter see Silver, Gold & Other Metals
ANT031000	ANTIQUES & COLLECTIBLES / Political
ANT052000	ANTIQUES & COLLECTIBLES / Popular Culture
ANT032000	ANTIQUES & COLLECTIBLES / Porcelain & China
ANT033000	ANTIQUES & COLLECTIBLES / Postcards
ANT034000	ANTIQUES & COLLECTIBLES / Posters
ANT035000	ANTIQUES & COLLECTIBLES / Pottery & Ceramics
ANT036000	ANTIQUES & COLLECTIBLES / Radios & Televisions (see also Performing Arts)
ANT037000	ANTIQUES & COLLECTIBLES / Records
ANT038000	ANTIQUES & COLLECTIBLES / Reference

ANTIQUES & COLLECTIBLES / Restoration see Care & Restoration
ANTIQUES & COLLECTIBLES / Royalty see Popular Culture
ANT040000   ANTIQUES & COLLECTIBLES / Rugs
ANT041000   ANTIQUES & COLLECTIBLES / Silver, Gold & Other Metals
ANT043000   ANTIQUES & COLLECTIBLES / Sports (see also headings under Sports Cards)
ANT042000   ANTIQUES & COLLECTIBLES / Sports Cards / General
ANT042010   ANTIQUES & COLLECTIBLES / Sports Cards / Baseball
ANTIQUES & COLLECTIBLES / Stained Glass see Glass & Glassware
ANT044000   ANTIQUES & COLLECTIBLES / Stamps
ANT045000   ANTIQUES & COLLECTIBLES / Teddy Bears
ANTIQUES & COLLECTIBLES / Televisions & Television-Related see Performing Arts or Radios & Televisions
ANT047000   ANTIQUES & COLLECTIBLES / Textiles & Costume
ANTIQUES & COLLECTIBLES / Theater see Performing Arts
ANT055000   ANTIQUES & COLLECTIBLES / Tobacco-Related
ANT049000   ANTIQUES & COLLECTIBLES / Toy Animals
ANT050000   ANTIQUES & COLLECTIBLES / Toys
ANT009000   ANTIQUES & COLLECTIBLES / Transportation
ANTIQUES & COLLECTIBLES / Watches see Clocks & Watches
ANTIQUES & COLLECTIBLES / Weapons see Firearms & Weapons
ANT051000   ANTIQUES & COLLECTIBLES / Wine

ARCHITECHTURE
ARC000000   ARCHITECTURE / General
ARC022000   ARCHITECTURE / Adaptive Reuse & Renovation
ARC023000   ARCHITECTURE / Annuals
ARC024000   ARCHITECTURE / Buildings / General
ARC024010   ARCHITECTURE / Buildings / Landmarks & Monuments
ARC011000   ARCHITECTURE / Buildings / Public, Commercial & Industrial
ARC016000   ARCHITECTURE / Buildings / Religious
ARC003000   ARCHITECTURE / Buildings / Residential
ARCHITECTURE / CAD (Computer Aided Design) see Design, Drafting, Drawing & Presentation
ARC019000   ARCHITECTURE / Codes & Standards
ARC001000   ARCHITECTURE / Criticism
ARC002000   ARCHITECTURE / Decoration & Ornament
ARC004000   ARCHITECTURE / Design, Drafting, Drawing & Presentation
ARCHITECTURE / Feng Shui see BODY, MIND & SPIRIT / Feng Shui
ARC014000   ARCHITECTURE / Historic Preservation / General
ARC014010   ARCHITECTURE / Historic Preservation / Restoration Techniques
ARC005000   ARCHITECTURE / History / General
ARC005010   ARCHITECTURE / History / Prehistoric & Primitive
ARC005020   ARCHITECTURE / History / Ancient & Classical
ARC005030   ARCHITECTURE / History / Medieval
ARC005040   ARCHITECTURE / History / Renaissance
ARC005050   ARCHITECTURE / History / Baroque & Rococo
ARC005060   ARCHITECTURE / History / Romanticism
ARC005070   ARCHITECTURE / History / Modern (late 19th Century to 1945)
ARC005080   ARCHITECTURE / History / Contemporary (1945-)
ARC006000   ARCHITECTURE / Individual Architects & Firms / General
ARC006010   ARCHITECTURE / Individual Architects & Firms / Essays
ARC006020   ARCHITECTURE / Individual Architects & Firms / Monographs
ARC007000   ARCHITECTURE / Interior Design / General
ARC007010   ARCHITECTURE / Interior Design / Lighting
ARC008000   ARCHITECTURE / Landscape
ARC009000   ARCHITECTURE / Methods & Materials
ARC015000   ARCHITECTURE / Professional Practice
ARC017000   ARCHITECTURE / Project Management

ARC012000	ARCHITECTURE / Reference
ARC020000	ARCHITECTURE / Regional
ARC021000	ARCHITECTURE / Security Design
ARC013000	ARCHITECTURE / Study & Teaching
ARC018000	ARCHITECTURE / Sustainability & Green Design
ARC010000	ARCHITECTURE / Urban & Land Use Planning

ART

ART000000	ART / General
ART015010	ART / African
ART015020	ART / American / General
ART038000	ART / American / African American
ART039000	ART / American / Asian American
ART040000	ART / American / Hispanic American
	ART / Animation see PERFORMING ARTS / Animation
ART054000	ART / Annuals
ART037000	ART / Art & Politics
ART019000	ART / Asian
ART042000	ART / Australian & Oceanian
	ART / Basic Techniques see headings under Techniques
ART055000	ART / Body Art & Tattooing
	ART / Book Design see DESIGN / Book
ART043000	ART / Business Aspects
ART015040	ART / Canadian
ART044000	ART / Caribbean & Latin American
ART045000	ART / Ceramics
ART006000	ART / Collections, Catalogs, Exhibitions / General
ART006010	ART / Collections, Catalogs, Exhibitions / Group Shows
ART006020	ART / Collections, Catalogs, Exhibitions / Permanent Collections
ART007000	ART / Color Theory
ART008000	ART / Conceptual
ART056000	ART / Conservation & Preservation
	ART / Costume Design see DESIGN / Textile & Costume
ART009000	ART / Criticism & Theory
	ART / Design see headings under DESIGN
ART046000	ART / Digital
	ART / Exhibitions see headings under Collections, Catalogs, Exhibitions
ART015030	ART / European
ART057000	ART / Film & Video
ART013000	ART / Folk & Outsider Art
	ART / Furniture Design see DESIGN / Furniture
ART058000	ART / Graffiti & Street Art
ART015000	ART / History / General
ART015050	ART / History / Prehistoric & Primitive
ART015060	ART / History / Ancient & Classical
ART015070	ART / History / Medieval
ART015080	ART / History / Renaissance
ART015090	ART / History / Baroque & Rococo
ART015120	ART / History / Romanticism
ART015100	ART / History / Modern (late 19th Century to 1945)
ART015110	ART / History / Contemporary (1945-)
ART016000	ART / Individual Artists / General
ART016010	ART / Individual Artists / Artists' Books
ART016020	ART / Individual Artists / Essays
ART016030	ART / Individual Artists / Monographs
	ART / Latin American see Caribbean & Latin American
ART047000	ART / Middle Eastern
ART017000	ART / Mixed Media

ART / Museum Administration & Museology see BUSINESS & ECONOMICS / Museum Administration & Museology

ART059000	ART / Museum Studies
ART041000	ART / Native American
	ART / Oceanian see Australian & Oceanian
	ART / Oriental see Asian
ART060000	ART / Performance
ART023000	ART / Popular Culture
ART048000	ART / Prints
	ART / Product Design see DESIGN / Product
ART025000	ART / Reference
ART049000	ART / Russian & Former Soviet Union
ART026000	ART / Sculpture & Installation
ART027000	ART / Study & Teaching
ART050000	ART / Subjects & Themes / General
ART050050	ART / Subjects & Themes / Erotica
ART050010	ART / Subjects & Themes / Human Figure
ART050020	ART / Subjects & Themes / Landscapes & Seascapes
ART050030	ART / Subjects & Themes / Plants & Animals
ART050040	ART / Subjects & Themes / Portraits
ART035000	ART / Subjects & Themes / Religious
ART050060	ART / Subjects & Themes / Science Fiction & Fantasy *
ART028000	ART / Techniques / General
ART031000	ART / Techniques / Acrylic Painting
ART002000	ART / Techniques / Airbrush
ART003000	ART / Techniques / Calligraphy
ART004000	ART / Techniques / Cartooning
ART051000	ART / Techniques / Color
ART010000	ART / Techniques / Drawing
ART052000	ART / Techniques / Life Drawing
ART018000	ART / Techniques / Oil Painting
ART020000	ART / Techniques / Painting
ART021000	ART / Techniques / Pastel Drawing
ART033000	ART / Techniques / Pen & Ink Drawing
ART034000	ART / Techniques / Pencil Drawing
ART024000	ART / Techniques / Printmaking
ART053000	ART / Techniques / Sculpting
ART029000	ART / Techniques / Watercolor Painting
	ART / Textile Design see DESIGN / Textile & Costume
	ART / Video see Film & Video

BIBLES

BIB000000	BIBLES / General
BIB001000	BIBLES / Christian Standard Bible / General
BIB001010	BIBLES / Christian Standard Bible / Children
BIB001020	BIBLES / Christian Standard Bible / Devotional
BIB001030	BIBLES / Christian Standard Bible / New Testament & Portions
BIB001040	BIBLES / Christian Standard Bible / Reference
BIB001050	BIBLES / Christian Standard Bible / Study
BIB001060	BIBLES / Christian Standard Bible / Text
BIB001070	BIBLES / Christian Standard Bible / Youth & Teen
BIB022000	BIBLES / Common English Bible / General
BIB022010	BIBLES / Common English Bible / Children
BIB022020	BIBLES / Common English Bible / Devotional
BIB022030	BIBLES / Common English Bible / New Testament & Portions
BIB022040	BIBLES / Common English Bible / Reference
BIB022050	BIBLES / Common English Bible / Study
BIB022060	BIBLES / Common English Bible / Text

BIB022070	BIBLES / Common English Bible / Youth & Teen
BIB002000	BIBLES / Contemporary English Version / General
BIB002010	BIBLES / Contemporary English Version / Children
BIB002020	BIBLES / Contemporary English Version / Devotional
BIB002030	BIBLES / Contemporary English Version / New Testament & Portions
BIB002040	BIBLES / Contemporary English Version / Reference
BIB002050	BIBLES / Contemporary English Version / Study
BIB002060	BIBLES / Contemporary English Version / Text
BIB002070	BIBLES / Contemporary English Version / Youth & Teen
BIB003000	BIBLES / English Standard Version / General
BIB003010	BIBLES / English Standard Version / Children
BIB003020	BIBLES / English Standard Version / Devotional
BIB003030	BIBLES / English Standard Version / New Testament & Portions
BIB003040	BIBLES / English Standard Version / Reference
BIB003050	BIBLES / English Standard Version / Study
BIB003060	BIBLES / English Standard Version / Text
BIB003070	BIBLES / English Standard Version / Youth & Teen
BIB004000	BIBLES / God's Word / General
BIB004010	BIBLES / God's Word / Children
BIB004020	BIBLES / God's Word / Devotional
BIB004030	BIBLES / God's Word / New Testament & Portions
BIB004040	BIBLES / God's Word / Reference
BIB004050	BIBLES / God's Word / Study
BIB004060	BIBLES / God's Word / Text
BIB004070	BIBLES / God's Word / Youth & Teen
BIB005000	BIBLES / International Children's Bible / General
BIB005010	BIBLES / International Children's Bible / Children
BIB005020	BIBLES / International Children's Bible / Devotional
BIB005030	BIBLES / International Children's Bible / New Testament & Portions
BIB005040	BIBLES / International Children's Bible / Reference
BIB005050	BIBLES / International Children's Bible / Study
BIB005060	BIBLES / International Children's Bible / Text
BIB005070	BIBLES / International Children's Bible / Youth & Teen
BIB006000	BIBLES / King James Version / General
BIB006010	BIBLES / King James Version / Children
BIB006020	BIBLES / King James Version / Devotional
BIB006030	BIBLES / King James Version / New Testament & Portions
BIB006040	BIBLES / King James Version / Reference
BIB006050	BIBLES / King James Version / Study
BIB006060	BIBLES / King James Version / Text
BIB006070	BIBLES / King James Version / Youth & Teen
BIB007000	BIBLES / La Biblia de las Americas / General
BIB007010	BIBLES / La Biblia de las Americas / Children
BIB007020	BIBLES / La Biblia de las Americas / Devotional
BIB007030	BIBLES / La Biblia de las Americas / New Testament & Portions
BIB007040	BIBLES / La Biblia de las Americas / Reference
BIB007050	BIBLES / La Biblia de las Americas / Study
BIB007060	BIBLES / La Biblia de las Americas / Text
BIB007070	BIBLES / La Biblia de las Americas / Youth & Teen
BIB008000	BIBLES / Multiple Translations / General
BIB008010	BIBLES / Multiple Translations / Children
BIB008020	BIBLES / Multiple Translations / Devotional
BIB008030	BIBLES / Multiple Translations / New Testament & Portions
BIB008040	BIBLES / Multiple Translations / Reference
BIB008050	BIBLES / Multiple Translations / Study
BIB008060	BIBLES / Multiple Translations / Text
BIB008070	BIBLES / Multiple Translations / Youth & Teen
BIB009000	BIBLES / New American Bible / General
BIB009010	BIBLES / New American Bible / Children

BIB009020	BIBLES / New American Bible / Devotional
BIB009030	BIBLES / New American Bible / New Testament & Portions
BIB009040	BIBLES / New American Bible / Reference
BIB009050	BIBLES / New American Bible / Study
BIB009060	BIBLES / New American Bible / Text
BIB009070	BIBLES / New American Bible / Youth & Teen
BIB010000	BIBLES / New American Standard Bible / General
BIB010010	BIBLES / New American Standard Bible / Children
BIB010020	BIBLES / New American Standard Bible / Devotional
BIB010030	BIBLES / New American Standard Bible / New Testament & Portions
BIB010040	BIBLES / New American Standard Bible / Reference
BIB010050	BIBLES / New American Standard Bible / Study
BIB010060	BIBLES / New American Standard Bible / Text
BIB010070	BIBLES / New American Standard Bible / Youth & Teen
BIB011000	BIBLES / New Century Version / General
BIB011010	BIBLES / New Century Version / Children
BIB011020	BIBLES / New Century Version / Devotional
BIB011030	BIBLES / New Century Version / New Testament & Portions
BIB011040	BIBLES / New Century Version / Reference
BIB011050	BIBLES / New Century Version / Study
BIB011060	BIBLES / New Century Version / Text
BIB011070	BIBLES / New Century Version / Youth & Teen
BIB012000	BIBLES / New International Reader's Version / General
BIB012010	BIBLES / New International Reader's Version / Children
BIB012020	BIBLES / New International Reader's Version / Devotional
BIB012030	BIBLES / New International Reader's Version / New Testament & Portions
BIB012040	BIBLES / New International Reader's Version / Reference
BIB012050	BIBLES / New International Reader's Version / Study
BIB012060	BIBLES / New International Reader's Version / Text
BIB012070	BIBLES / New International Reader's Version / Youth & Teen
BIB013000	BIBLES / New International Version / General
BIB013010	BIBLES / New International Version / Children
BIB013020	BIBLES / New International Version / Devotional
BIB013030	BIBLES / New International Version / New Testament & Portions
BIB013040	BIBLES / New International Version / Reference
BIB013050	BIBLES / New International Version / Study
BIB013060	BIBLES / New International Version / Text
BIB013070	BIBLES / New International Version / Youth & Teen
BIB014000	BIBLES / New King James Version / General
BIB014010	BIBLES / New King James Version / Children
BIB014020	BIBLES / New King James Version / Devotional
BIB014030	BIBLES / New King James Version / New Testament & Portions
BIB014040	BIBLES / New King James Version / Reference
BIB014050	BIBLES / New King James Version / Study
BIB014060	BIBLES / New King James Version / Text
BIB014070	BIBLES / New King James Version / Youth & Teen
BIB015000	BIBLES / New Living Translation / General
BIB015010	BIBLES / New Living Translation / Children
BIB015020	BIBLES / New Living Translation / Devotional
BIB015030	BIBLES / New Living Translation / New Testament & Portions
BIB015040	BIBLES / New Living Translation / Reference
BIB015050	BIBLES / New Living Translation / Study
BIB015060	BIBLES / New Living Translation / Text
BIB015070	BIBLES / New Living Translation / Youth & Teen
BIB016000	BIBLES / New Revised Standard Version / General
BIB016010	BIBLES / New Revised Standard Version / Children
BIB016020	BIBLES / New Revised Standard Version / Devotional
BIB016030	BIBLES / New Revised Standard Version / New Testament & Portions

BIB016040	BIBLES / New Revised Standard Version / Reference
BIB016050	BIBLES / New Revised Standard Version / Study
BIB016060	BIBLES / New Revised Standard Version / Text
BIB016070	BIBLES / New Revised Standard Version / Youth & Teen
BIB017000	BIBLES / Nueva Version International / General
BIB017010	BIBLES / Nueva Version International / Children
BIB017020	BIBLES / Nueva Version International / Devotional
BIB017030	BIBLES / Nueva Version International / New Testament & Portions
BIB017040	BIBLES / Nueva Version International / Reference
BIB017050	BIBLES / Nueva Version International / Study
BIB017060	BIBLES / Nueva Version International / Text
BIB017070	BIBLES / Nueva Version International / Youth & Teen
BIB018000	BIBLES / Other Translations / General
BIB018010	BIBLES / Other Translations / Children
BIB018020	BIBLES / Other Translations / Devotional
BIB018030	BIBLES / Other Translations / New Testament & Portions
BIB018040	BIBLES / Other Translations / Reference
BIB018050	BIBLES / Other Translations / Study
BIB018060	BIBLES / Other Translations / Text
BIB018070	BIBLES / Other Translations / Youth & Teen
BIB019000	BIBLES / Reina Valera / General
BIB019010	BIBLES / Reina Valera / Children
BIB019020	BIBLES / Reina Valera / Devotional
BIB019030	BIBLES / Reina Valera / New Testament & Portions
BIB019040	BIBLES / Reina Valera / Reference
BIB019050	BIBLES / Reina Valera / Study
BIB019060	BIBLES / Reina Valera / Text
BIB019070	BIBLES / Reina Valera / Youth & Teen
BIB023000	BIBLES / The Amplified Bible / General *
BIB023010	BIBLES / The Amplified Bible / Children *
BIB023020	BIBLES / The Amplified Bible / Devotional *
BIB023030	BIBLES / The Amplified Bible / New Testament & Portions *
BIB023040	BIBLES / The Amplified Bible / Reference *
BIB023050	BIBLES / The Amplified Bible / Study *
BIB023060	BIBLES / The Amplified Bible / Text *
BIB023070	BIBLES / The Amplified Bible / Youth & Teen *
BIB020000	BIBLES / The Message / General
BIB020010	BIBLES / The Message / Children
BIB020020	BIBLES / The Message / Devotional
BIB020030	BIBLES / The Message / New Testament & Portions
BIB020040	BIBLES / The Message / Reference
BIB020050	BIBLES / The Message / Study
BIB020060	BIBLES / The Message / Text
BIB020070	BIBLES / The Message / Youth & Teen

BIOGRAPHY & AUTOBIOGRAPHY

BIO000000	BIOGRAPHY & AUTOBIOGRAPHY / General
BIO023000	BIOGRAPHY & AUTOBIOGRAPHY / Adventurers & Explorers
	BIOGRAPHY & AUTOBIOGRAPHY / African American & Black see Cultural Heritage
BIO001000	BIOGRAPHY & AUTOBIOGRAPHY / Artists, Architects, Photographers
BIO003000	BIOGRAPHY & AUTOBIOGRAPHY / Business
BIO004000	BIOGRAPHY & AUTOBIOGRAPHY / Composers & Musicians
BIO024000	BIOGRAPHY & AUTOBIOGRAPHY / Criminals & Outlaws
BIO029000	BIOGRAPHY & AUTOBIOGRAPHY / Culinary
BIO002000	BIOGRAPHY & AUTOBIOGRAPHY / Cultural Heritage
	BIOGRAPHY & AUTOBIOGRAPHY / Doctors see Medical
BIO025000	BIOGRAPHY & AUTOBIOGRAPHY / Editors, Journalists, Publishers
BIO019000	BIOGRAPHY & AUTOBIOGRAPHY / Educators

BIO005000 BIOGRAPHY & AUTOBIOGRAPHY / Entertainment & Performing Arts

BIO030000 BIOGRAPHY & AUTOBIOGRAPHY / Environmentalists & Naturalists

BIOGRAPHY & AUTOBIOGRAPHY / Famous see Rich & Famous

BIO006000 BIOGRAPHY & AUTOBIOGRAPHY / Historical

BIOGRAPHY & AUTOBIOGRAPHY / Judges see Lawyers & Judges

BIO027000 BIOGRAPHY & AUTOBIOGRAPHY / Law Enforcement

BIO020000 BIOGRAPHY & AUTOBIOGRAPHY / Lawyers & Judges

BIO031000 BIOGRAPHY & AUTOBIOGRAPHY / LGBT

BIO007000 BIOGRAPHY & AUTOBIOGRAPHY / Literary

BIO017000 BIOGRAPHY & AUTOBIOGRAPHY / Medical

BIO008000 BIOGRAPHY & AUTOBIOGRAPHY / Military

BIOGRAPHY & AUTOBIOGRAPHY / Musicians see Composers & Musicians

BIO028000 BIOGRAPHY & AUTOBIOGRAPHY / Native Americans

BIOGRAPHY & AUTOBIOGRAPHY / Nurses see Medical

BIO033000 BIOGRAPHY & AUTOBIOGRAPHY / People with Disabilities

BIOGRAPHY & AUTOBIOGRAPHY / Performing Arts see Entertainment & Performing Arts

BIO026000 BIOGRAPHY & AUTOBIOGRAPHY / Personal Memoirs

BIO009000 BIOGRAPHY & AUTOBIOGRAPHY / Philosophers

BIOGRAPHY & AUTOBIOGRAPHY / Photographers see Artists, Architects, Photographers

BIOGRAPHY & AUTOBIOGRAPHY / Physicians see Medical

BIO010000 BIOGRAPHY & AUTOBIOGRAPHY / Political

BIO011000 BIOGRAPHY & AUTOBIOGRAPHY / Presidents & Heads of State

BIOGRAPHY & AUTOBIOGRAPHY / Psychologists see Social Scientists & Psychologists

BIO012000 BIOGRAPHY & AUTOBIOGRAPHY / Reference

BIO018000 BIOGRAPHY & AUTOBIOGRAPHY / Religious

BIO013000 BIOGRAPHY & AUTOBIOGRAPHY / Rich & Famous

BIO014000 BIOGRAPHY & AUTOBIOGRAPHY / Royalty

BIO015000 BIOGRAPHY & AUTOBIOGRAPHY / Science & Technology

BIO032000 BIOGRAPHY & AUTOBIOGRAPHY / Social Activists

BIO021000 BIOGRAPHY & AUTOBIOGRAPHY / Social Scientists & Psychologists

BIO016000 BIOGRAPHY & AUTOBIOGRAPHY / Sports

BIOGRAPHY & AUTOBIOGRAPHY / Surgeons see Medical

BIOGRAPHY & AUTOBIOGRAPHY / Teachers see Educators

BIO022000 BIOGRAPHY & AUTOBIOGRAPHY / Women

BODY, MIND & SPIRIT

OCC000000 BODY, MIND & SPIRIT / General

OCC022000 BODY, MIND & SPIRIT / Afterlife & Reincarnation

OCC031000 BODY, MIND & SPIRIT / Ancient Mysteries & Controversial Knowledge

OCC032000 BODY, MIND & SPIRIT / Angels & Spirit Guides

OCC002000 BODY, MIND & SPIRIT / Astrology / General

OCC030000 BODY, MIND & SPIRIT / Astrology / Eastern

OCC009000 BODY, MIND & SPIRIT / Astrology / Horoscopes

OCC036010 BODY, MIND & SPIRIT / Celtic Spirituality

OCC003000 BODY, MIND & SPIRIT / Channeling & Mediumship

OCC004000 BODY, MIND & SPIRIT / Crystals

OCC005000 BODY, MIND & SPIRIT / Divination / General

OCC008000 BODY, MIND & SPIRIT / Divination / Fortune Telling

OCC017000 BODY, MIND & SPIRIT / Divination / Palmistry

OCC024000 BODY, MIND & SPIRIT / Divination / Tarot

BODY, MIND & SPIRIT / Dowsing see Divination / General

OCC006000 BODY, MIND & SPIRIT / Dreams

OCC039000 BODY, MIND & SPIRIT / Entheogens & Visionary Substances

OCC037000 BODY, MIND & SPIRIT / Feng Shui

OCC033000   BODY, MIND & SPIRIT / Gaia & Earth Energies
BODY, MIND & SPIRIT / Gnosticism see RELIGION / Gnosticism
OCC036050   BODY, MIND & SPIRIT / Goddess Worship
OCC011000   BODY, MIND & SPIRIT / Healing / General
OCC011010   BODY, MIND & SPIRIT / Healing / Energy (Qigong, Reiki, Polarity)
OCC011020   BODY, MIND & SPIRIT / Healing / Prayer & Spiritual
OCC040000   BODY, MIND & SPIRIT / Hermetism & Rosicrucianism
OCC038000   BODY, MIND & SPIRIT / I Ching
OCC019000   BODY, MIND & SPIRIT / Inspiration & Personal Growth
OCC028000   BODY, MIND & SPIRIT / Magick Studies
OCC010000   BODY, MIND & SPIRIT / Mindfulness & Meditation
OCC012000   BODY, MIND & SPIRIT / Mysticism
BODY, MIND & SPIRIT / New Age see General
OCC014000   BODY, MIND & SPIRIT / New Thought
OCC015000   BODY, MIND & SPIRIT / Numerology
OCC016000   BODY, MIND & SPIRIT / Occultism
BODY, MIND & SPIRIT / Paganism & Neo-Paganism see RELIGION / Paganism &
Neo-Paganism
OCC018000   BODY, MIND & SPIRIT / Parapsychology / General
OCC007000   BODY, MIND & SPIRIT / Parapsychology / ESP (Clairvoyance,
Precognition, Telepathy)
OCC034000   BODY, MIND & SPIRIT / Parapsychology / Near-Death Experience
OCC035000   BODY, MIND & SPIRIT / Parapsychology / Out-of-Body Experience
OCC020000   BODY, MIND & SPIRIT / Prophecy
BODY, MIND & SPIRIT / Psychic Phenomena see headings under Parapsychology
OCC021000   BODY, MIND & SPIRIT / Reference
OCC041000   BODY, MIND & SPIRIT / Sacred Sexuality
OCC036030   BODY, MIND & SPIRIT / Shamanism
BODY, MIND & SPIRIT / Spiritual Healing see Healing / Prayer & Spiritual
OCC027000   BODY, MIND & SPIRIT / Spiritualism
OCC023000   BODY, MIND & SPIRIT / Supernatural
OCC025000   BODY, MIND & SPIRIT / UFOs & Extraterrestrials
OCC029000   BODY, MIND & SPIRIT / Unexplained Phenomena
OCC026000   BODY, MIND & SPIRIT / Witchcraft (see also RELIGION / Wicca)
BODY, MIND & SPIRIT / Yoga see HEALTH & FITNESS / Yoga
BODY, MIND & SPIRIT / Zen Buddhism see PHILOSOPHY / Zen or RELIGION /
Buddhism / Zen

BUSINESS & ECONOMICS
BUS000000   BUSINESS & ECONOMICS / General
BUS001000   BUSINESS & ECONOMICS / Accounting/General
BUS001010   BUSINESS & ECONOMICS / Accounting / Financial
BUS001020   BUSINESS & ECONOMICS / Accounting / Governmental
BUSINESS & ECONOMICS / Accounting / International see International / Accounting
BUS001040   BUSINESS & ECONOMICS / Accounting / Managerial
BUS001050   BUSINESS & ECONOMICS / Accounting / Standards (GAAP, IFRS,
etc.)
BUS002000   BUSINESS & ECONOMICS / Advertising & Promotion
BUS003000   BUSINESS & ECONOMICS / Auditing
BUS004000   BUSINESS & ECONOMICS / Banks & Banking
BUS005000   BUSINESS & ECONOMICS / Bookkeeping
BUS006000   BUSINESS & ECONOMICS / Budgeting
BUS007000   BUSINESS & ECONOMICS / Business Communication / General
BUS007010   BUSINESS & ECONOMICS / Business Communication / Meetings &
Presentations
BUS008000   BUSINESS & ECONOMICS / Business Ethics
BUS009000   BUSINESS & ECONOMICS / Business Etiquette
BUS010000   BUSINESS & ECONOMICS / Business Law
BUS091000   BUSINESS & ECONOMICS / Business Mathematics

BUSINESS & ECONOMICS / Business Travel see TRAVEL / Special Interest / Business

BUS011000	BUSINESS & ECONOMICS / Business Writing
BUS012000	BUSINESS & ECONOMICS / Careers / General
BUS012010	BUSINESS & ECONOMICS / Careers / Internships
BUS037020	BUSINESS & ECONOMICS / Careers / Job Hunting
BUS056030	BUSINESS & ECONOMICS / Careers / Resumes

BUSINESS & ECONOMICS / Charities see Nonprofit Organizations & Charities

BUS073000	BUSINESS & ECONOMICS / Commerce
BUS013000	BUSINESS & ECONOMICS / Commercial Policy
BUS110000	BUSINESS & ECONOMICS / Conflict Resolution & Mediation

BUSINESS & ECONOMICS / Consolidation & Merger see Mergers & Acquisitions

BUS075000	BUSINESS & ECONOMICS / Consulting
BUS016000	BUSINESS & ECONOMICS / Consumer Behavior
BUS077000	BUSINESS & ECONOMICS / Corporate & Business History
BUS017000	BUSINESS & ECONOMICS / Corporate Finance / General
BUS017010	BUSINESS & ECONOMICS / Corporate Finance / Private Equity
BUS017020	BUSINESS & ECONOMICS / Corporate Finance / Valuation
BUS017030	BUSINESS & ECONOMICS / Corporate Finance / Venture Capital
BUS104000	BUSINESS & ECONOMICS / Corporate Governance
BUS111000	BUSINESS & ECONOMICS / Crowdfunding
BUS018000	BUSINESS & ECONOMICS / Customer Relations
BUS019000	BUSINESS & ECONOMICS / Decision-Making & Problem Solving
BUS092000	BUSINESS & ECONOMICS / Development / General
BUS020000	BUSINESS & ECONOMICS / Development / Business Development
BUS068000	BUSINESS & ECONOMICS / Development / Economic Development
BUS072000	BUSINESS & ECONOMICS / Development / Sustainable Development
BUS078000	BUSINESS & ECONOMICS / Distribution
BUS090000	BUSINESS & ECONOMICS / E-Commerce / General (see also COMPUTERS / Electronic Commerce)
BUS090040	BUSINESS & ECONOMICS / E-Commerce / Auctions & Small Business
BUS090010	BUSINESS & ECONOMICS / E-Commerce / Internet Marketing
BUS090030	BUSINESS & ECONOMICS / E-Commerce / Online Trading
BUS021000	BUSINESS & ECONOMICS / Econometrics
BUS022000	BUSINESS & ECONOMICS / Economic Conditions

BUSINESS & ECONOMICS / Economic Development see Development / Economic Development

BUS023000	BUSINESS & ECONOMICS / Economic History
BUS069000	BUSINESS & ECONOMICS / Economics / General
BUS069010	BUSINESS & ECONOMICS / Economics / Comparative

BUSINESS & ECONOMICS / Economics / International see International / Economics

BUS039000	BUSINESS & ECONOMICS / Economics / Macroeconomics
BUS044000	BUSINESS & ECONOMICS / Economics / Microeconomics
BUS069030	BUSINESS & ECONOMICS / Economics / Theory
BUS024000	BUSINESS & ECONOMICS / Education
BUS025000	BUSINESS & ECONOMICS / Entrepreneurship
BUS099000	BUSINESS & ECONOMICS / Environmental Economics

BUSINESS & ECONOMICS / Etailing see headings under E-Commerce

BUS026000	BUSINESS & ECONOMICS / Exports & Imports
BUS093000	BUSINESS & ECONOMICS / Facility Management
BUS027000	BUSINESS & ECONOMICS / Finance / General
BUS027010	BUSINESS & ECONOMICS / Finance / Financial Engineering
BUS027020	BUSINESS & ECONOMICS / Finance / Financial Risk Management
BUS027030	BUSINESS & ECONOMICS / Finance / Wealth Management
BUS086000	BUSINESS & ECONOMICS / Forecasting
BUS028000	BUSINESS & ECONOMICS / Foreign Exchange
BUS105000	BUSINESS & ECONOMICS / Franchises
BUS029000	BUSINESS & ECONOMICS / Free Enterprise

BUS079000	BUSINESS & ECONOMICS / Government & Business
BUS094000	BUSINESS & ECONOMICS / Green Business
BUS080000	BUSINESS & ECONOMICS / Home-Based Businesses
	BUSINESS & ECONOMICS / Hospitality, Travel & Tourism see Industries / Hospitality, Travel & Tourism
BUS030000	BUSINESS & ECONOMICS / Human Resources & Personnel Management
	BUSINESS & ECONOMICS / Humor see HUMOR / Topic / Business & Professional
	BUSINESS & ECONOMICS / Imports see Exports & Imports
BUS082000	BUSINESS & ECONOMICS / Industrial Management
BUS070000	BUSINESS & ECONOMICS / Industries / General
BUS070010	BUSINESS & ECONOMICS / Industries / Agribusiness
BUS070020	BUSINESS & ECONOMICS / Industries / Automobile Industry
BUS070030	BUSINESS & ECONOMICS / Industries / Computers & Information Technology
BUS070040	BUSINESS & ECONOMICS / Industries / Energy
BUS070110	BUSINESS & ECONOMICS / Industries / Entertainment
BUS070090	BUSINESS & ECONOMICS / Industries / Fashion & Textile Industry
BUS070140	BUSINESS & ECONOMICS / Industries / Financial Services
BUS070120	BUSINESS & ECONOMICS / Industries / Food Industry
BUS081000	BUSINESS & ECONOMICS / Industries / Hospitality, Travel & Tourism
BUS070050	BUSINESS & ECONOMICS / Industries / Manufacturing
BUS070060	BUSINESS & ECONOMICS / Industries / Media & Communications
BUS070150	BUSINESS & ECONOMICS / Industries / Natural Resource Extraction
BUS070070	BUSINESS & ECONOMICS / Industries / Park & Recreation Management
BUS070130	BUSINESS & ECONOMICS / Industries / Pharmaceutical & Biotechnology
BUS057000	BUSINESS & ECONOMICS / Industries / Retailing
BUS070080	BUSINESS & ECONOMICS / Industries / Service
BUS070100	BUSINESS & ECONOMICS / Industries / Transportation
BUS031000	BUSINESS & ECONOMICS / Inflation
BUS083000	BUSINESS & ECONOMICS / Information Management
BUS032000	BUSINESS & ECONOMICS / Infrastructure
BUS033000	BUSINESS & ECONOMICS / Insurance / General
BUS033010	BUSINESS & ECONOMICS / Insurance / Automobile
BUS033020	BUSINESS & ECONOMICS / Insurance / Casualty
BUS033040	BUSINESS & ECONOMICS / Insurance / Health
BUS033050	BUSINESS & ECONOMICS / Insurance / Liability
BUS033060	BUSINESS & ECONOMICS / Insurance / Life
BUS033080	BUSINESS & ECONOMICS / Insurance / Property
BUS033070	BUSINESS & ECONOMICS / Insurance / Risk Assessment & Management
BUS034000	BUSINESS & ECONOMICS / Interest
BUS035000	BUSINESS & ECONOMICS / International / General
BUS001030	BUSINESS & ECONOMICS / International / Accounting
BUS069020	BUSINESS & ECONOMICS / International / Economics
BUS043030	BUSINESS & ECONOMICS / International / Marketing
BUS064020	BUSINESS & ECONOMICS / International / Taxation
BUS036000	BUSINESS & ECONOMICS / Investments & Securities / General
BUS036070	BUSINESS & ECONOMICS / Investments & Securities / Analysis & Trading Strategies
BUS036010	BUSINESS & ECONOMICS / Investments & Securities / Bonds
BUS014000	BUSINESS & ECONOMICS / Investments & Securities / Commodities/ General
BUS014010	BUSINESS & ECONOMICS / Investments & Securities / Commodities/ Energy
BUS014020	BUSINESS & ECONOMICS / Investments & Securities / Commodities/ Metals

BUS036080   BUSINESS & ECONOMICS / Investments & Securities / Derivatives
BUS036090   BUSINESS & ECONOMICS / Investments & Securities / Portfolio Management
BUS036020   BUSINESS & ECONOMICS / Investments & Securities / Futures
BUS036030   BUSINESS & ECONOMICS / Investments & Securities / Mutual Funds
BUS036040   BUSINESS & ECONOMICS / Investments & Securities / Options
BUS036050   BUSINESS & ECONOMICS / Investments & Securities / Real Estate
BUS036060   BUSINESS & ECONOMICS / Investments & Securities / Stocks
BUS112000   BUSINESS & ECONOMICS / Islamic Banking & Finance *
             BUSINESS & ECONOMICS / Job Hunting see Careers / Job Hunting
BUS098000   BUSINESS & ECONOMICS / Knowledge Capital
BUS038000   BUSINESS & ECONOMICS / Labor
BUS071000   BUSINESS & ECONOMICS / Leadership
             BUSINESS & ECONOMICS / Macroeconomics see Economics / Macroeconomics
BUS040000   BUSINESS & ECONOMICS / Mail Order
BUS041000   BUSINESS & ECONOMICS / Management
BUS042000   BUSINESS & ECONOMICS / Management Science
BUS043000   BUSINESS & ECONOMICS / Marketing / General
BUS043010   BUSINESS & ECONOMICS / Marketing / Direct
BUS043020   BUSINESS & ECONOMICS / Marketing / Industrial
             BUSINESS & ECONOMICS / Marketing / International see International / Marketing
             BUSINESS & ECONOMICS / Marketing / Internet see E-Commerce / Internet Marketing
BUS043040   BUSINESS & ECONOMICS / Marketing / Multilevel
BUS043060   BUSINESS & ECONOMICS / Marketing / Research
BUS043050   BUSINESS & ECONOMICS / Marketing / Telemarketing
BUS106000   BUSINESS & ECONOMICS / Mentoring & Coaching
BUS015000   BUSINESS & ECONOMICS / Mergers & Acquisitions
             BUSINESS & ECONOMICS / Microeconomics see Economics / Microeconomics
BUS045000   BUSINESS & ECONOMICS / Money & Monetary Policy
             BUSINESS & ECONOMICS / Money Management see Personal Finance / Money Management
BUS046000   BUSINESS & ECONOMICS / Motivational
BUS100000   BUSINESS & ECONOMICS / Museum Administration & Museology
BUS047000   BUSINESS & ECONOMICS / Negotiating
BUS048000   BUSINESS & ECONOMICS / New Business Enterprises
BUS074000   BUSINESS & ECONOMICS / Nonprofit Organizations & Charities / General
BUS074010   BUSINESS & ECONOMICS / Nonprofit Organizations & Charities / Finance & Accounting
BUS074020   BUSINESS & ECONOMICS / Nonprofit Organizations & Charities / Fundraising & Grants
BUS074030   BUSINESS & ECONOMICS / Nonprofit Organizations & Charities / Management & Leadership
BUS074040   BUSINESS & ECONOMICS / Nonprofit Organizations & Charities / Marketing & Communications
BUS084000   BUSINESS & ECONOMICS / Office Automation
BUS095000   BUSINESS & ECONOMICS / Office Equipment & Supplies
BUS096000   BUSINESS & ECONOMICS / Office Management
             BUSINESS & ECONOMICS / Operations Management see Production & Operations Management
BUS049000   BUSINESS & ECONOMICS / Operations Research
BUS085000   BUSINESS & ECONOMICS / Organizational Behavior
BUS103000   BUSINESS & ECONOMICS / Organizational Development
BUS102000   BUSINESS & ECONOMICS / Outsourcing
BUS050000   BUSINESS & ECONOMICS / Personal Finance / General
BUS050010   BUSINESS & ECONOMICS / Personal Finance / Budgeting
BUS050020   BUSINESS & ECONOMICS / Personal Finance / Investing
BUS050030   BUSINESS & ECONOMICS / Personal Finance / Money Management

BUS050040	BUSINESS & ECONOMICS / Personal Finance / Retirement Planning
BUS050050	BUSINESS & ECONOMICS / Personal Finance / Taxation
BUS107000	BUSINESS & ECONOMICS / Personal Success

BUSINESS & ECONOMICS / Personnel Management see Human Resources & Personnel Management

BUSINESS & ECONOMICS / Planning see Strategic Planning

BUS087000	BUSINESS & ECONOMICS / Production & Operations Management
BUS101000	BUSINESS & ECONOMICS / Project Management

BUSINESS & ECONOMICS / Promotion see Advertising & Promotion

BUS051000	BUSINESS & ECONOMICS / Public Finance
BUS052000	BUSINESS & ECONOMICS / Public Relations
BUS076000	BUSINESS & ECONOMICS / Purchasing & Buying
BUS053000	BUSINESS & ECONOMICS / Quality Control
BUS054000	BUSINESS & ECONOMICS / Real Estate / General
BUS054010	BUSINESS & ECONOMICS / Real Estate / Buying & Selling Homes
BUS054020	BUSINESS & ECONOMICS / Real Estate / Commercial
BUS054030	BUSINESS & ECONOMICS / Real Estate / Mortgages
BUS055000	BUSINESS & ECONOMICS / Reference
BUS108000	BUSINESS & ECONOMICS / Research & Development

BUSINESS & ECONOMICS / Resumes see Careers / Resumes

BUSINESS & ECONOMICS / Retailing see Industries / Retailing

BUSINESS & ECONOMICS / Risk Assessment & Management see Insurance / Risk Assessment & Management

BUS058000	BUSINESS & ECONOMICS / Sales & Selling / General
BUS058010	BUSINESS & ECONOMICS / Sales & Selling / Management
BUS089000	BUSINESS & ECONOMICS / Secretarial Aids & Training

BUSINESS & ECONOMICS / Securities see headings under Investments & Securities

BUS059000	BUSINESS & ECONOMICS / Skills
BUS060000	BUSINESS & ECONOMICS / Small Business
BUS061000	BUSINESS & ECONOMICS / Statistics
BUS063000	BUSINESS & ECONOMICS / Strategic Planning
BUS062000	BUSINESS & ECONOMICS / Structural Adjustment

BUSINESS & ECONOMICS / Sustainable Development see Development / Sustainable Development

BUS064000	BUSINESS & ECONOMICS / Taxation / General
BUS064010	BUSINESS & ECONOMICS / Taxation / Corporate

BUSINESS & ECONOMICS / Taxation / International see International / Taxation

BUSINESS & ECONOMICS / Taxation / Personal see Personal Finance / Taxation

BUS064030	BUSINESS & ECONOMICS / Taxation / Small Business
BUS088000	BUSINESS & ECONOMICS / Time Management
BUS065000	BUSINESS & ECONOMICS / Total Quality Management
BUS066000	BUSINESS & ECONOMICS / Training

BUSINESS & ECONOMICS / Travel & Tourism see Industries / Hospitality, Travel & Tourism

BUS067000	BUSINESS & ECONOMICS / Urban & Regional
BUS109000	BUSINESS & ECONOMICS / Women in Business
BUS097000	BUSINESS & ECONOMICS / Workplace Culture

COMICS & GRAPHIC NOVELS

CGN000000	COMICS & GRAPHIC NOVELS / General
CGN012000	COMICS & GRAPHIC NOVELS / Adaptations
CGN001000	COMICS & GRAPHIC NOVELS / Anthologies

COMICS & GRAPHIC NOVELS / Comics & Cartoons see HUMOR / Form / Comic Strips & Cartoons

CGN008000	COMICS & GRAPHIC NOVELS / Contemporary Women
CGN004010	COMICS & GRAPHIC NOVELS / Crime & Mystery
CGN013000	COMICS & GRAPHIC NOVELS / Dystopian *
CGN004020	COMICS & GRAPHIC NOVELS / Erotica
CGN004030	COMICS & GRAPHIC NOVELS / Fantasy
CGN010000	COMICS & GRAPHIC NOVELS / Historical Fiction

CGN004040   COMICS & GRAPHIC NOVELS / Horror
COMICS & GRAPHIC NOVELS / Juvenile Fiction see headings under JUVENILE FICTION / Comics & Graphic Novels
COMICS & GRAPHIC NOVELS / Juvenile Nonfiction see headings under JUVENILE NONFICTION / Comics & Graphic Novels
CGN009000   COMICS & GRAPHIC NOVELS / LGBT
CGN006000   COMICS & GRAPHIC NOVELS / Literary
CGN004050   COMICS & GRAPHIC NOVELS / Manga / General
CGN004100   COMICS & GRAPHIC NOVELS / Manga / Crime & Mystery
CGN004230   COMICS & GRAPHIC NOVELS / Manga / Dystopian *
CGN004110   COMICS & GRAPHIC NOVELS / Manga / Erotica & Hentai
CGN004120   COMICS & GRAPHIC NOVELS / Manga / Fantasy
CGN004140   COMICS & GRAPHIC NOVELS / Manga / Historical Fiction
CGN004150   COMICS & GRAPHIC NOVELS / Manga / Horror
CGN004130   COMICS & GRAPHIC NOVELS / Manga / LGBT
CGN004160   COMICS & GRAPHIC NOVELS / Manga / Media Tie-In
CGN004170   COMICS & GRAPHIC NOVELS / Manga / Nonfiction
CGN004180   COMICS & GRAPHIC NOVELS / Manga / Romance
CGN004190   COMICS & GRAPHIC NOVELS / Manga / Science Fiction
CGN004200   COMICS & GRAPHIC NOVELS / Manga / Sports
CGN004210   COMICS & GRAPHIC NOVELS / Manga / Yaoi
CGN004060   COMICS & GRAPHIC NOVELS / Media Tie-In
CGN007000   COMICS & GRAPHIC NOVELS / Nonfiction
CGN011000   COMICS & GRAPHIC NOVELS / Religious
CGN004090   COMICS & GRAPHIC NOVELS / Romance
CGN004070   COMICS & GRAPHIC NOVELS / Science Fiction
CGN004080   COMICS & GRAPHIC NOVELS / Superheroes
COMICS & GRAPHIC NOVELS / Techniques see ART / Techniques / Cartooning

COMPUTERS
COM000000   COMPUTERS / General
COM082000   COMPUTERS / Bioinformatics
COMPUTERS / Business Software see Enterprise Applications / Business Intelligence Tools
COM006000   COMPUTERS / Buyer's Guides
COM007000   COMPUTERS / CAD-CAM
COM008000   COMPUTERS / Calculators
COM009000   COMPUTERS / CD-DVD Technology
COM055000   COMPUTERS / Certification Guides / General
COM055010   COMPUTERS / Certification Guides / A+
COM055020   COMPUTERS / Certification Guides / MCSE
COM061000   COMPUTERS / Client-Server Computing
COM091000   COMPUTERS / Cloud Computing *
COM010000   COMPUTERS / Compilers
COM059000   COMPUTERS / Computer Engineering
COM012000   COMPUTERS / Computer Graphics
COMPUTERS / Computer Industry see BUSINESS & ECONOMICS / Industries / Computers & Information Technology
COM013000   COMPUTERS / Computer Literacy
COM014000   COMPUTERS / Computer Science
COM072000   COMPUTERS / Computer Simulation
COMPUTERS / Computer Viruses see Security / Viruses & Malware
COM016000   COMPUTERS / Computer Vision & Pattern Recognition
COM086000   COMPUTERS / Computerized Home & Entertainment
COM017000   COMPUTERS / Cybernetics
COM062000   COMPUTERS / Data Modeling & Design
COM018000   COMPUTERS / Data Processing
COMPUTERS / Data Recovery see System Administration / Disaster & Recovery
COM020000   COMPUTERS / Data Transmission Systems / General

COM020050	COMPUTERS / Data Transmission Systems / Broadband
COM020010	COMPUTERS / Data Transmission Systems / Electronic Data Interchange
COM020090	COMPUTERS / Data Transmission Systems / Wireless
COM089000	COMPUTERS / Data Visualization
COM021000	COMPUTERS / Databases / General
COM021030	COMPUTERS / Databases / Data Mining
COM021040	COMPUTERS / Databases / Data Warehousing
COM021050	COMPUTERS / Databases / Servers
COM084000	COMPUTERS / Desktop Applications / General
COM084010	COMPUTERS / Desktop Applications / Databases
COM087020	COMPUTERS / Desktop Applications / Design & Graphics
COM022000	COMPUTERS / Desktop Applications / Desktop Publishing
COM084020	COMPUTERS / Desktop Applications / Email Clients
COM027000	COMPUTERS / Desktop Applications / Personal Finance Applications
COM078000	COMPUTERS / Desktop Applications / Presentation Software
COM081000	COMPUTERS / Desktop Applications / Project Management Software
COM054000	COMPUTERS / Desktop Applications / Spreadsheets
COM084030	COMPUTERS / Desktop Applications / Suites
COM058000	COMPUTERS / Desktop Applications / Word Processing
COM087000	COMPUTERS / Digital Media / General
COM087010	COMPUTERS / Digital Media / Audio
COM087030	COMPUTERS / Digital Media / Photography (see also PHOTOGRAPHY / Techniques / Digital)
COM071000	COMPUTERS / Digital Media / Video & Animation
COM063000	COMPUTERS / Document Management
COM085000	COMPUTERS / Documentation & Technical Writing
COM023000	COMPUTERS / Educational Software
COM064000	COMPUTERS / Electronic Commerce (see also headings under BUSINESS & ECONOMICS / E-Commerce)
COM065000	COMPUTERS / Electronic Publishing
	COMPUTERS / Email see Desktop Applications / Email Clients or System Administration / Email Administration
COM005000	COMPUTERS / Enterprise Applications / General
COM005030	COMPUTERS / Enterprise Applications / Business Intelligence Tools
COM066000	COMPUTERS / Enterprise Applications / Collaboration Software
	COMPUTERS / Entertainment & Games see GAMES / Video & Electronic
COM025000	COMPUTERS / Expert Systems
	COMPUTERS / Financial Applications see Desktop Applications / Personal Finance Applications or Enterprise Applications / Business Intelligence Tools
	COMPUTERS / Games see Programming / Games or GAMES / Video & Electronic
COM067000	COMPUTERS / Hardware / General
COM038000	COMPUTERS / Hardware / Mainframes & Minicomputers
COM074000	COMPUTERS / Hardware / Mobile Devices
COM049000	COMPUTERS / Hardware / Peripherals
COM050000	COMPUTERS / Hardware / Personal Computers / General
COM050020	COMPUTERS / Hardware / Personal Computers / Macintosh
COM050010	COMPUTERS / Hardware / Personal Computers / PCs
COM090000	COMPUTERS / Hardware / Tablets
COM080000	COMPUTERS / History
	COMPUTERS / Hypertext Systems see Programming Languages / HTML
COM012050	COMPUTERS / Image Processing
	COMPUTERS / Information Storage & Retrieval see System Administration / Storage & Retrieval
COM032000	COMPUTERS / Information Technology
COM031000	COMPUTERS / Information Theory
	COMPUTERS / Input-Output Equipment see headings under Hardware
	COMPUTERS / Integrated Software see headings under Desktop Applications or headings under Enterprise Applications

COM004000   COMPUTERS / Intelligence (AI) & Semantics
COM034000   COMPUTERS / Interactive & Multimedia
COM060000   COMPUTERS / Internet / General
COM060090   COMPUTERS / Internet / Application Development
          COMPUTERS / Internet / Commercial Use see Electronic Commerce or headings under BUSINESS & ECONOMICS / E-Commerce
          COMPUTERS / Internet / Intranets see Networking / Intranets & Extranets
          COMPUTERS / Internet / Server Maintenance see Hardware / Network Hardware
COM035000   COMPUTERS / Keyboarding
          COMPUTERS / Languages see headings under Programming Languages
COM036000   COMPUTERS / Logic Design
COM037000   COMPUTERS / Machine Theory
          COMPUTERS / Mainframes & Minicomputers see Hardware / Mainframes & Minicomputers
COM039000   COMPUTERS / Management Information Systems
COM077000   COMPUTERS / Mathematical & Statistical Software
COM041000   COMPUTERS / Microprocessors
          COMPUTERS / Multimedia see Interactive & Multimedia
COM042000   COMPUTERS / Natural Language Processing
COM043000   COMPUTERS / Networking / General
COM060030   COMPUTERS / Networking / Intranets & Extranets
COM075000   COMPUTERS / Networking / Hardware
COM043020   COMPUTERS / Networking / Local Area Networks (LANs)
COM043040   COMPUTERS / Networking / Network Protocols
          COMPUTERS / Networking / Security see Security / Networking
COM043060   COMPUTERS / Networking / Vendor Specific
COM044000   COMPUTERS / Neural Networks
COM069000   COMPUTERS / Online Services
COM046000   COMPUTERS / Operating Systems / General
COM046060   COMPUTERS / Operating Systems / DOS
COM046070   COMPUTERS / Operating Systems / Linux
COM046020   COMPUTERS / Operating Systems / Macintosh
COM046080   COMPUTERS / Operating Systems / Mainframe & Midrange
COM046030   COMPUTERS / Operating Systems / UNIX
COM046090   COMPUTERS / Operating Systems / Virtualization
COM046040   COMPUTERS / Operating Systems / Windows Desktop
COM046050   COMPUTERS / Operating Systems / Windows Server
COM047000   COMPUTERS / Optical Data Processing
          COMPUTERS / Parallel Processing see Systems Architecture / Distributed Systems & Computing
          COMPUTERS / Peripherals see Hardware / Peripherals
          COMPUTERS / Personal Computers & Microcomputers see headings under Hardware / Personal Computers
COM051000   COMPUTERS / Programming / General
COM051300   COMPUTERS / Programming / Algorithms
COM012040   COMPUTERS / Programming / Games
COM051370   COMPUTERS / Programming / Macintosh
          COMPUTERS / Programming / Languages see headings under Programming Languages
COM051380   COMPUTERS / Programming / Microsoft
COM051460   COMPUTERS / Programming / Mobile Devices
COM051210   COMPUTERS / Programming / Object Oriented
COM051390   COMPUTERS / Programming / Open Source
COM051220   COMPUTERS / Programming / Parallel
COM051010   COMPUTERS / Programming Languages / General
COM051020   COMPUTERS / Programming Languages / Ada
COM051470   COMPUTERS / Programming Languages / ASP .NET
COM051040   COMPUTERS / Programming Languages / Assembly Language
COM051050   COMPUTERS / Programming Languages / BASIC
COM051060   COMPUTERS / Programming Languages / C

COM051070	COMPUTERS / Programming Languages / C++
COM051310	COMPUTERS / Programming Languages / C#
COM051080	COMPUTERS / Programming Languages / COBOL
COM051090	COMPUTERS / Programming Languages / FORTRAN
COM051270	COMPUTERS / Programming Languages / HTML
COM051280	COMPUTERS / Programming Languages / Java
COM051260	COMPUTERS / Programming Languages / JavaScript
COM051100	COMPUTERS / Programming Languages / LISP
COM051130	COMPUTERS / Programming Languages / Pascal
COM051350	COMPUTERS / Programming Languages / Perl
COM051400	COMPUTERS / Programming Languages / PHP
COM051140	COMPUTERS / Programming Languages / Prolog
COM051360	COMPUTERS / Programming Languages / Python
COM051290	COMPUTERS / Programming Languages / RPG
COM051410	COMPUTERS / Programming Languages / Ruby
COM051170	COMPUTERS / Programming Languages / SQL
COM051450	COMPUTERS / Programming Languages / UML
COM051420	COMPUTERS / Programming Languages / VBScript
COM051200	COMPUTERS / Programming Languages / Visual BASIC
COM051320	COMPUTERS / Programming Languages / XML
COM052000	COMPUTERS / Reference
COM053000	COMPUTERS / Security / General
COM083000	COMPUTERS / Security / Cryptography
COM043050	COMPUTERS / Security / Networking
COM060040	COMPUTERS / Security / Online Safety & Privacy
COM015000	COMPUTERS / Security / Viruses & Malware
COM079000	COMPUTERS / Social Aspects / General
COM079010	COMPUTERS / Social Aspects / Human-Computer Interaction
COM051230	COMPUTERS / Software Development & Engineering / General
COM051430	COMPUTERS / Software Development & Engineering / Project Management
COM051330	COMPUTERS / Software Development & Engineering / Quality Assurance & Testing
COM051240	COMPUTERS / Software Development & Engineering / Systems Analysis & Design
COM051440	COMPUTERS / Software Development & Engineering / Tools
COM073000	COMPUTERS / Speech & Audio Processing
COM088000	COMPUTERS / System Administration / General
COM019000	COMPUTERS / System Administration / Disaster & Recovery
COM020020	COMPUTERS / System Administration / Email Administration
COM088010	COMPUTERS / System Administration / Linux & UNIX Administration
COM030000	COMPUTERS / System Administration / Storage & Retrieval
COM088020	COMPUTERS / System Administration / Windows Administration
	COMPUTERS / Systems Analysis see Software Development & Engineering / Systems Analysis & Design
COM011000	COMPUTERS / Systems Architecture / General
COM048000	COMPUTERS / Systems Architecture / Distributed Systems & Computing
COM070000	COMPUTERS / User Interfaces
COM056000	COMPUTERS / Utilities
	COMPUTERS / Video Games see GAMES / Video & Electronic
COM057000	COMPUTERS / Virtual Worlds
	COMPUTERS / Viruses see Security / Viruses & Malware
COM060080	COMPUTERS / Web / General
COM060170	COMPUTERS / Web / Content Management Systems
COM060130	COMPUTERS / Web / Design
COM060100	COMPUTERS / Web / Blogs
COM060010	COMPUTERS / Web / Browsers
COM060110	COMPUTERS / Web / Podcasting & Webcasting

COM060120	COMPUTERS / Web / Search Engines
COM060070	COMPUTERS / Web / Site Directories
COM060140	COMPUTERS / Web / Social Networking
COM060150	COMPUTERS / Web / User Generated Content
COM060160	COMPUTERS / Web / Web Programming
COM060180	COMPUTERS / Web / Web Services & APIs

COOKING

CKB000000	COOKING / General
CKB107000	COOKING / Baby Food
CKB100000	COOKING / Beverages / General
CKB006000	COOKING / Beverages / Bartending
CKB007000	COOKING / Beverages / Beer
CKB019000	COOKING / Beverages / Coffee & Tea
CKB118000	COOKING / Beverages / Juices & Smoothies *
CKB008000	COOKING / Beverages / Non-Alcoholic
CKB088000	COOKING / Beverages / Wine & Spirits

COOKING / Cigars & Tobacco see Entertaining or ANTIQUES & COLLECTIBLES / Tobacco-Related

CKB119000	COOKING / Cooking for Kids *
CKB120000	COOKING / Cooking with Kids *
CKB101000	COOKING / Courses & Dishes / General
CKB003000	COOKING / Courses & Dishes / Appetizers
CKB009000	COOKING / Courses & Dishes / Bread
CKB010000	COOKING / Courses & Dishes / Breakfast
CKB012000	COOKING / Courses & Dishes / Brunch & Tea Time
CKB014000	COOKING / Courses & Dishes / Cakes
CKB112000	COOKING / Courses & Dishes / Casseroles
CKB018000	COOKING / Courses & Dishes / Chocolate
CKB095000	COOKING / Courses & Dishes / Confectionery
CKB021000	COOKING / Courses & Dishes / Cookies
CKB024000	COOKING / Courses & Dishes / Desserts
CKB062000	COOKING / Courses & Dishes / Pastry
CKB063000	COOKING / Courses & Dishes / Pies
CKB064000	COOKING / Courses & Dishes / Pizza
CKB073000	COOKING / Courses & Dishes / Salads
CKB121000	COOKING / Courses & Dishes / Sandwiches *
CKB102000	COOKING / Courses & Dishes / Sauces & Dressings
CKB079000	COOKING / Courses & Dishes / Soups & Stews
CKB029000	COOKING / Entertaining
CKB030000	COOKING / Essays & Narratives
CKB039000	COOKING / Health & Healing / General
CKB106000	COOKING / Health & Healing / Allergy
CKB103000	COOKING / Health & Healing / Cancer
CKB025000	COOKING / Health & Healing / Diabetic & Sugar-Free
CKB111000	COOKING / Health & Healing / Gluten-Free
CKB104000	COOKING / Health & Healing / Heart
CKB114000	COOKING / Health & Healing / High Protein
CKB108000	COOKING / Health & Healing / Low Carbohydrate
CKB050000	COOKING / Health & Healing / Low Cholesterol
CKB051000	COOKING / Health & Healing / Low Fat
CKB052000	COOKING / Health & Healing / Low Salt

COOKING / Health & Healing / Low Sugar see Health & Healing / Diabetic & Sugar-Free

CKB026000	COOKING / Health & Healing / Weight Control
CKB041000	COOKING / History
CKB042000	COOKING / Holiday
CKB115000	COOKING / Individual Chefs & Restaurants
CKB023000	COOKING / Methods / General

CKB004000	COOKING / Methods / Baking
CKB005000	COOKING / Methods / Barbecue & Grilling
CKB015000	COOKING / Methods / Canning & Preserving
CKB020000	COOKING / Methods / Cookery for One
CKB116000	COOKING / Methods / Frying
CKB033000	COOKING / Methods / Garnishing & Food Presentation
CKB037000	COOKING / Methods / Gourmet
CKB113000	COOKING / Methods / Low Budget
CKB057000	COOKING / Methods / Microwave
CKB060000	COOKING / Methods / Outdoor
CKB068000	COOKING / Methods / Professional
CKB069000	COOKING / Methods / Quantity
CKB070000	COOKING / Methods / Quick & Easy
CKB110000	COOKING / Methods / Raw Food
CKB109000	COOKING / Methods / Slow Cooking
CKB081000	COOKING / Methods / Special Appliances
CKB089000	COOKING / Methods / Wok
CKB117000	COOKING / Pet Food
CKB071000	COOKING / Reference
CKB031000	COOKING / Regional & Ethnic / General
CKB001000	COOKING / Regional & Ethnic / African
CKB002000	COOKING / Regional & Ethnic / American / General
CKB002010	COOKING / Regional & Ethnic / American / California Style
CKB002020	COOKING / Regional & Ethnic / American / Middle Atlantic States
CKB002030	COOKING / Regional & Ethnic / American / Middle Western States
CKB002040	COOKING / Regional & Ethnic / American / New England
CKB002050	COOKING / Regional & Ethnic / American / Northwestern States
CKB002060	COOKING / Regional & Ethnic / American / Southern States
CKB002070	COOKING / Regional & Ethnic / American / Southwestern States
CKB002080	COOKING / Regional & Ethnic / American / Western States
CKB090000	COOKING / Regional & Ethnic / Asian

COOKING / Regional & Ethnic / British see Regional & Ethnic / English, Scottish & Welsh

CKB013000	COOKING / Regional & Ethnic / Cajun & Creole
CKB091000	COOKING / Regional & Ethnic / Canadian
CKB016000	COOKING / Regional & Ethnic / Caribbean & West Indian
CKB099000	COOKING / Regional & Ethnic / Central American & South American
CKB017000	COOKING / Regional & Ethnic / Chinese

COOKING / Regional & Ethnic / Creole see Regional & Ethnic / Cajun & Creole

COOKING / Regional & Ethnic / Eastern European see Regional & Ethnic / European

CKB011000	COOKING / Regional & Ethnic / English, Scottish & Welsh
CKB092000	COOKING / Regional & Ethnic / European
CKB034000	COOKING / Regional & Ethnic / French
CKB036000	COOKING / Regional & Ethnic / German
CKB038000	COOKING / Regional & Ethnic / Greek
CKB043000	COOKING / Regional & Ethnic / Hungarian
CKB044000	COOKING / Regional & Ethnic / Indian & South Asian
CKB045000	COOKING / Regional & Ethnic / International
CKB046000	COOKING / Regional & Ethnic / Irish
CKB047000	COOKING / Regional & Ethnic / Italian
CKB048000	COOKING / Regional & Ethnic / Japanese
CKB049000	COOKING / Regional & Ethnic / Jewish & Kosher

COOKING / Regional & Ethnic / Latin American see Regional & Ethnic / Central American & South American

CKB055000	COOKING / Regional & Ethnic / Mediterranean
CKB056000	COOKING / Regional & Ethnic / Mexican
CKB093000	COOKING / Regional & Ethnic / Middle Eastern
CKB058000	COOKING / Regional & Ethnic / Native American
CKB097000	COOKING / Regional & Ethnic / Pacific Rim

CKB065000   COOKING / Regional & Ethnic / Polish
CKB066000   COOKING / Regional & Ethnic / Portuguese
CKB072000   COOKING / Regional & Ethnic / Russian
CKB074000   COOKING / Regional & Ethnic / Scandinavian
    COOKING / Regional & Ethnic / Scottish see Regional & Ethnic / English, Scottish & Welsh
CKB078000   COOKING / Regional & Ethnic / Soul Food
    COOKING / Regional & Ethnic / South American see Regional & Ethnic / Central American & South American
CKB080000   COOKING / Regional & Ethnic / Spanish
CKB083000   COOKING / Regional & Ethnic / Thai
CKB084000   COOKING / Regional & Ethnic / Turkish
CKB094000   COOKING / Regional & Ethnic / Vietnamese
    COOKING / Regional & Ethnic / Welsh see Regional & Ethnic / English, Scottish & Welsh
    COOKING / Regional & Ethnic / West Indian see Regional & Ethnic / Caribbean & West Indian
CKB077000   COOKING / Seasonal
CKB105000   COOKING / Specific Ingredients / General
CKB096000   COOKING / Specific Ingredients / Dairy
CKB035000   COOKING / Specific Ingredients / Fruit
CKB032000   COOKING / Specific Ingredients / Game
CKB040000   COOKING / Specific Ingredients / Herbs, Spices, Condiments
CKB054000   COOKING / Specific Ingredients / Meat
CKB059000   COOKING / Specific Ingredients / Natural Foods
CKB061000   COOKING / Specific Ingredients / Pasta
CKB067000   COOKING / Specific Ingredients / Poultry
CKB098000   COOKING / Specific Ingredients / Rice & Grains
CKB076000   COOKING / Specific Ingredients / Seafood
CKB085000   COOKING / Specific Ingredients / Vegetables
CKB082000   COOKING / Tablesetting
CKB086000   COOKING / Vegetarian & Vegan

CRAFTS & HOBBIES
CRA000000   CRAFTS & HOBBIES / General
CRA001000   CRAFTS & HOBBIES / Applique
CRA002000   CRAFTS & HOBBIES / Baskets
CRA048000   CRAFTS & HOBBIES / Beadwork
CRA046000   CRAFTS & HOBBIES / Book Printing & Binding
CRA049000   CRAFTS & HOBBIES / Candle & Soap Making
CRA003000   CRAFTS & HOBBIES / Carving
    CRAFTS & HOBBIES / Ceramics see Pottery & Ceramics
CRA043000   CRAFTS & HOBBIES / Crafts for Children
CRA005000   CRAFTS & HOBBIES / Decorating
CRA056000   CRAFTS & HOBBIES / Dollhouses
CRA057000   CRAFTS & HOBBIES / Dolls & Doll Clothing
CRA006000   CRAFTS & HOBBIES / Dough
CRA007000   CRAFTS & HOBBIES / Dye
CRA009000   CRAFTS & HOBBIES / Fashion
CRA060000   CRAFTS & HOBBIES / Felting *
CRA061000   CRAFTS & HOBBIES / Fiber Arts & Textiles *
CRA010000   CRAFTS & HOBBIES / Flower Arranging
CRA047000   CRAFTS & HOBBIES / Folkcrafts
CRA011000   CRAFTS & HOBBIES / Framing
CRA012000   CRAFTS & HOBBIES / Glass & Glassware
    CRAFTS & HOBBIES / Graphic Arts see headings under DESIGN / Graphic Arts
CRA014000   CRAFTS & HOBBIES / Jewelry
CRA055000   CRAFTS & HOBBIES / Knots, Macrame & Rope Work
CRA050000   CRAFTS & HOBBIES / Leatherwork

CRA017000	CRAFTS & HOBBIES / Metal Work
CRA018000	CRAFTS & HOBBIES / Miniatures
CRA054000	CRAFTS & HOBBIES / Mixed Media
CRA045000	CRAFTS & HOBBIES / Model Railroading
CRA020000	CRAFTS & HOBBIES / Models
CRA053000	CRAFTS & HOBBIES / Nature Crafts
CRA022000	CRAFTS & HOBBIES / Needlework / General
CRA004000	CRAFTS & HOBBIES / Needlework / Crocheting
CRA044000	CRAFTS & HOBBIES / Needlework / Cross-Stitch
CRA008000	CRAFTS & HOBBIES / Needlework / Embroidery
	CRAFTS & HOBBIES / Needlework / Felting see Felting
CRA015000	CRAFTS & HOBBIES / Needlework / Knitting
CRA016000	CRAFTS & HOBBIES / Needlework / Lace & Tatting
CRA021000	CRAFTS & HOBBIES / Needlework / Needlepoint
	CRAFTS & HOBBIES / Needlework / Tatting see Needlework / Lace & Tatting
CRA023000	CRAFTS & HOBBIES / Origami
CRA024000	CRAFTS & HOBBIES / Painting
CRA025000	CRAFTS & HOBBIES / Papercrafts
CRA026000	CRAFTS & HOBBIES / Patchwork
CRA051000	CRAFTS & HOBBIES / Polymer Clay
CRA027000	CRAFTS & HOBBIES / Potpourri
CRA028000	CRAFTS & HOBBIES / Pottery & Ceramics
CRA029000	CRAFTS & HOBBIES / Printmaking
CRA030000	CRAFTS & HOBBIES / Puppets & Puppetry
CRA031000	CRAFTS & HOBBIES / Quilts & Quilting
CRA032000	CRAFTS & HOBBIES / Reference
CRA058000	CRAFTS & HOBBIES / Ribbon Work
CRA033000	CRAFTS & HOBBIES / Rugs
CRA052000	CRAFTS & HOBBIES / Scrapbooking
CRA034000	CRAFTS & HOBBIES / Seasonal
CRA035000	CRAFTS & HOBBIES / Sewing
	CRAFTS & HOBBIES / Stained Glass see Glass & Glassware
CRA036000	CRAFTS & HOBBIES / Stenciling
CRA037000	CRAFTS & HOBBIES / Stuffed Animals
CRA039000	CRAFTS & HOBBIES / Toymaking
CRA040000	CRAFTS & HOBBIES / Weaving
CRA059000	CRAFTS & HOBBIES / Wirework
CRA041000	CRAFTS & HOBBIES / Wood Toys
CRA042000	CRAFTS & HOBBIES / Woodwork

DESIGN

DES000000	DESIGN / General
DES001000	DESIGN / Book
DES002000	DESIGN / Clip Art
DES003000	DESIGN / Decorative Arts
DES004000	DESIGN / Essays
DES005000	DESIGN / Fashion
	DESIGN / Feng Shui see BODY, MIND & SPIRIT / Feng Shui
DES006000	DESIGN / Furniture
DES007000	DESIGN / Graphic Arts / General
DES007010	DESIGN / Graphic Arts / Advertising
DES007020	DESIGN / Graphic Arts / Branding & Logo Design
DES007030	DESIGN / Graphic Arts / Commercial & Corporate
DES007040	DESIGN / Graphic Arts / Illustration
DES007050	DESIGN / Graphic Arts / Typography
DES008000	DESIGN / History & Criticism
DES009000	DESIGN / Industrial
DES010000	DESIGN / Interior Decorating
DES011000	DESIGN / Product

DES012000   DESIGN / Reference
DES013000   DESIGN / Textile & Costume

DRAMA
DRA000000   DRAMA / General
DRA011000   DRAMA / African
DRA001000   DRAMA / American / General
DRA001010   DRAMA / American / African American
DRA006000   DRAMA / Ancient & Classical
DRA002000   DRAMA / Anthologies (multiple authors)
DRA005000   DRAMA / Asian / General
DRA005010   DRAMA / Asian / Japanese
DRA012000   DRAMA / Australian & Oceanian
          DRAMA / Authorship & Technique see PERFORMING ARTS / Theater / Playwriting
DRA013000   DRAMA / Canadian
DRA014000   DRAMA / Caribbean & Latin American
DRA004000   DRAMA / European / General
DRA003000   DRAMA / European / English, Irish, Scottish, Welsh
DRA004010   DRAMA / European / French
DRA004020   DRAMA / European / German
DRA004030   DRAMA / European / Italian
DRA004040   DRAMA / European / Spanish & Portuguese
          DRAMA / History & Criticism see LITERARY CRITICISM / Drama
DRA017000   DRAMA / LGBT
DRA018000   DRAMA / Medieval
DRA015000   DRAMA / Middle Eastern
          DRAMA / Monologues see PERFORMING ARTS / Monologues & Scenes
DRA008000   DRAMA / Religious & Liturgical
DRA016000   DRAMA / Russian & Former Soviet Union
DRA010000   DRAMA / Shakespeare
DRA019000   DRAMA / Women Authors

EDUCATION
EDU000000   EDUCATION / General
EDU001000   EDUCATION / Administration / General
EDU001020   EDUCATION / Administration / Elementary & Secondary
EDU001010   EDUCATION / Administration / Facility Management
EDU001030   EDUCATION / Administration / Higher
EDU001040   EDUCATION / Administration / School Superintendents & Principals
EDU002000   EDUCATION / Adult & Continuing Education
          EDUCATION / Aids & Devices see headings under Teaching Methods & Materials
EDU003000   EDUCATION / Aims & Objectives
          EDUCATION / Alternative Education see Non-Formal Education
EDU057000   EDUCATION / Arts in Education
EDU049000   EDUCATION / Behavioral Management
EDU005000   EDUCATION / Bilingual Education
EDU044000   EDUCATION / Classroom Management
EDU050000   EDUCATION / Collaborative & Team Teaching
EDU043000   EDUCATION / Comparative
EDU039000   EDUCATION / Computers & Technology
EDU006000   EDUCATION / Counseling / General
EDU014000   EDUCATION / Counseling / Academic Development
EDU031000   EDUCATION / Counseling / Career Guidance
EDU045000   EDUCATION / Counseling / Crisis Management
EDU007000   EDUCATION / Curricula
EDU008000   EDUCATION / Decision-Making & Problem Solving
EDU041000   EDUCATION / Distance, Open & Online Education
          EDUCATION / Driver Education see TRANSPORTATION / Automotive / Driver
Education

EDU034000	EDUCATION / Educational Policy & Reform / General
EDU034020	EDUCATION / Educational Policy & Reform / Charter Schools
EDU034030	EDUCATION / Educational Policy & Reform / Federal Legislation
EDU034010	EDUCATION / Educational Policy & Reform / School Safety
EDU009000	EDUCATION / Educational Psychology
EDU010000	EDUCATION / Elementary
EDU042000	EDUCATION / Essays
EDU011000	EDUCATION / Evaluation & Assessment
EDU012000	EDUCATION / Experimental Methods
EDU013000	EDUCATION / Finance
	EDUCATION / Funding see Finance or STUDY AIDS / Financial Aid
EDU015000	EDUCATION / Higher
EDU016000	EDUCATION / History
EDU017000	EDUCATION / Home Schooling
EDU048000	EDUCATION / Inclusive Education
	EDUCATION / Institutions see Organizations & Institutions
EDU018000	EDUCATION / Language Experience Approach
EDU032000	EDUCATION / Leadership
EDU051000	EDUCATION / Learning Styles
	EDUCATION / Library & Information Science see headings under LANGUAGE ARTS & DISCIPLINES / Library & Information Science
	EDUCATION / Mainstreaming see Inclusive Education
EDU020000	EDUCATION / Multicultural Education
EDU021000	EDUCATION / Non-Formal Education
EDU036000	EDUCATION / Organizations & Institutions
	EDUCATION / Orientation see Guidance & Orientation
EDU022000	EDUCATION / Parent Participation
EDU040000	EDUCATION / Philosophy, Theory & Social Aspects
EDU033000	EDUCATION / Physical Education
EDU023000	EDUCATION / Preschool & Kindergarten
EDU046000	EDUCATION / Professional Development
EDU024000	EDUCATION / Reference
EDU037000	EDUCATION / Research
EDU052000	EDUCATION / Rural
EDU025000	EDUCATION / Secondary
	EDUCATION / Social Aspects see Philosophy, Theory & Social Aspects
EDU026000	EDUCATION / Special Education / General
EDU026050	EDUCATION / Special Education / Behavioral, Emotional & Social Disabilities
EDU026010	EDUCATION / Special Education / Communicative Disorders
EDU026030	EDUCATION / Special Education / Developmental & Intellectual Disabilities
EDU026060	EDUCATION / Special Education / Gifted
EDU026020	EDUCATION / Special Education / Learning Disabilities
EDU026040	EDUCATION / Special Education / Physical Disabilities
EDU027000	EDUCATION / Statistics
EDU058000	EDUCATION / Standards (incl. Common Core) *
	EDUCATION / Student Financial Aid see STUDY AIDS / Financial Aid
EDU038000	EDUCATION / Student Life & Student Affairs
EDU028000	EDUCATION / Study Skills
EDU059000	EDUCATION / Teacher & Student Mentoring *
EDU029000	EDUCATION / Teaching Methods & Materials / General
EDU029050	EDUCATION / Teaching Methods & Materials / Arts & Humanities
EDU029070	EDUCATION / Teaching Methods & Materials / Health & Sexuality
EDU029080	EDUCATION / Teaching Methods & Materials / Language Arts
EDU029060	EDUCATION / Teaching Methods & Materials / Library Skills
EDU029010	EDUCATION / Teaching Methods & Materials / Mathematics
EDU029020	EDUCATION / Teaching Methods & Materials / Reading & Phonics
EDU029030	EDUCATION / Teaching Methods & Materials / Science & Technology

EDU029040   EDUCATION / Teaching Methods & Materials / Social Science
EDU030000   EDUCATION / Testing & Measurement
EDU053000   EDUCATION / Training & Certification
EDU054000   EDUCATION / Urban
EDU055000   EDUCATION / Violence & Harassment
EDU056000   EDUCATION / Vocational

FAMILY & RELATIONSHIPS
FAM000000   FAMILY & RELATIONSHIPS / General
FAM001000   FAMILY & RELATIONSHIPS / Abuse / General
FAM001010   FAMILY & RELATIONSHIPS / Abuse / Child Abuse
FAM001030   FAMILY & RELATIONSHIPS / Abuse / Domestic Partner Abuse
FAM001020   FAMILY & RELATIONSHIPS / Abuse / Elder Abuse
FAM002000   FAMILY & RELATIONSHIPS / Activities
FAM004000   FAMILY & RELATIONSHIPS / Adoption & Fostering
FAM006000   FAMILY & RELATIONSHIPS / Alternative Family
FAM007000   FAMILY & RELATIONSHIPS / Anger (see also SELF-HELP / Anger Management)
FAM047000   FAMILY & RELATIONSHIPS / Attention Deficit Disorder (ADD-ADHD)
FAM048000   FAMILY & RELATIONSHIPS / Autism Spectrum Disorders
FAM050000   FAMILY & RELATIONSHIPS / Babysitting, Day Care & Child Care
FAM008000   FAMILY & RELATIONSHIPS / Baby Names
    FAMILY & RELATIONSHIPS / Bereavement see Death, Grief, Bereavement
    FAMILY & RELATIONSHIPS / Breastfeeding see HEALTH & FITNESS / Breastfeeding
FAM049000   FAMILY & RELATIONSHIPS / Bullying
FAM012000   FAMILY & RELATIONSHIPS / Children with Special Needs
FAM013000   FAMILY & RELATIONSHIPS / Conflict Resolution
FAM051000   FAMILY & RELATIONSHIPS / Dating
FAM014000   FAMILY & RELATIONSHIPS / Death, Grief, Bereavement
FAM015000   FAMILY & RELATIONSHIPS / Divorce & Separation
FAM052000   FAMILY & RELATIONSHIPS / Dysfunctional Families
FAM016000   FAMILY & RELATIONSHIPS / Education
FAM017000   FAMILY & RELATIONSHIPS / Eldercare
FAM053000   FAMILY & RELATIONSHIPS / Extended Family
FAM021000   FAMILY & RELATIONSHIPS / Friendship
    FAMILY & RELATIONSHIPS / Grief see Death, Grief, Bereavement
    FAMILY & RELATIONSHIPS / Humorous see HUMOR / Topic / Marriage & Family or HUMOR / Topic / Relationships
    FAMILY & RELATIONSHIPS / Infertility see HEALTH & FITNESS / Infertility
FAM028000   FAMILY & RELATIONSHIPS / Learning Disabilities
FAM046000   FAMILY & RELATIONSHIPS / Life Stages / General
FAM003000   FAMILY & RELATIONSHIPS / Life Stages / Adolescence
FAM025000   FAMILY & RELATIONSHIPS / Life Stages / Infants & Toddlers
FAM005000   FAMILY & RELATIONSHIPS / Life Stages / Later Years
FAM054000   FAMILY & RELATIONSHIPS / Life Stages / Mid-Life
FAM039000   FAMILY & RELATIONSHIPS / Life Stages / School Age
FAM043000   FAMILY & RELATIONSHIPS / Life Stages / Teenagers
FAM029000   FAMILY & RELATIONSHIPS / Love & Romance
FAM030000   FAMILY & RELATIONSHIPS / Marriage & Long Term Relationships
FAM055000   FAMILY & RELATIONSHIPS / Military Families
FAM034000   FAMILY & RELATIONSHIPS / Parenting / General
FAM020000   FAMILY & RELATIONSHIPS / Parenting / Fatherhood
FAM022000   FAMILY & RELATIONSHIPS / Parenting / Grandparenting
FAM032000   FAMILY & RELATIONSHIPS / Parenting / Motherhood
FAM033000   FAMILY & RELATIONSHIPS / Parenting / Parent & Adult Child
FAM034010   FAMILY & RELATIONSHIPS / Parenting / Single Parent
FAM042000   FAMILY & RELATIONSHIPS / Parenting / Stepparenting

FAM035000 FAMILY & RELATIONSHIPS / Peer Pressure
  FAMILY & RELATIONSHIPS / Pregnancy & Childbirth see HEALTH & FITNESS /
Pregnancy & Childbirth
FAM037000 FAMILY & RELATIONSHIPS / Prejudice
FAM038000 FAMILY & RELATIONSHIPS / Reference
  FAMILY & RELATIONSHIPS / Romance see Love & Romance
  FAMILY & RELATIONSHIPS / Sexuality see HEALTH & FITNESS / Sexuality or
RELIGION / Sexuality & Gender Studies or SELF-HELP / Sexual Instruction
FAM041000 FAMILY & RELATIONSHIPS / Siblings
FAM044000 FAMILY & RELATIONSHIPS / Toilet Training

FICTION
FIC000000 FICTION / General
FIC002000 FICTION / Action & Adventure
  FICTION / Adventure see Action & Adventure
FIC049000 FICTION / African American / General
FIC049010 FICTION / African American / Christian
FIC049020 FICTION / African American / Contemporary Women
FIC049030 FICTION / African American / Erotica
FIC049040 FICTION / African American / Historical
FIC049050 FICTION / African American / Mystery & Detective
FIC049070 FICTION / African American / Urban
FIC040000 FICTION / Alternative History
FIC053000 FICTION / Amish & Mennonite
FIC003000 FICTION / Anthologies (multiple authors)
FIC054000 FICTION / Asian American
FIC041000 FICTION / Biographical
FIC060000 FICTION / Black Humor
FIC042000 FICTION / Christian / General
FIC042010 FICTION / Christian / Classic & Allegory
FIC042050 FICTION / Christian / Collections & Anthologies
FIC042080 FICTION / Christian / Fantasy
FIC042020 FICTION / Christian / Futuristic
FIC042030 FICTION / Christian / Historical
FIC042040 FICTION / Christian / Romance
FIC042060 FICTION / Christian / Suspense
FIC042070 FICTION / Christian / Western
FIC004000 FICTION / Classics
FIC043000 FICTION / Coming of Age
FIC044000 FICTION / Contemporary Women
FIC050000 FICTION / Crime
FIC051000 FICTION / Cultural Heritage
FIC055000 FICTION / Dystopian
FIC005000 FICTION / Erotica / General
FIC005010 FICTION / Erotica / BDSM *
FIC005020 FICTION / Erotica / Collections & Anthologies *
FIC005030 FICTION / Erotica / Gay *
FIC005040 FICTION / Erotica / Lesbian *
FIC005050 FICTION / Erotica / Science Fiction, Fantasy & Horror *
FIC005060 FICTION / Erotica / Traditional Victorian *
FIC010000 FICTION / Fairy Tales, Folk Tales, Legends & Mythology
FIC045000 FICTION / Family Life
  FICTION / Family Saga see Sagas
FIC009000 FICTION / Fantasy / General
FIC009040 FICTION / Fantasy / Collections & Anthologies
FIC009010 FICTION / Fantasy / Contemporary
FIC009070 FICTION / Fantasy / Dark Fantasy
FIC009020 FICTION / Fantasy / Epic
FIC009030 FICTION / Fantasy / Historical

FIC009080   FICTION / Fantasy / Humorous *
FIC009050   FICTION / Fantasy / Paranormal
FIC009060   FICTION / Fantasy / Urban
    FICTION / Folklore see Fairy Tales, Folk Tales, Legends & Mythology
FIC011000   FICTION / Gay
FIC012000   FICTION / Ghost
FIC027040   FICTION / Gothic
    FICTION / Graphic Novels see headings under COMICS & GRAPHIC NOVELS
FIC056000   FICTION / Hispanic & Latino
FIC014000   FICTION / Historical
FIC058000   FICTION / Holidays
FIC015000   FICTION / Horror
FIC016000   FICTION / Humorous
FIC046000   FICTION / Jewish
FIC034000   FICTION / Legal
FIC018000   FICTION / Lesbian
FIC019000   FICTION / Literary
FIC061000   FICTION / Magical Realism
FIC05700 FICTION / Mashups
FIC021000   FICTION / Media Tie-In
FIC035000   FICTION / Medical
    FICTION / Metaphysical see Visionary & Metaphysical
FIC022000   FICTION / Mystery & Detective / General
FIC022100   FICTION / Mystery & Detective / Amateur Sleuth *
FIC022050   FICTION / Mystery & Detective / Collections & Anthologies
FIC022070   FICTION / Mystery & Detective / Cozy
FIC022010   FICTION / Mystery & Detective / Hard-Boiled
FIC022060   FICTION / Mystery & Detective / Historical
FIC022080   FICTION / Mystery & Detective / International Mystery & Crime
FIC022020   FICTION / Mystery & Detective / Police Procedural
FIC022090   FICTION / Mystery & Detective / Private Investigators
FIC022030   FICTION / Mystery & Detective / Traditional
FIC022040   FICTION / Mystery & Detective / Women Sleuths
    FICTION / Mythology see Fairy Tales, Folk Tales, Legends & Mythology
FIC059000   FICTION / Native American & Aboriginal
FIC062000   FICTION / Noir
FIC024000   FICTION / Occult & Supernatural
FIC037000   FICTION / Political
FIC025000   FICTION / Psychological
FIC026000   FICTION / Religious
FIC027000   FICTION / Romance / General
FIC027260   FICTION / Romance / Action & Adventure *
FIC049060   FICTION / Romance / African American
FIC027270   FICTION / Romance / Clean & Wholesome *
FIC027080   FICTION / Romance / Collections & Anthologies
FIC027020   FICTION / Romance / Contemporary
FIC027010   FICTION / Romance / Erotica
FIC027030   FICTION / Romance / Fantasy
FIC027190   FICTION / Romance / Gay
FIC027050   FICTION / Romance / Historical / General
FIC027140   FICTION / Romance / Historical / Ancient World
FIC027150   FICTION / Romance / Historical / Medieval
FIC027070   FICTION / Romance / Historical / Regency
FIC027160   FICTION / Romance / Historical / Scottish
FIC027200   FICTION / Romance / Historical / 20th Century
FIC027170   FICTION / Romance / Historical / Victorian
FIC027180   FICTION / Romance / Historical / Viking
FIC027210   FICTION / Romance / Lesbian
FIC027220   FICTION / Romance / Military

FIC027230	FICTION / Romance / Multicultural & Interracial
FIC027240	FICTION / Romance / New Adult
FIC027120	FICTION / Romance / Paranormal
FIC027250	FICTION / Romance / Romantic Comedy
FIC027130	FICTION / Romance / Science Fiction
FIC027110	FICTION / Romance / Suspense
FIC027090	FICTION / Romance / Time Travel
FIC027100	FICTION / Romance / Western
FIC008000	FICTION / Sagas
FIC052000	FICTION / Satire
FIC028000	FICTION / Science Fiction / General
FIC028010	FICTION / Science Fiction / Action & Adventure
FIC028090	FICTION / Science Fiction / Alien Contact
FIC028070	FICTION / Science Fiction / Apocalyptic & Post-Apocalyptic
	FICTION / Science Fiction / Alternative History see Alternative History
FIC028040	FICTION / Science Fiction / Collections & Anthologies
FIC028100	FICTION / Science Fiction / Cyberpunk
FIC028110	FICTION / Science Fiction / Genetic Engineering
FIC028020	FICTION / Science Fiction / Hard Science Fiction
FIC028050	FICTION / Science Fiction / Military
FIC028030	FICTION / Science Fiction / Space Opera
FIC028060	FICTION / Science Fiction / Steampunk
FIC028080	FICTION / Science Fiction / Time Travel
FIC047000	FICTION / Sea Stories
	FICTION / Short Stories (multiple authors) see Anthologies (multiple authors)
FIC029000	FICTION / Short Stories (single author)
FIC038000	FICTION / Sports
FIC063000	FICTION / Superheroes
	FICTION / Television Tie-in see Media Tie-In
FIC031000	FICTION / Thrillers / General
FIC031010	FICTION / Thrillers / Crime
FIC006000	FICTION / Thrillers / Espionage
FIC031020	FICTION / Thrillers / Historical
FIC031030	FICTION / Thrillers / Legal
FIC031040	FICTION / Thrillers / Medical
FIC031050	FICTION / Thrillers / Military
FIC031060	FICTION / Thrillers / Political
FIC031080	FICTION / Thrillers / Psychological *
FIC031070	FICTION / Thrillers / Supernatural
FIC030000	FICTION / Thrillers / Suspense
FIC036000	FICTION / Thrillers / Technological
FIC048000	FICTION / Urban
FIC039000	FICTION / Visionary & Metaphysical
FIC032000	FICTION / War & Military
FIC033000	FICTION / Westerns

FOREIGN LANGUAGE STUDY

FOR000000	FOREIGN LANGUAGE STUDY / General
FOR001000	FOREIGN LANGUAGE STUDY / African Languages (see also Swahili)
FOR033000	FOREIGN LANGUAGE STUDY / Ancient Languages (see also Latin)
FOR002000	FOREIGN LANGUAGE STUDY / Arabic
	FOREIGN LANGUAGE STUDY / Australian Languages see Oceanic & Australian Languages
FOR034000	FOREIGN LANGUAGE STUDY / Baltic Languages
FOR029000	FOREIGN LANGUAGE STUDY / Celtic Languages
FOR003000	FOREIGN LANGUAGE STUDY / Chinese
FOR035000	FOREIGN LANGUAGE STUDY / Creole Languages
FOR036000	FOREIGN LANGUAGE STUDY / Czech
FOR004000	FOREIGN LANGUAGE STUDY / Danish

FOR006000	FOREIGN LANGUAGE STUDY / Dutch
FOR007000	FOREIGN LANGUAGE STUDY / English as a Second Language
FOR037000	FOREIGN LANGUAGE STUDY / Finnish
FOR008000	FOREIGN LANGUAGE STUDY / French
FOR009000	FOREIGN LANGUAGE STUDY / German
FOR010000	FOREIGN LANGUAGE STUDY / Greek (Modern)
FOR011000	FOREIGN LANGUAGE STUDY / Hebrew
FOR038000	FOREIGN LANGUAGE STUDY / Hindi
FOR012000	FOREIGN LANGUAGE STUDY / Hungarian
FOR030000	FOREIGN LANGUAGE STUDY / Indic Languages
FOR013000	FOREIGN LANGUAGE STUDY / Italian
FOR014000	FOREIGN LANGUAGE STUDY / Japanese
FOR015000	FOREIGN LANGUAGE STUDY / Korean
FOR016000	FOREIGN LANGUAGE STUDY / Latin
FOR017000	FOREIGN LANGUAGE STUDY / Miscellaneous
FOR005000	FOREIGN LANGUAGE STUDY / Multi-Language Dictionaries
FOR018000	FOREIGN LANGUAGE STUDY / Multi-Language Phrasebooks
FOR031000	FOREIGN LANGUAGE STUDY / Native American Languages
FOR039000	FOREIGN LANGUAGE STUDY / Norwegian
FOR032000	FOREIGN LANGUAGE STUDY / Oceanic & Australian Languages
FOR045000	FOREIGN LANGUAGE STUDY / Old & Middle English
FOR040000	FOREIGN LANGUAGE STUDY / Persian
FOR019000	FOREIGN LANGUAGE STUDY / Polish
FOR020000	FOREIGN LANGUAGE STUDY / Portuguese
FOR041000	FOREIGN LANGUAGE STUDY / Romance Languages (Other)
FOR021000	FOREIGN LANGUAGE STUDY / Russian
FOR022000	FOREIGN LANGUAGE STUDY / Scandinavian Languages (Other)
FOR023000	FOREIGN LANGUAGE STUDY / Serbian & Croatian
FOR024000	FOREIGN LANGUAGE STUDY / Slavic Languages (Other)
FOR025000	FOREIGN LANGUAGE STUDY / Southeast Asian Languages (see also Vietnamese)
FOR026000	FOREIGN LANGUAGE STUDY / Spanish
FOR042000	FOREIGN LANGUAGE STUDY / Swahili
FOR043000	FOREIGN LANGUAGE STUDY / Swedish
FOR027000	FOREIGN LANGUAGE STUDY / Turkish & Turkic Languages
FOR044000	FOREIGN LANGUAGE STUDY / Vietnamese
FOR028000	FOREIGN LANGUAGE STUDY / Yiddish

GAMES

GAM000000	GAMES / General
GAM001010	GAMES / Backgammon
GAM001000	GAMES / Board Games
	GAMES / Bridge see Card Games / Bridge
GAM002000	GAMES / Card Games / General
GAM002030	GAMES / Card Games / Blackjack
GAM002010	GAMES / Card Games / Bridge
GAM002040	GAMES / Card Games / Poker
GAM001030	GAMES / Chess
GAM003000	GAMES / Crosswords / General
GAM003040	GAMES / Crosswords / Dictionaries
	GAMES / Fantasy Games see Role Playing & Fantasy
GAM016000	GAMES / Fantasy Sports
GAM004000	GAMES / Gambling / General (see also SELF-HELP / Compulsive Behavior / Gambling)
	GAMES / Gambling / Card Games see headings under Card Games
GAM004020	GAMES / Gambling / Lotteries
GAM004050	GAMES / Gambling / Sports
GAM004030	GAMES / Gambling / Table
GAM004040	GAMES / Gambling / Track Betting

GAM005000 GAMES / Logic & Brain Teasers
GAM006000 GAMES / Magic
GAM018000 GAMES / Optical Illusions
GAM007000 GAMES / Puzzles
GAM008000 GAMES / Quizzes
GAM009000 GAMES / Reference
GAM010000 GAMES / Role Playing & Fantasy
GAM017000 GAMES / Sudoku
GAM011000 GAMES / Travel Games
GAM012000 GAMES / Trivia
GAM013000 GAMES / Video & Electronic
GAM014000 GAMES / Word & Word Search

GARDENING
GAR000000 GARDENING / General
GAR027000 GARDENING / Climatic / General
GAR027010 GARDENING / Climatic / Desert
GAR027020 GARDENING / Climatic / Temperate
GAR027030 GARDENING / Climatic / Tropical
GAR001000 GARDENING / Container
GAR002000 GARDENING / Essays & Narratives
    GARDENING / Flower Arranging see CRAFTS & HOBBIES / Flower Arranging
GAR004000 GARDENING / Flowers / General
GAR004010 GARDENING / Flowers / Annuals
    GARDENING / Flowers / Azaleas see Shrubs
GAR004030 GARDENING / Flowers / Bulbs
GAR004040 GARDENING / Flowers / Orchids
GAR004050 GARDENING / Flowers / Perennials
GAR004060 GARDENING / Flowers / Roses
    GARDENING / Flowers / Violets see Flowers / Annuals
GAR004080 GARDENING / Flowers / Wildflowers
GAR005000 GARDENING / Fruit
GAR006000 GARDENING / Garden Design
GAR007000 GARDENING / Garden Furnishings
GAR008000 GARDENING / Greenhouses
GAR009000 GARDENING / Herbs
GAR010000 GARDENING / House Plants & Indoor
    GARDENING / Hydroponics see Techniques
    GARDENING / Indoor see House Plants & Indoor
GAR013000 GARDENING / Japanese Gardens
GAR014000 GARDENING / Landscape
GAR015000 GARDENING / Lawns
GAR016000 GARDENING / Organic
GAR017000 GARDENING / Ornamental Plants
GAR018000 GARDENING / Reference
GAR019000 GARDENING / Regional / General
GAR019010 GARDENING / Regional / Canada
GAR019020 GARDENING / Regional / Middle Atlantic (DC, DE, MD, NJ, NY, PA)
GAR019030 GARDENING / Regional / Midwest (IA, IL, IN, KS, MI, MN, MO, ND, NE, OH, SD, WI)
GAR019040 GARDENING / Regional / New England (CT, MA, ME, NH, RI, VT)
GAR019050 GARDENING / Regional / Pacific Northwest (OR, WA)
GAR019060 GARDENING / Regional / South (AL, AR, FL, GA, KY, LA, MS, NC, SC, TN, VA, WV)
GAR019070 GARDENING / Regional / Southwest (AZ, NM, OK, TX)
GAR019080 GARDENING / Regional / West (AK, CA, CO, HI, ID, MT, NV, UT, WY)
GAR020000 GARDENING / Shade
GAR021000 GARDENING / Shrubs

GAR022000 GARDENING / Techniques
GAR023000 GARDENING / Topiary
GAR024000 GARDENING / Trees
GAR028000 GARDENING / Urban
GAR025000 GARDENING / Vegetables
GAR029000 GARDENING / Water Gardens *
     GARDENING / Xeriscaping see Techniques

HEALTH & FITNESS

HEA000000 HEALTH & FITNESS / General
HEA001000 HEALTH & FITNESS / Acupressure & Acupuncture (see also MEDICAL / Acupuncture)
HEA002000 HEALTH & FITNESS / Aerobics
HEA027000 HEALTH & FITNESS / Allergies
HEA032000 HEALTH & FITNESS / Alternative Therapies
HEA029000 HEALTH & FITNESS / Aromatherapy
HEA003000 HEALTH & FITNESS / Beauty & Grooming
HEA047000 HEALTH & FITNESS / Body Cleansing & Detoxification
HEA044000 HEALTH & FITNESS / Breastfeeding
    HEALTH & FITNESS / Childbirth see Pregnancy & Childbirth
HEA046000 HEALTH & FITNESS / Children's Health
HEA048000 HEALTH & FITNESS / Diet & Nutrition / General
HEA006000 HEALTH & FITNESS / Diet & Nutrition / Diets
HEA034000 HEALTH & FITNESS / Diet & Nutrition / Food Content Guides
HEA013000 HEALTH & FITNESS / Diet & Nutrition / Macrobiotics
HEA017000 HEALTH & FITNESS / Diet & Nutrition / Nutrition
HEA023000 HEALTH & FITNESS / Diet & Nutrition / Vitamins
HEA019000 HEALTH & FITNESS / Diet & Nutrition / Weight Loss
HEA039000 HEALTH & FITNESS / Diseases / General
HEA039020 HEALTH & FITNESS / Diseases / AIDS & HIV
HEA039140 HEALTH & FITNESS / Diseases / Alzheimer's & Dementia
    HEALTH & FITNESS / Diseases / Brain see Diseases / Nervous System
HEA039030 HEALTH & FITNESS / Diseases / Cancer
HEA039150 HEALTH & FITNESS / Diseases / Chronic Fatigue Syndrome
HEA039040 HEALTH & FITNESS / Diseases / Contagious
HEA039050 HEALTH & FITNESS / Diseases / Diabetes
HEA039160 HEALTH & FITNESS / Diseases / Endocrine System
HEA039010 HEALTH & FITNESS / Diseases / Gastrointestinal
HEA039060 HEALTH & FITNESS / Diseases / Genetic
HEA039070 HEALTH & FITNESS / Diseases / Genitourinary & STDs
HEA039080 HEALTH & FITNESS / Diseases / Heart
HEA039090 HEALTH & FITNESS / Diseases / Immune & Autoimmune
HEA039100 HEALTH & FITNESS / Diseases / Musculoskeletal
HEA039110 HEALTH & FITNESS / Diseases / Nervous System (incl. Brain)
HEA039120 HEALTH & FITNESS / Diseases / Respiratory
HEA039130 HEALTH & FITNESS / Diseases / Skin
HEA007000 HEALTH & FITNESS / Exercise
HEA033000 HEALTH & FITNESS / First Aid
HEA009000 HEALTH & FITNESS / Healing
HEA028000 HEALTH & FITNESS / Health Care Issues
HEA010000 HEALTH & FITNESS / Healthy Living
HEA035000 HEALTH & FITNESS / Hearing & Speech
HEA011000 HEALTH & FITNESS / Herbal Medications
HEA012000 HEALTH & FITNESS / Holism
HEA030000 HEALTH & FITNESS / Homeopathy
HEA045000 HEALTH & FITNESS / Infertility
HEA049000 HEALTH & FITNESS / Longevity *
HEA014000 HEALTH & FITNESS / Massage & Reflexotherapy
HEA015000 HEALTH & FITNESS / Men's Health

HEA016000	HEALTH & FITNESS / Naturopathy
HEA040000	HEALTH & FITNESS / Oral Health
HEA036000	HEALTH & FITNESS / Pain Management
HEA018000	HEALTH & FITNESS / Physical Impairments
HEA041000	HEALTH & FITNESS / Pregnancy & Childbirth
HEA020000	HEALTH & FITNESS / Reference
	HEALTH & FITNESS / Reflexotherapy see Massage & Reflexotherapy
HEA021000	HEALTH & FITNESS / Safety
HEA042000	HEALTH & FITNESS / Sexuality
HEA043000	HEALTH & FITNESS / Sleep & Sleep Disorders
	HEALTH & FITNESS / Stretching see Exercise
HEA037000	HEALTH & FITNESS / Vision
HEA024000	HEALTH & FITNESS / Women's Health
HEA038000	HEALTH & FITNESS / Work-Related Health
HEA025000	HEALTH & FITNESS / Yoga

HISTORY

HIS000000	HISTORY / General
HIS001000	HISTORY / Africa / General
HIS001010	HISTORY / Africa / Central
HIS001020	HISTORY / Africa / East
	HISTORY / Africa / Egypt see Middle East / Egypt or Ancient / Egypt
HIS001030	HISTORY / Africa / North
HIS001040	HISTORY / Africa / South / General
HIS047000	HISTORY / Africa / South / Republic of South Africa
HIS001050	HISTORY / Africa / West
HIS056000	HISTORY / African American *
HIS038000	HISTORY / Americas (North, Central, South, West Indies)
HIS002000	HISTORY / Ancient / General
HIS002030	HISTORY / Ancient / Egypt
HIS002010	HISTORY / Ancient / Greece
HIS002020	HISTORY / Ancient / Rome
HIS003000	HISTORY / Asia / General
HIS050000	HISTORY / Asia / Central Asia
HIS008000	HISTORY / Asia / China
HIS017000	HISTORY / Asia / India & South Asia
HIS021000	HISTORY / Asia / Japan
HIS023000	HISTORY / Asia / Korea
HIS048000	HISTORY / Asia / Southeast Asia
HIS004000	HISTORY / Australia & New Zealand
HIS006000	HISTORY / Canada / General
HIS006010	HISTORY / Canada / Pre-Confederation (to 1867)
HIS006020	HISTORY / Canada / Post-Confederation (1867-)
HIS041000	HISTORY / Caribbean & West Indies / General
HIS041010	HISTORY / Caribbean & West Indies / Cuba
HIS039000	HISTORY / Civilization
HIS049000	HISTORY / Essays
HIS010000	HISTORY / Europe / General
HIS040000	HISTORY / Europe / Austria & Hungary
HIS005000	HISTORY / Europe / Baltic States
HIS010010	HISTORY / Europe / Eastern
HIS012000	HISTORY / Europe / Former Soviet Republics
HIS013000	HISTORY / Europe / France
HIS014000	HISTORY / Europe / Germany
HIS015000	HISTORY / Europe / Great Britain
HIS042000	HISTORY / Europe / Greece (see also Ancient / Greece)
	HISTORY / Europe / Hungary see Europe / Austria & Hungary
HIS018000	HISTORY / Europe / Ireland
HIS020000	HISTORY / Europe / Italy

HISTORY / Europe / Portugal see Europe / Spain & Portugal
HIS032000   HISTORY / Europe / Russia & the Former Soviet Union
HIS044000   HISTORY / Europe / Scandinavia
    HISTORY / Europe / Soviet Union see Europe / Russia & the Former Soviet Union
HIS045000   HISTORY / Europe / Spain & Portugal
HIS010020   HISTORY / Europe / Western
HIS051000   HISTORY / Expeditions & Discoveries
    HISTORY / Far East see headings under Asia
HIS052000   HISTORY / Historical Geography
HIS016000   HISTORY / Historiography
HIS043000   HISTORY / Holocaust
HIS022000   HISTORY / Jewish
    HISTORY / Labor see POLITICAL SCIENCE / Labor & Industrial Relations
HIS024000   HISTORY / Latin America / General
HIS007000   HISTORY / Latin America / Central America
HIS025000   HISTORY / Latin America / Mexico
HIS033000   HISTORY / Latin America / South America
HIS057000   HISTORY / Maritime History & Piracy *
HIS037010   HISTORY / Medieval
HIS026000   HISTORY / Middle East / General
HIS026010   HISTORY / Middle East / Arabian Peninsula
HIS009000   HISTORY / Middle East / Egypt (see also Ancient / Egypt)
HIS026020   HISTORY / Middle East / Iran
HIS026030   HISTORY / Middle East / Iraq
HIS019000   HISTORY / Middle East / Israel & Palestine
HIS055000   HISTORY / Middle East / Turkey & Ottoman Empire
HIS027000   HISTORY / Military / General
HIS027190   HISTORY / Military / Afghan War (2001-)
HIS027140   HISTORY / Military / Aviation
HIS027010   HISTORY / Military / Biological & Chemical Warfare
HIS027160   HISTORY / Military / Canada
HIS027170   HISTORY / Military / Iraq War (2003-2011)
HIS027020   HISTORY / Military / Korean War
HIS027200   HISTORY / Military / Napoleonic Wars *
HIS027150   HISTORY / Military / Naval
HIS027030   HISTORY / Military / Nuclear Warfare
HIS027040   HISTORY / Military / Persian Gulf War (1991)
HIS027050   HISTORY / Military / Pictorial
HIS027180   HISTORY / Military / Special Forces
HIS027060   HISTORY / Military / Strategy
HIS027110   HISTORY / Military / United States
    HISTORY / Military / United States / Civil War see United States / Civil War Period
(1850-1877)
HIS027120   HISTORY / Military / Veterans
HIS027070   HISTORY / Military / Vietnam War
HIS027210   HISTORY / Military / War of 1812 *
HIS027080   HISTORY / Military / Weapons
HIS027090   HISTORY / Military / World War I
HIS027100   HISTORY / Military / World War II
HIS027130   HISTORY / Military / Other
HIS037030   HISTORY / Modern / General
HIS037090   HISTORY / Modern / 16th Century
HIS037040   HISTORY / Modern / 17th Century
HIS037050   HISTORY / Modern / 18th Century
HIS037060   HISTORY / Modern / 19th Century
HIS037070   HISTORY / Modern / 20th Century
HIS037080   HISTORY / Modern / 21st Century
HIS028000   HISTORY / Native American
HIS029000   HISTORY / North America

HIS053000	HISTORY / Oceania
HIS046000	HISTORY / Polar Regions
HIS030000	HISTORY / Reference
HIS037020	HISTORY / Renaissance
HIS031000	HISTORY / Revolutionary
HIS054000	HISTORY / Social History
HIS035000	HISTORY / Study & Teaching
HIS036000	HISTORY / United States / General
HIS036020	HISTORY / United States / Colonial Period (1600-1775)
HIS036030	HISTORY / United States / Revolutionary Period (1775-1800)
HIS036040	HISTORY / United States / 19th Century
HIS036050	HISTORY / United States / Civil War Period (1850-1877)
HIS036060	HISTORY / United States / 20th Century
HIS036070	HISTORY / United States / 21st Century
HIS036010	HISTORY / United States / State & Local / General

HIS036080 HISTORY / United States / State & Local / Middle Atlantic (DC, DE, MD, NJ, NY, PA)

HIS036090 HISTORY / United States / State & Local / Midwest (IA, IL, IN, KS, MI, MN, MO, ND, NE, OH, SD, WI)

HIS036100 HISTORY / United States / State & Local / New England (CT, MA, ME, NH, RI, VT)

HIS036110 HISTORY / United States / State & Local / Pacific Northwest (OR, WA)

HIS036120 HISTORY / United States / State & Local / South (AL, AR, FL, GA, KY, LA, MS, NC, SC, TN, VA, WV)

HIS036130 HISTORY / United States / State & Local / Southwest (AZ, NM, OK, TX)

HIS036140 HISTORY / United States / State & Local / West (AK, CA, CO, HI, ID, MT, NV, UT, WY)

HISTORY / West Indies see headings under Caribbean & West Indies

HIS058000	HISTORY / Women *
HIS037000	HISTORY / World

HISTORY / World / Ancient see headings under Ancient

HISTORY / World / Medieval see Medieval

HISTORY / World / Renaissance see Renaissance

HISTORY / World / Modern see headings under Modern

HOUSE & HOME

HOM000000	HOUSE & HOME / General
HOM019000	HOUSE & HOME / Cleaning, Caretaking & Organizing

HOUSE & HOME / Contracting see TECHNOLOGY & ENGINEERING / Construction / Contracting

HOM003000	HOUSE & HOME / Decorating
HOM004000	HOUSE & HOME / Design & Construction
HOM005000	HOUSE & HOME / Do-It-Yourself / General
HOM001000	HOUSE & HOME / Do-It-Yourself / Carpentry
HOM006000	HOUSE & HOME / Do-It-Yourself / Electrical
HOM012000	HOUSE & HOME / Do-It-Yourself / Masonry
HOM014000	HOUSE & HOME / Do-It-Yourself / Plumbing
HOM020000	HOUSE & HOME / Equipment, Appliances & Supplies

HOUSE & HOME / Estimating see TECHNOLOGY & ENGINEERING / Construction / Estimating

HOM008000	HOUSE & HOME / Furniture
HOM009000	HOUSE & HOME / Hand Tools
HOM011000	HOUSE & HOME / House Plans
HOM013000	HOUSE & HOME / Outdoor & Recreational Areas
HOM015000	HOUSE & HOME / Power Tools
HOM016000	HOUSE & HOME / Reference
HOM017000	HOUSE & HOME / Remodeling & Renovation

HOM010000   HOUSE & HOME / Repair
HOM021000   HOUSE & HOME / Security
HOM022000   HOUSE & HOME / Sustainable Living
HOM018000   HOUSE & HOME / Woodworking

HUMOR

HUM000000   HUMOR / General
HUM015000   HUMOR / Form / Anecdotes & Quotations
HUM001000   HUMOR / Form / Comic Strips & Cartoons
HUM003000   HUMOR / Form / Essays
HUM004000   HUMOR / Form / Jokes & Riddles
HUM005000   HUMOR / Form / Limericks & Verse
HUM007000   HUMOR / Form / Parodies
HUM017000   HUMOR / Form / Pictorial
HUM018000   HUMOR / Form / Puns & Word Play
HUM016000   HUMOR / Form / Trivia
HUM008000   HUMOR / Topic / Adult
HUM009000   HUMOR / Topic / Animals
HUM010000   HUMOR / Topic / Business & Professional
HUM019000   HUMOR / Topic / Language
HUM011000   HUMOR / Topic / Marriage & Family
HUM006000   HUMOR / Topic / Political
HUM012000   HUMOR / Topic / Relationships
HUM014000   HUMOR / Topic / Religion
HUM013000   HUMOR / Topic / Sports

JUV000000   JUVENILE FICTION / General
JUV001000   JUVENILE FICTION / Action & Adventure / General
JUV001020   JUVENILE FICTION / Action & Adventure / Pirates
JUV001010   JUVENILE FICTION / Action & Adventure / Survival Stories
JUV054000   JUVENILE FICTION / Activity Books
JUV002000   JUVENILE FICTION / Animals / General
JUV002010   JUVENILE FICTION / Animals / Alligators & Crocodiles
JUV002020   JUVENILE FICTION / Animals / Apes, Monkeys, etc.
JUV002370   JUVENILE FICTION / Animals / Baby Animals
JUV002030   JUVENILE FICTION / Animals / Bears
JUV002040   JUVENILE FICTION / Animals / Birds
JUV002300   JUVENILE FICTION / Animals / Butterflies, Moths & Caterpillars
JUV002050   JUVENILE FICTION / Animals / Cats
JUV002310   JUVENILE FICTION / Animals / Cows
JUV002290   JUVENILE FICTION / Animals / Deer, Moose & Caribou
JUV002060   JUVENILE FICTION / Animals / Dinosaurs & Prehistoric Creatures
JUV002070   JUVENILE FICTION / Animals / Dogs
JUV002270   JUVENILE FICTION / Animals / Dragons, Unicorns & Mythical
JUV002280   JUVENILE FICTION / Animals / Ducks, Geese, etc.
JUV002080   JUVENILE FICTION / Animals / Elephants
JUV002090   JUVENILE FICTION / Animals / Farm Animals
JUV002100   JUVENILE FICTION / Animals / Fishes
JUV002110   JUVENILE FICTION / Animals / Foxes
JUV002120   JUVENILE FICTION / Animals / Frogs & Toads
JUV002320   JUVENILE FICTION / Animals / Giraffes
JUV002330   JUVENILE FICTION / Animals / Hippos & Rhinos
JUV002130   JUVENILE FICTION / Animals / Horses
JUV002140   JUVENILE FICTION / Animals / Insects, Spiders, etc.
JUV002340   JUVENILE FICTION / Animals / Jungle Animals
JUV002350   JUVENILE FICTION / Animals / Kangaroos

JUV002150   JUVENILE FICTION / Animals / Lions, Tigers, Leopards, etc.
JUV002160   JUVENILE FICTION / Animals / Mammals
JUV002170   JUVENILE FICTION / Animals / Marine Life
JUV002180   JUVENILE FICTION / Animals / Mice, Hamsters, Guinea Pigs, etc.
JUV002360   JUVENILE FICTION / Animals / Nocturnal
JUV002190   JUVENILE FICTION / Animals / Pets
JUV002200   JUVENILE FICTION / Animals / Pigs
JUV002210   JUVENILE FICTION / Animals / Rabbits
JUV002220   JUVENILE FICTION / Animals / Reptiles & Amphibians
JUV002230   JUVENILE FICTION / Animals / Squirrels
JUV002240   JUVENILE FICTION / Animals / Turtles
JUV002250   JUVENILE FICTION / Animals / Wolves & Coyotes
JUV002260   JUVENILE FICTION / Animals / Zoos
JUV003000   JUVENILE FICTION / Art & Architecture
JUV010000   JUVENILE FICTION / Bedtime & Dreams
JUV004000   JUVENILE FICTION / Biographical / General
JUV004040   JUVENILE FICTION / Biographical / Canada
JUV004010   JUVENILE FICTION / Biographical / European
JUV004020   JUVENILE FICTION / Biographical / United States
JUV004030   JUVENILE FICTION / Biographical / Other
JUV047000   JUVENILE FICTION / Books & Libraries
JUV005000   JUVENILE FICTION / Boys & Men
JUV006000   JUVENILE FICTION / Business, Careers, Occupations
               JUVENILE FICTION / Celebrations see headings under Holidays & Celebrations
               JUVENILE FICTION / Circus see Performing Arts / Circus
               JUVENILE FICTION / City Life see Lifestyles / City & Town Life
JUV007000   JUVENILE FICTION / Classics
JUV048000   JUVENILE FICTION / Clothing & Dress
JUV008000   JUVENILE FICTION / Comics & Graphic Novels / General
JUV008010   JUVENILE FICTION / Comics & Graphic Novels / Manga
JUV008030   JUVENILE FICTION / Comics & Graphic Novels / Media Tie-In
JUV008020   JUVENILE FICTION / Comics & Graphic Novels / Superheroes
JUV049000   JUVENILE FICTION / Computers
JUV009000   JUVENILE FICTION / Concepts / General
JUV009010   JUVENILE FICTION / Concepts / Alphabet
JUV009120   JUVENILE FICTION / Concepts / Body
JUV009020   JUVENILE FICTION / Concepts / Colors
JUV009030   JUVENILE FICTION / Concepts / Counting & Numbers
JUV009070   JUVENILE FICTION / Concepts / Date & Time
JUV009090   JUVENILE FICTION / Concepts / Money
JUV009040   JUVENILE FICTION / Concepts / Opposites
JUV009100   JUVENILE FICTION / Concepts / Seasons
JUV009050   JUVENILE FICTION / Concepts / Senses & Sensation
JUV009060   JUVENILE FICTION / Concepts / Size & Shape
JUV009110   JUVENILE FICTION / Concepts / Sounds
JUV009080   JUVENILE FICTION / Concepts / Words
JUV050000   JUVENILE FICTION / Cooking & Food
               JUVENILE FICTION / Country Life see Lifestyles / Country Life
               JUVENILE FICTION / Crime see Law & Crime
               JUVENILE FICTION / Detective Stories see Mysteries & Detective Stories
               JUVENILE FICTION / Dolls see Toys, Dolls & Puppets
               JUVENILE FICTION / Dreams see Bedtime & Dreams
JUV059000   JUVENILE FICTION / Dystopian
               JUVENILE FICTION / Education see School & Education
               JUVENILE FICTION / Ethnic see headings under People & Places
               JUVENILE FICTION / Fables see headings under Legends, Myths, Fables
JUV012030   JUVENILE FICTION / Fairy Tales & Folklore / General
JUV012040   JUVENILE FICTION / Fairy Tales & Folklore / Adaptations
JUV012000   JUVENILE FICTION / Fairy Tales & Folklore / Anthologies

JUV012020 JUVENILE FICTION / Fairy Tales & Folklore / Country & Ethnic
JUV013000 JUVENILE FICTION / Family / General (see also headings under Social Issues)
 JUVENILE FICTION / Family / Abuse see Social Issues / Physical & Emotional Abuse or Social Issues / Sexual Abuse
JUV013010 JUVENILE FICTION / Family / Adoption
JUV013090 JUVENILE FICTION / Family / Alternative Family
JUV013020 JUVENILE FICTION / Family / Marriage & Divorce
JUV013030 JUVENILE FICTION / Family / Multigenerational
JUV013040 JUVENILE FICTION / Family / New Baby
JUV013050 JUVENILE FICTION / Family / Orphans & Foster Homes
JUV013060 JUVENILE FICTION / Family / Parents
JUV013070 JUVENILE FICTION / Family / Siblings
JUV013080 JUVENILE FICTION / Family / Stepfamilies
JUV037000 JUVENILE FICTION / Fantasy & Magic
 JUVENILE FICTION / Farm Life see Lifestyles / Farm & Ranch Life
 JUVENILE FICTION / Folklore see headings under Fairy Tales & Folklore
 JUVENILE FICTION / Games see Sports & Recreation / Games
 JUVENILE FICTION / Ghost Stories see Horror & Ghost Stories
JUV014000 JUVENILE FICTION / Girls & Women
 JUVENILE FICTION / Graphic Novels see headings under Comics & Graphic Novels
JUV015000 JUVENILE FICTION / Health & Daily Living / General
JUV015010 JUVENILE FICTION / Health & Daily Living / Daily Activities
 JUVENILE FICTION / Health & Daily Living / Depression & Mental Illness see Social Issues / Depression & Mental Illness
JUV015020 JUVENILE FICTION / Health & Daily Living / Diseases, Illnesses & Injuries
JUV039170 JUVENILE FICTION / Health & Daily Living / Toilet Training
JUV016000 JUVENILE FICTION / Historical / General
JUV016010 JUVENILE FICTION / Historical / Africa
JUV016020 JUVENILE FICTION / Historical / Ancient Civilizations
JUV016030 JUVENILE FICTION / Historical / Asia
JUV016160 JUVENILE FICTION / Historical / Canada / General
JUV016170 JUVENILE FICTION / Historical / Canada / Pre-Confederation (to 1867)
JUV016180 JUVENILE FICTION / Historical / Canada / Post-Confederation (1867-)
JUV016040 JUVENILE FICTION / Historical / Europe
JUV016050 JUVENILE FICTION / Historical / Exploration & Discovery
JUV016060 JUVENILE FICTION / Historical / Holocaust
JUV016070 JUVENILE FICTION / Historical / Medieval
JUV016210 JUVENILE FICTION / Historical / Middle East
JUV016080 JUVENILE FICTION / Historical / Military & Wars
JUV016090 JUVENILE FICTION / Historical / Prehistory
JUV016100 JUVENILE FICTION / Historical / Renaissance
JUV016110 JUVENILE FICTION / Historical / United States / General
JUV016120 JUVENILE FICTION / Historical / United States / Colonial & Revolutionary Periods
JUV016140 JUVENILE FICTION / Historical / United States / 19th Century
JUV016200 JUVENILE FICTION / Historical / United States / Civil War Period (1850-1877)
JUV016150 JUVENILE FICTION / Historical / United States / 20th Century
JUV016190 JUVENILE FICTION / Historical / United States / 21st Century
JUV016130 JUVENILE FICTION / Historical / Other
JUV017000 JUVENILE FICTION / Holidays & Celebrations / General (see also Religious / Christian / Holidays & Celebrations)
JUV017100 JUVENILE FICTION / Holidays & Celebrations / Birthdays
JUV017010 JUVENILE FICTION / Holidays & Celebrations / Christmas & Advent
JUV017020 JUVENILE FICTION / Holidays & Celebrations / Easter & Lent

JUV017030   JUVENILE FICTION / Holidays & Celebrations / Halloween
JUV017110   JUVENILE FICTION / Holidays & Celebrations / Hanukkah
JUV017050   JUVENILE FICTION / Holidays & Celebrations / Kwanzaa
JUV017120   JUVENILE FICTION / Holidays & Celebrations / Passover
JUV017130   JUVENILE FICTION / Holidays & Celebrations / Patriotic Holidays
JUV017060   JUVENILE FICTION / Holidays & Celebrations / Thanksgiving
JUV017070   JUVENILE FICTION / Holidays & Celebrations / Valentine's Day
JUV017080   JUVENILE FICTION / Holidays & Celebrations / Other, Non-Religious
JUV017090   JUVENILE FICTION / Holidays & Celebrations / Other, Religious
JUV018000   JUVENILE FICTION / Horror & Ghost Stories
JUV019000   JUVENILE FICTION / Humorous Stories
JUV051000   JUVENILE FICTION / Imagination & Play
JUV020000   JUVENILE FICTION / Interactive Adventures
JUV021000   JUVENILE FICTION / Law & Crime
JUV022000   JUVENILE FICTION / Legends, Myths, Fables / General
JUV012050   JUVENILE FICTION / Legends, Myths, Fables / African *
JUV022010   JUVENILE FICTION / Legends, Myths, Fables / Arthurian
JUV012060   JUVENILE FICTION / Legends, Myths, Fables / Asian *
JUV012070   JUVENILE FICTION / Legends, Myths, Fables / Caribbean & Latin
American *
JUV022020   JUVENILE FICTION / Legends, Myths, Fables / Greek & Roman
JUV012080   JUVENILE FICTION / Legends, Myths, Fables / Native American *
JUV022030   JUVENILE FICTION / Legends, Myths, Fables / Norse
JUV022040   JUVENILE FICTION / Legends, Myths, Fables / Other
JUV060000   JUVENILE FICTION / LGBT
JUV023000   JUVENILE FICTION / Lifestyles / City & Town Life
JUV024000   JUVENILE FICTION / Lifestyles / Country Life
JUV025000   JUVENILE FICTION / Lifestyles / Farm & Ranch Life
JUV065000   JUVENILE FICTION / Light Novel (Ranobe) *
JUV026000   JUVENILE FICTION / Love & Romance
           JUVENILE FICTION / Magic see Fantasy & Magic
JUV027000   JUVENILE FICTION / Media Tie-In
           JUVENILE FICTION / Medicine see headings under Health & Daily Living
           JUVENILE FICTION / Men see Boys & Men
JUV066000   JUVENILE FICTION / Mermaids *
JUV052000   JUVENILE FICTION / Monsters
           JUVENILE FICTION / Music see Performing Arts / Music
JUV028000   JUVENILE FICTION / Mysteries & Detective Stories
           JUVENILE FICTION / Myths see headings under Legends, Myths, Fables
JUV029000   JUVENILE FICTION / Nature & the Natural World / General (see also
headings under Animals)
JUV029010   JUVENILE FICTION / Nature & the Natural World / Environment
JUV029020   JUVENILE FICTION / Nature & the Natural World / Weather
           JUVENILE FICTION / Night see Bedtime & Dreams
JUV055000   JUVENILE FICTION / Nursery Rhymes
           JUVENILE FICTION / Occupations see Business, Careers, Occupations
JUV058000   JUVENILE FICTION / Paranormal
JUV030000   JUVENILE FICTION / People & Places / General
JUV030010   JUVENILE FICTION / People & Places / Africa
JUV030020   JUVENILE FICTION / People & Places / Asia
JUV030080   JUVENILE FICTION / People & Places / Australia & Oceania
JUV030030   JUVENILE FICTION / People & Places / Canada / General
JUV030090   JUVENILE FICTION / People & Places / Canada / Native Canadian
JUV030040   JUVENILE FICTION / People & Places / Caribbean & Latin America
JUV030050   JUVENILE FICTION / People & Places / Europe
JUV030100   JUVENILE FICTION / People & Places / Mexico
JUV030110   JUVENILE FICTION / People & Places / Middle East
JUV030120   JUVENILE FICTION / People & Places / Polar Regions
JUV030060   JUVENILE FICTION / People & Places / United States / General

JUV011010   JUVENILE FICTION / People & Places / United States / African American
JUV011020   JUVENILE FICTION / People & Places / United States / Asian American
JUV011030   JUVENILE FICTION / People & Places / United States / Hispanic & Latino
JUV011040   JUVENILE FICTION / People & Places / United States / Native American
JUV011050   JUVENILE FICTION / People & Places / United States / Other
JUV030070   JUVENILE FICTION / People & Places / Other
JUV031000   JUVENILE FICTION / Performing Arts / General
JUV031010   JUVENILE FICTION / Performing Arts / Circus
JUV031020   JUVENILE FICTION / Performing Arts / Dance
JUV031030   JUVENILE FICTION / Performing Arts / Film
JUV031040   JUVENILE FICTION / Performing Arts / Music
JUV031050   JUVENILE FICTION / Performing Arts / Television & Radio
JUV031060   JUVENILE FICTION / Performing Arts / Theater
            JUVENILE FICTION / Play see Imagination & Play
            JUVENILE FICTION / Poetry see Stories in Verse or headings under JUVENILE NONFICTION / Poetry
JUV061000   JUVENILE FICTION / Politics & Government
            JUVENILE FICTION / Puppets see Toys, Dolls & Puppets
JUV043000   JUVENILE FICTION / Readers / Beginner
JUV044000   JUVENILE FICTION / Readers / Intermediate
JUV045000   JUVENILE FICTION / Readers / Chapter Books
            JUVENILE FICTION / Recreation see headings under Sports & Recreation
JUV063000   JUVENILE FICTION / Recycling & Green Living
JUV033000   JUVENILE FICTION / Religious / General
JUV033010   JUVENILE FICTION / Religious / Christian / General
JUV033040   JUVENILE FICTION / Religious / Christian / Action & Adventure
JUV033050   JUVENILE FICTION / Religious / Christian / Animals
JUV033060   JUVENILE FICTION / Religious / Christian / Bedtime & Dreams
JUV033070   JUVENILE FICTION / Religious / Christian / Comics & Graphic Novels
JUV033080   JUVENILE FICTION / Religious / Christian / Early Readers
JUV033090   JUVENILE FICTION / Religious / Christian / Emotions & Feelings
JUV033100   JUVENILE FICTION / Religious / Christian / Family
JUV033110   JUVENILE FICTION / Religious / Christian / Fantasy
JUV033120   JUVENILE FICTION / Religious / Christian / Friendship
JUV033140   JUVENILE FICTION / Religious / Christian / Historical
JUV033150   JUVENILE FICTION / Religious / Christian / Holidays & Celebrations
JUV033160   JUVENILE FICTION / Religious / Christian / Humorous
JUV033170   JUVENILE FICTION / Religious / Christian / Learning Concepts
JUV033180   JUVENILE FICTION / Religious / Christian / Mysteries & Detective Stories
JUV033190   JUVENILE FICTION / Religious / Christian / People & Places
JUV033200   JUVENILE FICTION / Religious / Christian / Relationships
JUV033210   JUVENILE FICTION / Religious / Christian / Science Fiction
JUV033220   JUVENILE FICTION / Religious / Christian / Social Issues
JUV033230   JUVENILE FICTION / Religious / Christian / Sports & Recreation
JUV033240   JUVENILE FICTION / Religious / Christian / Values & Virtues
JUV033020   JUVENILE FICTION / Religious / Jewish
JUV033030   JUVENILE FICTION / Religious / Other
JUV056000   JUVENILE FICTION / Robots
            JUVENILE FICTION / Romance see Love & Romance
JUV034000   JUVENILE FICTION / Royalty
JUV035000   JUVENILE FICTION / School & Education
JUV036000   JUVENILE FICTION / Science & Technology
JUV053000   JUVENILE FICTION / Science Fiction

JUV038000   JUVENILE FICTION / Short Stories
JUVENILE FICTION / Sleeping see Bedtime & Dreams
JUV039000   JUVENILE FICTION / Social Issues / General (see also headings under Family)
JUVENILE FICTION / Social Issues / Abuse see Social Issues / Physical & Emotional Abuse or Social Issues / Sexual Abuse
JUV039020   JUVENILE FICTION / Social Issues / Adolescence
JUVENILE FICTION
JUV039230   JUVENILE FICTION / Social Issues / Bullying
JUV039190   JUVENILE FICTION / Social Issues / Dating & Sex
JUV039030   JUVENILE FICTION / Social Issues / Death & Dying
JUV039240   JUVENILE FICTION / Social Issues / Depression & Mental Illness
JUV039040   JUVENILE FICTION / Social Issues / Drugs, Alcohol, Substance Abuse
JUV039250   JUVENILE FICTION / Social Issues / Emigration & Immigration
JUV039050   JUVENILE FICTION / Social Issues / Emotions & Feelings
JUV039060   JUVENILE FICTION / Social Issues / Friendship
JUV039070   JUVENILE FICTION / Social Issues / Homelessness & Poverty
JUV039080   JUVENILE FICTION / Social Issues / Homosexuality
JUV039200   JUVENILE FICTION / Social Issues / Manners & Etiquette
JUV039090   JUVENILE FICTION / Social Issues / New Experience
JUV039100   JUVENILE FICTION / Social Issues / Peer Pressure
JUV039010   JUVENILE FICTION / Social Issues / Physical & Emotional Abuse (see also Social Issues / Sexual Abuse)
JUV039110   JUVENILE FICTION / Social Issues / Pregnancy
JUV039120   JUVENILE FICTION / Social Issues / Prejudice & Racism
JUV039130   JUVENILE FICTION / Social Issues / Runaways
JUV039140   JUVENILE FICTION / Social Issues / Self-Esteem & Self-Reliance
JUV039260   JUVENILE FICTION / Social Issues / Self-Mutilation
JUV039210   JUVENILE FICTION / Social Issues / Sexual Abuse
JUVENILE FICTION / Social Issues / Sexuality see Social Issues / Dating & Sex
JUV039150   JUVENILE FICTION / Social Issues / Special Needs
JUV039270   JUVENILE FICTION / Social Issues / Strangers
JUVENILE FICTION / Social Issues / Substance Abuse see Social Issues / Drugs, Alcohol, Substance Abuse
JUV039160   JUVENILE FICTION / Social Issues / Suicide
JUV039220   JUVENILE FICTION / Social Issues / Values & Virtues
JUV039180   JUVENILE FICTION / Social Issues / Violence
JUV032000   JUVENILE FICTION / Sports & Recreation / General
JUV032010   JUVENILE FICTION / Sports & Recreation / Baseball & Softball
JUV032020   JUVENILE FICTION / Sports & Recreation / Basketball
JUV032170   JUVENILE FICTION / Sports & Recreation / Camping & Outdoor Activities
JUV032180   JUVENILE FICTION / Sports & Recreation / Cycling
JUV032090   JUVENILE FICTION / Sports & Recreation / Equestrian
JUV032100   JUVENILE FICTION / Sports & Recreation / Extreme Sports
JUV032030   JUVENILE FICTION / Sports & Recreation / Football
JUV032040   JUVENILE FICTION / Sports & Recreation / Games
JUV032190   JUVENILE FICTION / Sports & Recreation / Golf
JUV032110   JUVENILE FICTION / Sports & Recreation / Hockey
JUV032120   JUVENILE FICTION / Sports & Recreation / Ice Skating
JUV032070   JUVENILE FICTION / Sports & Recreation / Martial Arts
JUV032140   JUVENILE FICTION / Sports & Recreation / Skateboarding
JUV032150   JUVENILE FICTION / Sports & Recreation / Soccer
JUV032060   JUVENILE FICTION / Sports & Recreation / Water Sports
JUV032080   JUVENILE FICTION / Sports & Recreation / Winter Sports
JUV032160   JUVENILE FICTION / Sports & Recreation / Wrestling
JUV062000   JUVENILE FICTION / Steampunk
JUV057000   JUVENILE FICTION / Stories in Verse
JUVENILE FICTION / Technology see Science & Technology

JUVENILE FICTION / Television Tie-In see Media Tie-In
JUV067000   JUVENILE FICTION / Thrillers & Suspense *
JUV064000   JUVENILE FICTION / Time Travel
JUVENILE FICTION / Town Life see Lifestyles / City & Town Life
JUV040000   JUVENILE FICTION / Toys, Dolls & Puppets
JUV041000   JUVENILE FICTION / Transportation / General
JUV041010   JUVENILE FICTION / Transportation / Aviation
JUV041020   JUVENILE FICTION / Transportation / Boats, Ships & Underwater
Craft
JUV041030   JUVENILE FICTION / Transportation / Cars & Trucks
JUV041040   JUVENILE FICTION / Transportation / Motorcycles
JUV041050   JUVENILE FICTION / Transportation / Railroads & Trains
JUV068000   JUVENILE FICTION / Travel *
JUV046000   JUVENILE FICTION / Visionary & Metaphysical
JUV042000   JUVENILE FICTION / Westerns
JUVENILE FICTION / Women see Girls & Women
JUVENILE FICTION / Work see Business, Careers, Occupations

JUVENILE NONFICTION
JNF000000   JUVENILE NONFICTION / General
JUVENILE NONFICTION / Activities see headings under Games & Activities
JNF001000   JUVENILE NONFICTION / Activity Books
JNF002000   JUVENILE NONFICTION / Adventure & Adventurers
JUVENILE NONFICTION / Alphabet see Concepts / Alphabet
JNF003000   JUVENILE NONFICTION / Animals / General
JNF003220   JUVENILE NONFICTION / Animals / Animal Welfare
JNF003010   JUVENILE NONFICTION / Animals / Apes, Monkeys, etc.
JNF003330   JUVENILE NONFICTION / Animals / Baby Animals
JNF003020   JUVENILE NONFICTION / Animals / Bears
JNF003030   JUVENILE NONFICTION / Animals / Birds
JNF003250   JUVENILE NONFICTION / Animals / Butterflies, Moths & Caterpillars
JNF003040   JUVENILE NONFICTION / Animals / Cats
JNF003260   JUVENILE NONFICTION / Animals / Cows
JNF003230   JUVENILE NONFICTION / Animals / Deer, Moose & Caribou
JNF003050   JUVENILE NONFICTION / Animals / Dinosaurs & Prehistoric
Creatures
JNF003060   JUVENILE NONFICTION / Animals / Dogs
JNF003210   JUVENILE NONFICTION / Animals / Ducks, Geese, etc.
JNF003070   JUVENILE NONFICTION / Animals / Elephants
JNF003270   JUVENILE NONFICTION / Animals / Endangered
JNF003080   JUVENILE NONFICTION / Animals / Farm Animals
JNF003090   JUVENILE NONFICTION / Animals / Fishes
JNF003100   JUVENILE NONFICTION / Animals / Foxes
JNF003280   JUVENILE NONFICTION / Animals / Giraffes
JNF003290   JUVENILE NONFICTION / Animals / Hippos & Rhinos
JNF003110   JUVENILE NONFICTION / Animals / Horses
JNF003120   JUVENILE NONFICTION / Animals / Insects, Spiders, etc.
JNF003300   JUVENILE NONFICTION / Animals / Jungle Animals
JNF003310   JUVENILE NONFICTION / Animals / Kangaroos
JNF003130   JUVENILE NONFICTION / Animals / Lions, Tigers, Leopards, etc.
JNF003140   JUVENILE NONFICTION / Animals / Mammals
JNF003150   JUVENILE NONFICTION / Animals / Marine Life
JNF003160   JUVENILE NONFICTION / Animals / Mice, Hamsters, Guinea Pigs,
Squirrels, etc.
JNF003320   JUVENILE NONFICTION / Animals / Nocturnal
JNF003170   JUVENILE NONFICTION / Animals / Pets
JNF003180   JUVENILE NONFICTION / Animals / Rabbits
JNF003190   JUVENILE NONFICTION / Animals / Reptiles & Amphibians

JNF003240   JUVENILE NONFICTION / Animals / Wolves & Coyotes
JNF003200   JUVENILE NONFICTION / Animals / Zoos
JNF004000   JUVENILE NONFICTION / Antiques & Collectibles
JNF005000   JUVENILE NONFICTION / Architecture
JNF006000   JUVENILE NONFICTION / Art / General
JNF006010   JUVENILE NONFICTION / Art / Cartooning
JNF006020   JUVENILE NONFICTION / Art / Drawing
JNF006030   JUVENILE NONFICTION / Art / Fashion
JNF006040   JUVENILE NONFICTION / Art / History
JNF006050   JUVENILE NONFICTION / Art / Painting
JNF006060   JUVENILE NONFICTION / Art / Sculpture
JNF006070   JUVENILE NONFICTION / Art / Techniques
JNF007000   JUVENILE NONFICTION / Biography & Autobiography / General
JNF007010   JUVENILE NONFICTION / Biography & Autobiography / Art
JNF007050   JUVENILE NONFICTION / Biography & Autobiography / Cultural
Heritage
JNF007020   JUVENILE NONFICTION / Biography & Autobiography / Historical
JNF007030   JUVENILE NONFICTION / Biography & Autobiography / Literary
JNF007040   JUVENILE NONFICTION / Biography & Autobiography / Music
    JUVENILE NONFICTION / Biography & Autobiography / People of Color see
Biography & Autobiography / Cultural Heritage
JNF007060   JUVENILE NONFICTION / Biography & Autobiography / Performing
Arts
JNF007070   JUVENILE NONFICTION / Biography & Autobiography / Political
JNF007130   JUVENILE NONFICTION / Biography & Autobiography / Presidents
and First Families (U.S.)
JNF007080   JUVENILE NONFICTION / Biography & Autobiography / Religious
(see also Religious / Christian / Biography & Autobiography)
JNF007140   JUVENILE NONFICTION / Biography & Autobiography / Royalty
JNF007090   JUVENILE NONFICTION / Biography & Autobiography / Science &
Technology
JNF007110   JUVENILE NONFICTION / Biography & Autobiography / Social
Activists
JNF007100   JUVENILE NONFICTION / Biography & Autobiography / Sports &
Recreation
JNF007120   JUVENILE NONFICTION / Biography & Autobiography / Women
JNF008000   JUVENILE NONFICTION / Body, Mind & Spirit
JNF063000   JUVENILE NONFICTION / Books & Libraries
JNF009000   JUVENILE NONFICTION / Boys & Men
JNF010000   JUVENILE NONFICTION / Business & Economics
JNF011000   JUVENILE NONFICTION / Careers
    JUVENILE NONFICTION / Celebrations see headings under Holidays & Celebrations
    JUVENILE NONFICTION / City Life see Lifestyles / City & Town Life
JNF059000   JUVENILE NONFICTION / Clothing & Dress
    JUVENILE NONFICTION / Collectibles see Antiques & Collectibles
JNF062000   JUVENILE NONFICTION / Comics & Graphic Novels / General
JNF062010   JUVENILE NONFICTION / Comics & Graphic Novels / Biography
JNF062020   JUVENILE NONFICTION / Comics & Graphic Novels / History
JNF012000   JUVENILE NONFICTION / Computers / General
JNF012010   JUVENILE NONFICTION / Computers / Entertainment & Games
JNF012030   JUVENILE NONFICTION / Computers / Internet
JNF012040   JUVENILE NONFICTION / Computers / Programming
JNF012050   JUVENILE NONFICTION / Computers / Software
JNF013000   JUVENILE NONFICTION / Concepts / General
JNF013010   JUVENILE NONFICTION / Concepts / Alphabet
JNF013110   JUVENILE NONFICTION / Concepts / Body
JNF013020   JUVENILE NONFICTION / Concepts / Colors
JNF013030   JUVENILE NONFICTION / Concepts / Counting & Numbers
JNF013080   JUVENILE NONFICTION / Concepts / Date & Time

139

JNF013040   JUVENILE NONFICTION / Concepts / Money
JNF013050   JUVENILE NONFICTION / Concepts / Opposites
JNF013090   JUVENILE NONFICTION / Concepts / Seasons
JNF013060   JUVENILE NONFICTION / Concepts / Senses & Sensation
JNF013070   JUVENILE NONFICTION / Concepts / Size & Shape
JNF013100   JUVENILE NONFICTION / Concepts / Sounds
    JUVENILE NONFICTION / Concepts / Words see headings under Language Arts
JNF014000   JUVENILE NONFICTION / Cooking & Food
    JUVENILE NONFICTION / Counting & Numbers see Concepts / Counting & Numbers
    JUVENILE NONFICTION / Country Life see Lifestyles / Country Life
JNF015000   JUVENILE NONFICTION / Crafts & Hobbies
    JUVENILE NONFICTION / Crime see Law & Crime
JNF016000   JUVENILE NONFICTION / Curiosities & Wonders
    JUVENILE NONFICTION / Dolls see Toys, Dolls & Puppets
JNF017000   JUVENILE NONFICTION / Drama
    JUVENILE NONFICTION / Economics see Business & Economics
    JUVENILE NONFICTION / Education see School & Education
    JUVENILE NONFICTION / Ethnic see headings under People & Places
JNF019000   JUVENILE NONFICTION / Family / General (see also headings under Social Issues)
    JUVENILE NONFICTION / Family / Abuse see Social Issues / Physical & Emotional Abuse or Social Issues / Sexual Abuse
JNF019010   JUVENILE NONFICTION / Family / Adoption
JNF019090   JUVENILE NONFICTION / Family / Alternative Family
JNF019020   JUVENILE NONFICTION / Family / Marriage & Divorce
JNF019030   JUVENILE NONFICTION / Family / Multigenerational
JNF019040   JUVENILE NONFICTION / Family / New Baby
JNF019050   JUVENILE NONFICTION / Family / Orphans & Foster Homes
JNF019060   JUVENILE NONFICTION / Family / Parents
JNF019070   JUVENILE NONFICTION / Family / Siblings
JNF019080   JUVENILE NONFICTION / Family / Stepfamilies
    JUVENILE NONFICTION / Farm Life see Lifestyles / Farm & Ranch Life
JNF020000   JUVENILE NONFICTION / Foreign Language Study / General
JNF020010   JUVENILE NONFICTION / Foreign Language Study / English as a Second Language
JNF020020   JUVENILE NONFICTION / Foreign Language Study / French
JNF020030   JUVENILE NONFICTION / Foreign Language Study / Spanish
JNF021000   JUVENILE NONFICTION / Games & Activities / General
JNF021010   JUVENILE NONFICTION / Games & Activities / Board Games
JNF021020   JUVENILE NONFICTION / Games & Activities / Card Games
JNF021030   JUVENILE NONFICTION / Games & Activities / Magic
JNF021040   JUVENILE NONFICTION / Games & Activities / Puzzles
JNF021050   JUVENILE NONFICTION / Games & Activities / Questions & Answers
JNF021060   JUVENILE NONFICTION / Games & Activities / Video & Electronic Games
JNF021070   JUVENILE NONFICTION / Games & Activities / Word Games
JNF022000   JUVENILE NONFICTION / Gardening
JNF023000   JUVENILE NONFICTION / Girls & Women
    JUVENILE NONFICTION / Government see Social Science / Politics & Government
JNF024000   JUVENILE NONFICTION / Health & Daily Living / General
    JUVENILE NONFICTION / Health & Daily Living / Bodily Functions see Health & Daily Living / Personal Hygiene
JNF024120   JUVENILE NONFICTION / Health & Daily Living / Daily Activities
    JUVENILE NONFICTION / Health & Daily Living / Depression & Mental Illness see Social Issues / Depression & Mental Illness
JNF024010   JUVENILE NONFICTION / Health & Daily Living / Diet & Nutrition
JNF024020   JUVENILE NONFICTION / Health & Daily Living / Diseases, Illnesses

& Injuries
JNF024030	JUVENILE NONFICTION / Health & Daily Living / First Aid
JNF024040	JUVENILE NONFICTION / Health & Daily Living / Fitness & Exercise
JNF024050	JUVENILE NONFICTION / Health & Daily Living / Maturing
JNF024060	JUVENILE NONFICTION / Health & Daily Living / Personal Hygiene
JNF024070	JUVENILE NONFICTION / Health & Daily Living / Physical

Impairments
JNF024080	JUVENILE NONFICTION / Health & Daily Living / Safety
JNF024090	JUVENILE NONFICTION / Health & Daily Living / Sexuality &

Pregnancy
JNF024100	JUVENILE NONFICTION / Health & Daily Living / Substance Abuse
JNF024110	JUVENILE NONFICTION / Health & Daily Living / Toilet Training
JNF025000	JUVENILE NONFICTION / History / General
JNF025010	JUVENILE NONFICTION / History / Africa
JNF025020	JUVENILE NONFICTION / History / Ancient
JNF025030	JUVENILE NONFICTION / History / Asia
JNF025040	JUVENILE NONFICTION / History / Australia & Oceania
JNF025050	JUVENILE NONFICTION / History / Canada / General
JNF025230	JUVENILE NONFICTION / History / Canada / Pre-Confederation (to

1867)
JNF025240	JUVENILE NONFICTION / History / Canada / Post-Confederation

(1867-)
JNF025060	JUVENILE NONFICTION / History / Central & South America
JNF025070	JUVENILE NONFICTION / History / Europe
JNF025080	JUVENILE NONFICTION / History / Exploration & Discovery
JNF025090	JUVENILE NONFICTION / History / Holocaust
JNF025100	JUVENILE NONFICTION / History / Medieval
JNF025110	JUVENILE NONFICTION / History / Mexico
JNF025120	JUVENILE NONFICTION / History / Middle East
JNF025130	JUVENILE NONFICTION / History / Military & Wars
JNF025140	JUVENILE NONFICTION / History / Modern
JNF025150	JUVENILE NONFICTION / History / Prehistoric
JNF025160	JUVENILE NONFICTION / History / Renaissance
JNF025260	JUVENILE NONFICTION / History / Symbols, Monuments, National

Parks, etc.
JNF025170	JUVENILE NONFICTION / History / United States / General
JNF025180	JUVENILE NONFICTION / History / United States / State & Local
JNF025190	JUVENILE NONFICTION / History / United States / Colonial &

Revolutionary Periods
JNF025200	JUVENILE NONFICTION / History / United States / 19th Century
JNF025270	JUVENILE NONFICTION / History / United States / Civil War Period

(1850-1877)
JNF025210	JUVENILE NONFICTION / History / United States / 20th Century
JNF025250	JUVENILE NONFICTION / History / United States / 21st Century
JNF025220	JUVENILE NONFICTION / History / Other
JNF026000	JUVENILE NONFICTION / Holidays & Celebrations / General (see

also Religious / Christian / Holidays & Celebrations)
JNF026100	JUVENILE NONFICTION / Holidays & Celebrations / Birthdays
JNF026010	JUVENILE NONFICTION / Holidays & Celebrations / Christmas &

Advent
JNF026020	JUVENILE NONFICTION / Holidays & Celebrations / Easter & Lent
JNF026030	JUVENILE NONFICTION / Holidays & Celebrations / Halloween
JNF026110	JUVENILE NONFICTION / Holidays & Celebrations / Hanukkah
JNF026050	JUVENILE NONFICTION / Holidays & Celebrations / Kwanzaa
JNF026120	JUVENILE NONFICTION / Holidays & Celebrations / Passover
JNF026130	JUVENILE NONFICTION / Holidays & Celebrations / Patriotic

Holidays
JNF026060	JUVENILE NONFICTION / Holidays & Celebrations / Thanksgiving
JNF026070	JUVENILE NONFICTION / Holidays & Celebrations / Valentine's Day

JNF026080   JUVENILE NONFICTION / Holidays & Celebrations / Other, Non-Religious

JNF026090   JUVENILE NONFICTION / Holidays & Celebrations / Other, Religious

JNF027000   JUVENILE NONFICTION / House & Home

JNF028000   JUVENILE NONFICTION / Humor / General

JNF028010   JUVENILE NONFICTION / Humor / Comic Strips & Cartoons

JNF028020   JUVENILE NONFICTION / Humor / Jokes & Riddles

JNF029000   JUVENILE NONFICTION / Language Arts / General

JUVENILE NONFICTION / Language Arts / Alphabet see Concepts / Alphabet

JNF029010   JUVENILE NONFICTION / Language Arts / Composition & Creative Writing

JNF029020   JUVENILE NONFICTION / Language Arts / Grammar

JNF029030   JUVENILE NONFICTION / Language Arts / Handwriting

JNF029060   JUVENILE NONFICTION / Language Arts / Journal Writing

JUVENILE NONFICTION / Language Arts / Readers see headings under Readers

JNF029050   JUVENILE NONFICTION / Language Arts / Sign Language

JNF029040   JUVENILE NONFICTION / Language Arts / Vocabulary & Spelling

JNF030000   JUVENILE NONFICTION / Law & Crime

JNF031000   JUVENILE NONFICTION / Lifestyles / City & Town Life

JNF032000   JUVENILE NONFICTION / Lifestyles / Country Life

JNF033000   JUVENILE NONFICTION / Lifestyles / Farm & Ranch Life

JNF034000   JUVENILE NONFICTION / Literary Criticism & Collections

JNF035000   JUVENILE NONFICTION / Mathematics / General

JNF035010   JUVENILE NONFICTION / Mathematics / Advanced

JNF035020   JUVENILE NONFICTION / Mathematics / Algebra

JNF035030   JUVENILE NONFICTION / Mathematics / Arithmetic

JUVENILE NONFICTION / Mathematics / Counting & Numbers see Concepts / Counting & Numbers

JNF035040   JUVENILE NONFICTION / Mathematics / Fractions

JNF035050   JUVENILE NONFICTION / Mathematics / Geometry

JNF060000   JUVENILE NONFICTION / Media Studies

JNF064000   JUVENILE NONFICTION / Media Tie-In

JUVENILE NONFICTION / Medicine see headings under Health & Daily Living

JUVENILE NONFICTION / Men see Boys & Men

JUVENILE NONFICTION / Metaphysical see Body, Mind & Spirit

JNF036000   JUVENILE NONFICTION / Music / General

JNF036010   JUVENILE NONFICTION / Music / Classical

JNF036020   JUVENILE NONFICTION / Music / History

JNF036030   JUVENILE NONFICTION / Music / Instruction & Study

JNF036090   JUVENILE NONFICTION / Music / Instruments

JNF036040   JUVENILE NONFICTION / Music / Jazz

JNF036050   JUVENILE NONFICTION / Music / Popular

JNF036060   JUVENILE NONFICTION / Music / Rap & Hip Hop

JNF036070   JUVENILE NONFICTION / Music / Rock

JNF036080   JUVENILE NONFICTION / Music / Songbooks

JUVENILE NONFICTION / Nature see headings under Animals or Science & Nature

JNF038000   JUVENILE NONFICTION / People & Places / General

JNF038010   JUVENILE NONFICTION / People & Places / Africa

JNF038020   JUVENILE NONFICTION / People & Places / Asia

JNF038030   JUVENILE NONFICTION / People & Places / Australia & Oceania

JNF038040   JUVENILE NONFICTION / People & Places / Canada / General

JNF038120   JUVENILE NONFICTION / People & Places / Canada / Native Canadian

JNF038050   JUVENILE NONFICTION / People & Places / Caribbean & Latin America

JNF038060   JUVENILE NONFICTION / People & Places / Europe

JNF038070   JUVENILE NONFICTION / People & Places / Mexico

JNF038080   JUVENILE NONFICTION / People & Places / Middle East

JNF038090   JUVENILE NONFICTION / People & Places / Polar Regions

JNF038100   JUVENILE NONFICTION / People & Places / United States / General
JNF018010   JUVENILE NONFICTION / People & Places / United States / African American
JNF018020   JUVENILE NONFICTION / People & Places / United States / Asian American
JNF018030   JUVENILE NONFICTION / People & Places / United States / Hispanic & Latino
JNF018040   JUVENILE NONFICTION / People & Places / United States / Native American
JNF018050   JUVENILE NONFICTION / People & Places / United States / Other
JNF038110   JUVENILE NONFICTION / People & Places / Other
JNF039000   JUVENILE NONFICTION / Performing Arts / General
JNF039010   JUVENILE NONFICTION / Performing Arts / Circus
JNF039020   JUVENILE NONFICTION / Performing Arts / Dance
JNF039030   JUVENILE NONFICTION / Performing Arts / Film
              JUVENILE NONFICTION / Performing Arts / Music see headings under Music
JNF039040   JUVENILE NONFICTION / Performing Arts / Television & Radio
JNF039050   JUVENILE NONFICTION / Performing Arts / Theater
              JUVENILE NONFICTION / Pets see Animals / Pets
JNF040000   JUVENILE NONFICTION / Philosophy
JNF041000   JUVENILE NONFICTION / Photography
JNF066000   JUVENILE NONFICTION / Pirates *
JNF042000   JUVENILE NONFICTION / Poetry / General
JNF042010   JUVENILE NONFICTION / Poetry / Humorous
              JUVENILE NONFICTION / Politics & Government see Social Science / Politics & Government
              JUVENILE NONFICTION / Psychology see Social Science / Psychology
              JUVENILE NONFICTION / Puppets see Toys, Dolls & Puppets
JNF045000   JUVENILE NONFICTION / Readers / Beginner
JNF046000   JUVENILE NONFICTION / Readers / Intermediate
JNF047000   JUVENILE NONFICTION / Readers / Chapter Books
              JUVENILE NONFICTION / Recreation see headings under Sports & Recreation
JNF065000   JUVENILE NONFICTION / Recycling & Green Living
JNF048000   JUVENILE NONFICTION / Reference / General
JNF048010   JUVENILE NONFICTION / Reference / Almanacs
JNF048020   JUVENILE NONFICTION / Reference / Atlases
JNF048030   JUVENILE NONFICTION / Reference / Dictionaries
JNF048040   JUVENILE NONFICTION / Reference / Encyclopedias
JNF048050   JUVENILE NONFICTION / Reference / Thesauri
JNF049000   JUVENILE NONFICTION / Religion / General
JNF049040   JUVENILE NONFICTION / Religion / Bible Stories / General
JNF049140   JUVENILE NONFICTION / Religion / Bible Stories / Old Testament
JNF049150   JUVENILE NONFICTION / Religion / Bible Stories / New Testament
JNF049020   JUVENILE NONFICTION / Religion / Biblical Biography
JNF049030   JUVENILE NONFICTION / Religion / Biblical Commentaries & Interpretation
JNF049170   JUVENILE NONFICTION / Religion / Biblical Reference
JNF049010   JUVENILE NONFICTION / Religion / Biblical Studies
JNF049080   JUVENILE NONFICTION / Religion / Christianity
JNF049090   JUVENILE NONFICTION / Religion / Eastern
JNF049100   JUVENILE NONFICTION / Religion / Islam
JNF049110   JUVENILE NONFICTION / Religion / Judaism
JNF049130   JUVENILE NONFICTION / Religious / Christian / General
JNF049180   JUVENILE NONFICTION / Religious / Christian / Biography & Autobiography (see also Biography & Autobiography / Religious)
JNF049190   JUVENILE NONFICTION / Religious / Christian / Comics & Graphic Novels
JNF049120   JUVENILE NONFICTION / Religious / Christian / Devotional & Prayer

143

JNF049200   JUVENILE NONFICTION / Religious / Christian / Early Readers
JNF049210   JUVENILE NONFICTION / Religious / Christian / Family & Relationships
JNF049220   JUVENILE NONFICTION / Religious / Christian / Games & Activities
JNF049230   JUVENILE NONFICTION / Religious / Christian / Health & Daily Living
JNF049240   JUVENILE NONFICTION / Religious / Christian / Holidays & Celebrations
JNF049250   JUVENILE NONFICTION / Religious / Christian / Inspirational
JNF049260   JUVENILE NONFICTION / Religious / Christian / Learning Concepts
JNF049280   JUVENILE NONFICTION / Religious / Christian / Science & Nature
JNF049290   JUVENILE NONFICTION / Religious / Christian / Social Issues
JNF049310   JUVENILE NONFICTION / Religious / Christian / Values & Virtues
JNF050000   JUVENILE NONFICTION / School & Education
JNF051000   JUVENILE NONFICTION / Science & Nature / General (see also headings under Animals or Technology)
JNF051030   JUVENILE NONFICTION / Science & Nature / Anatomy & Physiology
JNF051040   JUVENILE NONFICTION / Science & Nature / Astronomy
JNF051050   JUVENILE NONFICTION / Science & Nature / Biology
JNF051060   JUVENILE NONFICTION / Science & Nature / Botany
JNF051070   JUVENILE NONFICTION / Science & Nature / Chemistry
JNF051160   JUVENILE NONFICTION / Science & Nature / Disasters
JNF051170   JUVENILE NONFICTION / Science & Nature / Discoveries
JNF051080   JUVENILE NONFICTION / Science & Nature / Earth Sciences / General
JNF037010   JUVENILE NONFICTION / Science & Nature / Earth Sciences / Earthquakes & Volcanoes
JNF051180   JUVENILE NONFICTION / Science & Nature / Earth Sciences / Geography
JNF037060   JUVENILE NONFICTION / Science & Nature / Earth Sciences / Rocks & Minerals
JNF037070   JUVENILE NONFICTION / Science & Nature / Earth Sciences / Water (Oceans, Lakes, etc.)
JNF037080   JUVENILE NONFICTION / Science & Nature / Earth Sciences / Weather
JNF037020   JUVENILE NONFICTION / Science & Nature / Environmental Conservation & Protection
JNF051100   JUVENILE NONFICTION / Science & Nature / Environmental Science & Ecosystems
JNF051110   JUVENILE NONFICTION / Science & Nature / Experiments & Projects
JNF037030   JUVENILE NONFICTION / Science & Nature / Flowers & Plants
JNF037050   JUVENILE NONFICTION / Science & Nature / Fossils
JNF051190   JUVENILE NONFICTION / Science & Nature / History of Science
JNF051140   JUVENILE NONFICTION / Science & Nature / Physics
JNF037040   JUVENILE NONFICTION / Science & Nature / Trees & Forests
JNF051200   JUVENILE NONFICTION / Science & Nature / Weights & Measures
JNF051150   JUVENILE NONFICTION / Science & Nature / Zoology
JNF053000   JUVENILE NONFICTION / Social Issues / General (see also headings under Family)
            JUVENILE NONFICTION / Social Issues / Abuse see Social Issues / Physical & Emotional Abuse or Social Issues / Sexual Abuse
JNF053010   JUVENILE NONFICTION / Social Issues / Adolescence
JNF053220   JUVENILE NONFICTION / Social Issues / Bullying
JNF053020   JUVENILE NONFICTION / Social Issues / Dating & Sex
JNF053030   JUVENILE NONFICTION / Social Issues / Death & Dying
JNF053230   JUVENILE NONFICTION / Social Issues / Depression & Mental Illness
JNF053040   JUVENILE NONFICTION / Social Issues / Drugs, Alcohol, Substance Abuse

JNF053240   JUVENILE NONFICTION / Social Issues / Emigration & Immigration
JNF053050   JUVENILE NONFICTION / Social Issues / Emotions & Feelings
JNF053060   JUVENILE NONFICTION / Social Issues / Friendship
JNF053070   JUVENILE NONFICTION / Social Issues / Homelessness & Poverty
JNF053080   JUVENILE NONFICTION / Social Issues / Homosexuality
JNF053090   JUVENILE NONFICTION / Social Issues / Manners & Etiquette
JNF053100   JUVENILE NONFICTION / Social Issues / New Experience
JNF053110   JUVENILE NONFICTION / Social Issues / Peer Pressure
JNF053120   JUVENILE NONFICTION / Social Issues / Physical & Emotional
Abuse (see also Social Issues / Sexual Abuse)
JNF053130   JUVENILE NONFICTION / Social Issues / Pregnancy
JNF053140   JUVENILE NONFICTION / Social Issues / Prejudice & Racism
JNF053150   JUVENILE NONFICTION / Social Issues / Runaways
JNF053160   JUVENILE NONFICTION / Social Issues / Self-Esteem & Self-Reliance
JNF053250   JUVENILE NONFICTION / Social Issues / Self-Mutilation
JNF053170   JUVENILE NONFICTION / Social Issues / Sexual Abuse
             JUVENILE NONFICTION / Social Issues / Sexuality see Social Issues / Dating & Sex
JNF053180   JUVENILE NONFICTION / Social Issues / Special Needs
JNF053260   JUVENILE NONFICTION / Social Issues / Strangers
             JUVENILE NONFICTION / Social Issues / Substance Abuse see Social Issues / Drugs,
Alcohol, Substance Abuse
JNF053190   JUVENILE NONFICTION / Social Issues / Suicide
JNF053200   JUVENILE NONFICTION / Social Issues / Values & Virtues
JNF053210   JUVENILE NONFICTION / Social Issues / Violence
JNF052000   JUVENILE NONFICTION / Social Science / General
JNF052010   JUVENILE NONFICTION / Social Science / Archaeology
JNF052020   JUVENILE NONFICTION / Social Science / Customs, Traditions,
Anthropology
JNF052030   JUVENILE NONFICTION / Social Science / Folklore & Mythology
JNF043000   JUVENILE NONFICTION / Social Science / Politics & Government
JNF044000   JUVENILE NONFICTION / Social Science / Psychology
JNF052040   JUVENILE NONFICTION / Social Science / Sociology
             JUVENILE NONFICTION / Social Studies see headings under Social Science
JNF054000   JUVENILE NONFICTION / Sports & Recreation / General
JNF054010   JUVENILE NONFICTION / Sports & Recreation / Baseball & Softball
JNF054020   JUVENILE NONFICTION / Sports & Recreation / Basketball
JNF054030   JUVENILE NONFICTION / Sports & Recreation / Camping &
Outdoor Activities
JNF054040   JUVENILE NONFICTION / Sports & Recreation / Cycling
JNF054170   JUVENILE NONFICTION / Sports & Recreation / Equestrian
JNF054180   JUVENILE NONFICTION / Sports & Recreation / Extreme Sports
JNF054050   JUVENILE NONFICTION / Sports & Recreation / Football
             JUVENILE NONFICTION / Sports & Recreation / Games see headings under Games
& Activities
JNF054230   JUVENILE NONFICTION / Sports & Recreation / Golf
JNF054060   JUVENILE NONFICTION / Sports & Recreation / Gymnastics
JNF054070   JUVENILE NONFICTION / Sports & Recreation / Hockey
JNF054190   JUVENILE NONFICTION / Sports & Recreation / Ice Skating
JNF054080   JUVENILE NONFICTION / Sports & Recreation / Martial Arts
JNF054100   JUVENILE NONFICTION / Sports & Recreation / Motor Sports
JNF054110   JUVENILE NONFICTION / Sports & Recreation / Olympics
JNF054120   JUVENILE NONFICTION / Sports & Recreation / Racket Sports
JNF054200   JUVENILE NONFICTION / Sports & Recreation / Roller & In-Line
Skating
JNF054210   JUVENILE NONFICTION / Sports & Recreation / Skateboarding
JNF054130   JUVENILE NONFICTION / Sports & Recreation / Soccer
JNF054140   JUVENILE NONFICTION / Sports & Recreation / Track & Field
JNF054150   JUVENILE NONFICTION / Sports & Recreation / Water Sports
JNF054160   JUVENILE NONFICTION / Sports & Recreation / Winter Sports

JNF054220   JUVENILE NONFICTION / Sports & Recreation / Wrestling
JNF055000   JUVENILE NONFICTION / Study Aids / General
JNF055010   JUVENILE NONFICTION / Study Aids / Book Notes (see also STUDY AIDS / Book Notes)
JUVENILE NONFICTION / Study Aids / College Guides see STUDY AIDS / College Guides
JNF055030   JUVENILE NONFICTION / Study Aids / Test Preparation
JNF061000   JUVENILE NONFICTION / Technology / General
JNF051010   JUVENILE NONFICTION / Technology / Aeronautics, Astronautics & Space Science
JNF051020   JUVENILE NONFICTION / Technology / Agriculture
JUVENILE NONFICTION / Technology / Computers see headings under Computers
JNF051090   JUVENILE NONFICTION / Technology / Electricity & Electronics
JNF051120   JUVENILE NONFICTION / Technology / How Things Work-Are Made
JNF061010   JUVENILE NONFICTION / Technology / Inventions
JNF051130   JUVENILE NONFICTION / Technology / Machinery & Tools
JUVENILE NONFICTION / Town Life see Lifestyles / City & Town Life
JNF056000   JUVENILE NONFICTION / Toys, Dolls & Puppets
JNF057000   JUVENILE NONFICTION / Transportation / General
JNF057010   JUVENILE NONFICTION / Transportation / Aviation
JNF057020   JUVENILE NONFICTION / Transportation / Boats, Ships & Underwater Craft
JNF057030   JUVENILE NONFICTION / Transportation / Cars & Trucks
JNF057040   JUVENILE NONFICTION / Transportation / Motorcycles
JNF057050   JUVENILE NONFICTION / Transportation / Railroads & Trains
JNF058000   JUVENILE NONFICTION / Travel
JUVENILE NONFICTION / Vocational Guidance see Careers
JUVENILE NONFICTION / Women see Girls & Women

LANGUAGE ARTS & DISCIPLINES

LAN000000   LANGUAGE ARTS & DISCIPLINES / General
LAN001000   LANGUAGE ARTS & DISCIPLINES / Alphabets & Writing Systems
LAN002000   LANGUAGE ARTS & DISCIPLINES / Authorship
LAN004000   LANGUAGE ARTS & DISCIPLINES / Communication Studies
LAN005000   LANGUAGE ARTS & DISCIPLINES / Composition & Creative Writing
LAN022000   LANGUAGE ARTS & DISCIPLINES / Editing & Proofreading
LAN006000   LANGUAGE ARTS & DISCIPLINES / Grammar & Punctuation
LAN007000   LANGUAGE ARTS & DISCIPLINES / Handwriting
LAN008000   LANGUAGE ARTS & DISCIPLINES / Journalism
LAN029000   LANGUAGE ARTS & DISCIPLINES / Lexicography
LAN025000   LANGUAGE ARTS & DISCIPLINES / Library & Information Science / General
LAN025010   LANGUAGE ARTS & DISCIPLINES / Library & Information Science / Administration & Management
LAN025020   LANGUAGE ARTS & DISCIPLINES / Library & Information Science / Archives & Special Libraries
LAN025030   LANGUAGE ARTS & DISCIPLINES / Library & Information Science / Cataloging & Classification
LAN025040   LANGUAGE ARTS & DISCIPLINES / Library & Information Science / Collection Development
LAN025060   LANGUAGE ARTS & DISCIPLINES / Library & Information Science / Digital & Online Resources
LAN025050   LANGUAGE ARTS & DISCIPLINES / Library & Information Science / School Media
LAN009000   LANGUAGE ARTS & DISCIPLINES / Linguistics / General
LANGUAGE ARTS & DISCIPLINES / Linguistics / Computational see COMPUTERS / Natural Language Processing
LAN024000   LANGUAGE ARTS & DISCIPLINES / Linguistics / Etymology

LAN009010	LANGUAGE ARTS & DISCIPLINES / Linguistics / Historical & Comparative
LAN009020	LANGUAGE ARTS & DISCIPLINES / Linguistics / Morphology
LAN011000	LANGUAGE ARTS & DISCIPLINES / Linguistics / Phonetics & Phonology
LAN009030	LANGUAGE ARTS & DISCIPLINES / Linguistics / Pragmatics
LAN009040	LANGUAGE ARTS & DISCIPLINES / Linguistics / Psycholinguistics
LAN016000	LANGUAGE ARTS & DISCIPLINES / Linguistics / Semantics
LAN009050	LANGUAGE ARTS & DISCIPLINES / Linguistics / Sociolinguistics
LAN009060	LANGUAGE ARTS & DISCIPLINES / Linguistics / Syntax
LAN010000	LANGUAGE ARTS & DISCIPLINES / Literacy
	LANGUAGE ARTS & DISCIPLINES / Proofreading see Editing & Proofreading
LAN026000	LANGUAGE ARTS & DISCIPLINES / Public Speaking
LAN027000	LANGUAGE ARTS & DISCIPLINES / Publishing
LAN012000	LANGUAGE ARTS & DISCIPLINES / Readers
LAN013000	LANGUAGE ARTS & DISCIPLINES / Reading Skills
LAN014000	LANGUAGE ARTS & DISCIPLINES / Reference
LAN015000	LANGUAGE ARTS & DISCIPLINES / Rhetoric
LAN017000	LANGUAGE ARTS & DISCIPLINES / Sign Language
LAN018000	LANGUAGE ARTS & DISCIPLINES / Speech
LAN019000	LANGUAGE ARTS & DISCIPLINES / Spelling
LAN020000	LANGUAGE ARTS & DISCIPLINES / Study & Teaching
LAN028000	LANGUAGE ARTS & DISCIPLINES / Style Manuals
LAN023000	LANGUAGE ARTS & DISCIPLINES / Translating & Interpreting
LAN021000	LANGUAGE ARTS & DISCIPLINES / Vocabulary

LAW

LAW000000	LAW / General
LAW001000	LAW / Administrative Law & Regulatory Practice
	LAW / Admiralty see Maritime
LAW102000	LAW / Agricultural
LAW002000	LAW / Air & Space
LAW003000	LAW / Alternative Dispute Resolution
LAW004000	LAW / Annotations & Citations
LAW005000	LAW / Antitrust
LAW006000	LAW / Arbitration, Negotiation, Mediation
LAW007000	LAW / Banking
LAW008000	LAW / Bankruptcy & Insolvency
LAW009000	LAW / Business & Financial
LAW010000	LAW / Child Advocacy
	LAW / Children see Family Law / Children
LAW011000	LAW / Civil Law
LAW012000	LAW / Civil Procedure
LAW013000	LAW / Civil Rights
LAW014000	LAW / Commercial / General
LAW014010	LAW / Commercial / International Trade
LAW103000	LAW / Common
LAW015000	LAW / Communications
LAW016000	LAW / Comparative
LAW104000	LAW / Computer & Internet
LAW017000	LAW / Conflict of Laws
LAW018000	LAW / Constitutional
LAW019000	LAW / Construction
LAW020000	LAW / Consumer
LAW021000	LAW / Contracts
	LAW / Copyright see Intellectual Property / Copyright
LAW022000	LAW / Corporate
	LAW / Corporate Governance see Corporate or BUSINESS & ECONOMICS / Corporate Governance

Bo Bryant & Thax Turner

LAW023000   LAW / Court Records
LAW024000   LAW / Court Rules
LAW025000   LAW / Courts
LAW026000   LAW / Criminal Law / General
LAW026010   LAW / Criminal Law / Juvenile Offenders
LAW026020   LAW / Criminal Law / Sentencing
LAW027000   LAW / Criminal Procedure
LAW028000   LAW / Customary
LAW106000   LAW / Defamation
LAW029000   LAW / Depositions
LAW030000   LAW / Dictionaries & Terminology
LAW031000   LAW / Disability
LAW094000   LAW / Discrimination
         LAW / Divorce see Family Law / Divorce & Separation
         LAW / Domestic Relations see headings under Family Law
LAW092000   LAW / Educational Law & Legislation
LAW107000   LAW / Elder Law
LAW108000   LAW / Election Law
LAW032000   LAW / Emigration & Immigration
         LAW / Employment see Labor & Employment
LAW033000   LAW / Entertainment
LAW034000   LAW / Environmental
LAW101000   LAW / Essays
LAW035000   LAW / Estates & Trusts
LAW036000   LAW / Ethics & Professional Responsibility
LAW037000   LAW / Evidence
LAW038000   LAW / Family Law / General
LAW038010   LAW / Family Law / Children
LAW038020   LAW / Family Law / Divorce & Separation
LAW038030   LAW / Family Law / Marriage
LAW041000   LAW / Forensic Science
         LAW / Franchising see Business & Financial
LAW043000   LAW / Gender & the Law
LAW044000   LAW / General Practice
LAW109000   LAW / Government / General
LAW039000   LAW / Government / Federal
LAW089000   LAW / Government / State, Provincial & Municipal
LAW046000   LAW / Health
LAW047000   LAW / Housing & Urban Development
         LAW / Human Rights see POLITICAL SCIENCE / Human Rights
         LAW / Immigration see Emigration & Immigration
LAW110000   LAW / Indigenous Peoples
LAW049000   LAW / Insurance
LAW050000   LAW / Intellectual Property / General
LAW050010   LAW / Intellectual Property / Copyright
LAW050020   LAW / Intellectual Property / Patent
LAW050030   LAW / Intellectual Property / Trademark
LAW051000   LAW / International
LAW111000   LAW / Judicial Power
LAW052000   LAW / Jurisprudence
LAW053000   LAW / Jury
LAW054000   LAW / Labor & Employment
LAW055000   LAW / Land Use
LAW112000   LAW / Landlord & Tenant
LAW056000   LAW / Law Office Management
         LAW / Legal Assistants see Paralegals & Paralegalism
LAW059000   LAW / Legal Education
LAW060000   LAW / Legal History
LAW061000   LAW / Legal Profession

148

LAW062000   LAW / Legal Services
LAW063000   LAW / Legal Writing
LAW113000   LAW / Liability
    LAW / Libel & Slander see Defamation
LAW064000   LAW / Litigation
LAW100000   LAW / Living Trusts
    LAW / Living Wills see Right to Die
LAW095000   LAW / Malpractice
LAW066000   LAW / Maritime
    LAW / Marriage see Family Law / Marriage
LAW096000   LAW / Media & the Law
    LAW / Mediation see Arbitration, Negotiation, Mediation
LAW093000   LAW / Medical Law & Legislation
LAW067000   LAW / Mental Health
LAW114000   LAW / Mergers & Acquisitions
LAW068000   LAW / Military
LAW069000   LAW / Natural Law
LAW070000   LAW / Natural Resources
    LAW / Negotiation see Arbitration, Negotiation, Mediation
LAW071000   LAW / Paralegals & Paralegalism
    LAW / Patent see Intellectual Property / Patent
LAW115000   LAW / Pension Law
LAW097000   LAW / Personal Injury
LAW098000   LAW / Practical Guides
LAW116000   LAW / Privacy
    LAW / Professional Responsibility see Ethics & Professional Responsibility
LAW074000   LAW / Property
LAW075000   LAW / Public
LAW076000   LAW / Public Contract
LAW077000   LAW / Public Utilities
LAW078000   LAW / Real Estate
LAW079000   LAW / Reference
LAW080000   LAW / Remedies & Damages
LAW081000   LAW / Research
LAW082000   LAW / Right to Die
LAW099000   LAW / Science & Technology
LAW083000   LAW / Securities
    LAW / Separation see Family Law / Divorce & Separation
LAW084000   LAW / Sports
    LAW / Study & Teaching see Legal Education
LAW086000   LAW / Taxation
    LAW / Technology see Science & Technology
LAW087000   LAW / Torts
    LAW / Trademark see Intellectual Property / Trademark
LAW117000   LAW / Transportation
LAW088000   LAW / Trial Practice
    LAW / Urban Development see Housing & Urban Development
LAW090000   LAW / Wills
LAW091000   LAW / Witnesses

LITERARY COLLECTIONS
LCO000000   LITERARY COLLECTIONS / General
LCO001000   LITERARY COLLECTIONS / African
LCO002000   LITERARY COLLECTIONS / American / General
LCO002010   LITERARY COLLECTIONS / American / African American
LCO003000   LITERARY COLLECTIONS / Ancient & Classical
LCO004000   LITERARY COLLECTIONS / Asian / General
LCO004010   LITERARY COLLECTIONS / Asian / Chinese
LCO004020   LITERARY COLLECTIONS / Asian / Indic

LCO004030   LITERARY COLLECTIONS / Asian / Japanese
LCO005000   LITERARY COLLECTIONS / Australian & Oceanian
LCO006000   LITERARY COLLECTIONS / Canadian
LCO007000   LITERARY COLLECTIONS / Caribbean & Latin American
LCO015000   LITERARY COLLECTIONS / Diaries & Journals
LCO010000   LITERARY COLLECTIONS / Essays
LCO008000   LITERARY COLLECTIONS / European / General
LCO008010   LITERARY COLLECTIONS / European / Eastern (see also Russian & Former Soviet Union)
LCO009000   LITERARY COLLECTIONS / European / English, Irish, Scottish, Welsh
LCO008020   LITERARY COLLECTIONS / European / French
LCO008030   LITERARY COLLECTIONS / European / German
LCO008040   LITERARY COLLECTIONS / European / Italian
LCO008050   LITERARY COLLECTIONS / European / Scandinavian
LCO008060   LITERARY COLLECTIONS / European / Spanish & Portuguese
LCO011000   LITERARY COLLECTIONS / Letters
LCO016000   LITERARY COLLECTIONS / LGBT
LCO017000   LITERARY COLLECTIONS / Medieval
LCO012000   LITERARY COLLECTIONS / Middle Eastern
LCO013000   LITERARY COLLECTIONS / Native American
LCO014000   LITERARY COLLECTIONS / Russian & Former Soviet Union
LCO018000   LITERARY COLLECTIONS / Speeches
LCO019000   LITERARY COLLECTIONS / Women Authors

LITERARY CRITICISM
LIT000000   LITERARY CRITICISM / General
LIT004010   LITERARY CRITICISM / African
LIT004020   LITERARY CRITICISM / American / General
LIT004040   LITERARY CRITICISM / American / African American
LIT004030   LITERARY CRITICISM / American / Asian American
LIT004050   LITERARY CRITICISM / American / Hispanic American
LIT023000   LITERARY CRITICISM / American / Regional *
LIT004190   LITERARY CRITICISM / Ancient & Classical
LIT008000   LITERARY CRITICISM / Asian / General
LIT008010   LITERARY CRITICISM / Asian / Chinese
LIT008020   LITERARY CRITICISM / Asian / Indic
LIT008030   LITERARY CRITICISM / Asian / Japanese
LIT004070   LITERARY CRITICISM / Australian & Oceanian
LIT007000   LITERARY CRITICISM / Books & Reading
LIT004080   LITERARY CRITICISM / Canadian
LIT004100   LITERARY CRITICISM / Caribbean & Latin American
              LITERARY CRITICISM / Central American & South American see Caribbean & Latin American
LIT009000   LITERARY CRITICISM / Children's & Young Adult Literature
              LITERARY CRITICISM / Classical see Ancient & Classical
LIT017000   LITERARY CRITICISM / Comics & Graphic Novels
LIT020000   LITERARY CRITICISM / Comparative Literature
LIT013000   LITERARY CRITICISM / Drama
LIT004130   LITERARY CRITICISM / European / General
LIT004110   LITERARY CRITICISM / European / Eastern (see also Russian & Former Soviet Union)
LIT004120   LITERARY CRITICISM / European / English, Irish, Scottish, Welsh
              LITERARY CRITICISM / European / English, Irish, Scottish, Welsh / Shakespeare see Shakespeare
LIT004150   LITERARY CRITICISM / European / French
LIT004170   LITERARY CRITICISM / European / German
LIT004200   LITERARY CRITICISM / European / Italian
LIT004250   LITERARY CRITICISM / European / Scandinavian

LIT004280   LITERARY CRITICISM / European / Spanish & Portuguese
LIT022000   LITERARY CRITICISM / Fairy Tales, Folk Tales, Legends & Mythology
            LITERARY CRITICISM / Fantasy see Science Fiction & Fantasy
            LITERARY CRITICISM / Far Eastern see headings under Asian
LIT003000   LITERARY CRITICISM / Feminist
LIT004180   LITERARY CRITICISM / Gothic & Romance
LIT021000   LITERARY CRITICISM / Horror & Supernatural
LIT016000   LITERARY CRITICISM / Humor
LIT004210   LITERARY CRITICISM / Jewish
LIT004160   LITERARY CRITICISM / LGBT
LIT011000   LITERARY CRITICISM / Medieval
LIT004220   LITERARY CRITICISM / Middle Eastern
LIT024000   LITERARY CRITICISM / Modern / General *
LIT024010   LITERARY CRITICISM / Modern / 16th Century *
LIT024020   LITERARY CRITICISM / Modern / 17th Century *
LIT024030   LITERARY CRITICISM / Modern / 18th Century *
LIT024040   LITERARY CRITICISM / Modern / 19th Century *
LIT024050   LITERARY CRITICISM / Modern / 20th Century *
LIT024060   LITERARY CRITICISM / Modern / 21st Century *
LIT004230   LITERARY CRITICISM / Mystery & Detective
LIT004060   LITERARY CRITICISM / Native American
            LITERARY CRITICISM / Oceanian see Australian & Oceanian
            LITERARY CRITICISM / Oriental see headings under Asian
LIT014000   LITERARY CRITICISM / Poetry
LIT012000   LITERARY CRITICISM / Reference
LIT019000   LITERARY CRITICISM / Renaissance
LIT004240   LITERARY CRITICISM / Russian & Former Soviet Union
LIT004260   LITERARY CRITICISM / Science Fiction & Fantasy
LIT006000   LITERARY CRITICISM / Semiotics & Theory
LIT015000   LITERARY CRITICISM / Shakespeare
LIT018000   LITERARY CRITICISM / Short Stories
            LITERARY CRITICISM / South & Southeast Asian see headings under Asian
LIT025000   LITERARY CRITICISM / Subjects & Themes / General *
LIT025010   LITERARY CRITICISM / Subjects & Themes / Historical Events *
LIT025020   LITERARY CRITICISM / Subjects & Themes / Nature *
LIT025030   LITERARY CRITICISM / Subjects & Themes / Politics *
LIT025040   LITERARY CRITICISM / Subjects & Themes / Religion *
LIT025050   LITERARY CRITICISM / Subjects & Themes / Women *
            LITERARY CRITICISM / Theory see Semiotics & Theory
LIT004290   LITERARY CRITICISM / Women Authors

MATHEMATICS
MAT000000   MATHEMATICS / General
MAT002000   MATHEMATICS / Algebra / General
MAT002010   MATHEMATICS / Algebra / Abstract
MAT002030   MATHEMATICS / Algebra / Elementary
MAT002040   MATHEMATICS / Algebra / Intermediate
MAT002050   MATHEMATICS / Algebra / Linear
MAT003000   MATHEMATICS / Applied
MAT004000   MATHEMATICS / Arithmetic
MAT005000   MATHEMATICS / Calculus
MAT036000   MATHEMATICS / Combinatorics
MAT040000   MATHEMATICS / Complex Analysis
            MATHEMATICS / Computer Mathematics see Discrete Mathematics
MAT006000   MATHEMATICS / Counting & Numeration
MAT007000   MATHEMATICS / Differential Equations / General
MAT007010   MATHEMATICS / Differential Equations / Ordinary
MAT007020   MATHEMATICS / Differential Equations / Partial
MAT008000   MATHEMATICS / Discrete Mathematics

MAT039000	MATHEMATICS / Essays
MAT009000	MATHEMATICS / Finite Mathematics
	MATHEMATICS / Fractions see Arithmetic
MAT037000	MATHEMATICS / Functional Analysis
MAT011000	MATHEMATICS / Game Theory
	MATHEMATICS / Games see Recreations & Games
MAT012000	MATHEMATICS / Geometry / General
MAT012010	MATHEMATICS / Geometry / Algebraic
MAT012020	MATHEMATICS / Geometry / Analytic
MAT012030	MATHEMATICS / Geometry / Differential
MAT012040	MATHEMATICS / Geometry / Non-Euclidean
MAT013000	MATHEMATICS / Graphic Methods
MAT014000	MATHEMATICS / Group Theory
MAT015000	MATHEMATICS / History & Philosophy
MAT016000	MATHEMATICS / Infinity
MAT017000	MATHEMATICS / Linear & Nonlinear Programming
MAT018000	MATHEMATICS / Logic
MAT034000	MATHEMATICS / Mathematical Analysis
MAT019000	MATHEMATICS / Matrices
MAT020000	MATHEMATICS / Measurement
MAT021000	MATHEMATICS / Number Systems
MAT022000	MATHEMATICS / Number Theory
MAT041000	MATHEMATICS / Numerical Analysis
MAT042000	MATHEMATICS / Optimization
MAT023000	MATHEMATICS / Pre-Calculus
MAT029000	MATHEMATICS / Probability & Statistics / General
MAT029010	MATHEMATICS / Probability & Statistics / Bayesian Analysis
MAT029020	MATHEMATICS / Probability & Statistics / Multivariate Analysis
MAT029030	MATHEMATICS / Probability & Statistics / Regression Analysis
MAT029040	MATHEMATICS / Probability & Statistics / Stochastic Processes
MAT029050	MATHEMATICS / Probability & Statistics / Time Series
MAT025000	MATHEMATICS / Recreations & Games
MAT026000	MATHEMATICS / Reference
MAT027000	MATHEMATICS / Research
MAT028000	MATHEMATICS / Set Theory
	MATHEMATICS / Statistics see headings under Probability & Statistics
MAT030000	MATHEMATICS / Study & Teaching
MAT038000	MATHEMATICS / Topology
MAT031000	MATHEMATICS / Transformations
MAT032000	MATHEMATICS / Trigonometry
MAT033000	MATHEMATICS / Vector Analysis

MEDICAL

MED000000	MEDICAL / General
MED001000	MEDICAL / Acupuncture
MED002000	MEDICAL / Administration
MED022020	MEDICAL / AIDS & HIV
MED003000	MEDICAL / Allied Health Services / General
MED003010	MEDICAL / Allied Health Services / Emergency Medical Services
MED003020	MEDICAL / Allied Health Services / Hypnotherapy
MED003070	MEDICAL / Allied Health Services / Imaging Technologies
MED003090	MEDICAL / Allied Health Services / Massage Therapy
MED003030	MEDICAL / Allied Health Services / Medical Assistants
MED003040	MEDICAL / Allied Health Services / Medical Technology
MED003050	MEDICAL / Allied Health Services / Occupational Therapy
MED003060	MEDICAL / Allied Health Services / Physical Therapy
MED003080	MEDICAL / Allied Health Services / Respiratory Therapy
MED004000	MEDICAL / Alternative & Complementary Medicine
MED005000	MEDICAL / Anatomy

MED006000   MEDICAL / Anesthesiology
MED101000   MEDICAL / Atlases
MED007000   MEDICAL / Audiology & Speech Pathology
MED111000   MEDICAL / Bariatrics
MED008000   MEDICAL / Biochemistry
MED090000   MEDICAL / Biostatistics
MED009000   MEDICAL / Biotechnology
   MEDICAL / Cancer see Oncology
MED010000   MEDICAL / Cardiology
MED011000   MEDICAL / Caregiving
MED012000   MEDICAL / Chemotherapy
MED013000   MEDICAL / Chiropractic
MED014000   MEDICAL / Clinical Medicine
   MEDICAL / Communicable Diseases see Infectious Diseases
   MEDICAL / Complementary Medicine see Alternative & Complementary Medicine
   MEDICAL / Cosmetic Surgery see Surgery / Plastic & Cosmetic
MED015000   MEDICAL / Critical Care
MED016000   MEDICAL / Dentistry / General
MED016010   MEDICAL / Dentistry / Dental Assisting
MED016020   MEDICAL / Dentistry / Dental Hygiene
MED016080   MEDICAL / Dentistry / Dental Implants
MED016060   MEDICAL / Dentistry / Endodontics
MED016050   MEDICAL / Dentistry / Oral Surgery
MED016030   MEDICAL / Dentistry / Orthodontics
MED016040   MEDICAL / Dentistry / Periodontics
MED016090   MEDICAL / Dentistry / Practice Management
MED016070   MEDICAL / Dentistry / Prosthodontics
MED017000   MEDICAL / Dermatology
MED018000   MEDICAL / Diagnosis
MED019000   MEDICAL / Diagnostic Imaging / General
MED019010   MEDICAL / Diagnostic Imaging / Radiography *
MED098000   MEDICAL / Diagnostic Imaging / Ultrasonography
MED020000   MEDICAL / Dictionaries & Terminology
MED021000   MEDICAL / Diet Therapy
MED022000   MEDICAL / Diseases
   MEDICAL / Diseases / Abdominal see Gastroenterology
   MEDICAL / Diseases / AIDS & HIV see AIDS & HIV
   MEDICAL / Diseases / Bacterial see Infectious Diseases
   MEDICAL / Diseases / Brain see Neurology
   MEDICAL / Diseases / Cancer see Oncology
   MEDICAL / Diseases / Cardiopulmonary see Cardiology
   MEDICAL / Diseases / Cardiovascular see Cardiology
   MEDICAL / Diseases / Cerebrovascular see Neurology
   MEDICAL / Diseases / Communicable see Infectious Diseases
   MEDICAL / Diseases / Cutaneous see Dermatology
   MEDICAL / Diseases / Diabetes see Endocrinology & Metabolism
   MEDICAL / Diseases / Digestive Organs see Gastroenterology
   MEDICAL / Diseases / Endocrine Glands see Endocrinology & Metabolism
   MEDICAL / Diseases / Gastrointestinal see Gastroenterology
   MEDICAL / Diseases / Genetic see Genetics
   MEDICAL / Diseases / Genitourinary see Urology
   MEDICAL / Diseases / Immunological see Immunology
   MEDICAL / Diseases / Infectious see Infectious Diseases
   MEDICAL / Diseases / Neuromuscular see Anatomy or Neurology or Physical Medicine
& Rehabilitation or Physiology
   MEDICAL / Diseases / Nutritional see Nutrition
   MEDICAL / Diseases / Respiratory see Pulmonary & Thoracic Medicine
   MEDICAL / Diseases / Viral see Infectious Diseases
MED023000   MEDICAL / Drug Guides

MED024000   MEDICAL / Education & Training
MED025000   MEDICAL / Embryology
MED026000   MEDICAL / Emergency Medicine
MED027000   MEDICAL / Endocrinology & Metabolism
MED028000   MEDICAL / Epidemiology
          MEDICAL / Equipment see Instruments & Supplies
MED109000   MEDICAL / Essays
MED050000   MEDICAL / Ethics
MED112000   MEDICAL / Evidence-Based Medicine
MED029000   MEDICAL / Family & General Practice
MED030000   MEDICAL / Forensic Medicine
MED031000   MEDICAL / Gastroenterology
          MEDICAL / General Practice see Family & General Practice
MED107000   MEDICAL / Genetics
MED032000   MEDICAL / Geriatrics
MED033000   MEDICAL / Gynecology & Obstetrics
MED034000   MEDICAL / Healing
MED035000   MEDICAL / Health Care Delivery
MED036000   MEDICAL / Health Policy
MED037000   MEDICAL / Health Risk Assessment
          MEDICAL / Hearing see Audiology & Speech Pathology
MED038000   MEDICAL / Hematology
MED114000   MEDICAL / Hepatology
MED110000   MEDICAL / Histology
MED039000   MEDICAL / History
MED040000   MEDICAL / Holistic Medicine
MED041000   MEDICAL / Home Care
          MEDICAL / Hospice Care see Terminal Care
MED043000   MEDICAL / Hospital Administration & Care
MED044000   MEDICAL / Immunology
          MEDICAL / Industrial Medicine see Occupational & Industrial Medicine
MED115000   MEDICAL / Infection Control
MED022090   MEDICAL / Infectious Diseases
MED108000   MEDICAL / Instruments & Supplies
MED045000   MEDICAL / Internal Medicine
          MEDICAL / Iridology see Alternative & Complementary Medicine
MED047000   MEDICAL / Laboratory Medicine
MED048000   MEDICAL / Lasers in Medicine
MED113000   MEDICAL / Long-Term Care
MED049000   MEDICAL / Medicaid & Medicare
          MEDICAL / Medical Ethics see Ethics
MED051000   MEDICAL / Medical History & Records
MED102000   MEDICAL / Mental Health
          MEDICAL / Metabolism see Endocrinology & Metabolism
MED052000   MEDICAL / Microbiology
          MEDICAL / Mind-Body Medicine (Psychoneuroimmunology) see Alternative & Complementary Medicine
          MEDICAL / Naturopathy see HEALTH & FITNESS / Naturopathy
          MEDICAL / Neonatology see Perinatology & Neonatology
MED055000   MEDICAL / Nephrology
MED056000   MEDICAL / Neurology
MED057000   MEDICAL / Neuroscience
          MEDICAL / Neurosurgery see Surgery / Neurosurgery
MED091000   MEDICAL / Nosology
          MEDICAL / Nuclear Medicine see Radiology, Radiotherapy & Nuclear Medicine
MED058000   MEDICAL / Nursing / General
MED058010   MEDICAL / Nursing / Anesthesia
MED058020   MEDICAL / Nursing / Assessment & Diagnosis
MED058030   MEDICAL / Nursing / Critical & Intensive Care

MED058040	MEDICAL / Nursing / Emergency
MED058050	MEDICAL / Nursing / Fundamentals & Skills
MED058060	MEDICAL / Nursing / Gerontology
MED058070	MEDICAL / Nursing / Home & Community Care
MED058090	MEDICAL / Nursing / Issues
MED058100	MEDICAL / Nursing / LPN & LVN
MED058110	MEDICAL / Nursing / Management & Leadership
MED058120	MEDICAL / Nursing / Maternity, Perinatal, Women's Health
MED058220	MEDICAL / Nursing / Medical & Surgical
MED058130	MEDICAL / Nursing / Mental Health
MED058140	MEDICAL / Nursing / Nurse & Patient
MED058150	MEDICAL / Nursing / Nutrition
MED058160	MEDICAL / Nursing / Oncology & Cancer
MED058080	MEDICAL / Nursing / Pediatric & Neonatal
MED058170	MEDICAL / Nursing / Pharmacology
MED058180	MEDICAL / Nursing / Psychiatric
MED058190	MEDICAL / Nursing / Reference
MED058200	MEDICAL / Nursing / Research & Theory
MED058210	MEDICAL / Nursing / Test Preparation & Review
MED059000	MEDICAL / Nursing Home Care
MED060000	MEDICAL / Nutrition
	MEDICAL / Obstetrics see Gynecology & Obstetrics
MED061000	MEDICAL / Occupational & Industrial Medicine
MED062000	MEDICAL / Oncology
MED063000	MEDICAL / Ophthalmology
MED064000	MEDICAL / Optometry
	MEDICAL / Oral & Maxillofacial Surgery see Surgery / Oral & Maxillofacial
MED065000	MEDICAL / Orthopedics
MED092000	MEDICAL / Osteopathy
MED066000	MEDICAL / Otorhinolaryngology
MED093000	MEDICAL / Pain Medicine
MED103000	MEDICAL / Parasitology
MED067000	MEDICAL / Pathology
MED068000	MEDICAL / Pathophysiology
	MEDICAL / Patients see Physician & Patient
MED094000	MEDICAL / Pediatric Emergencies
MED069000	MEDICAL / Pediatrics
MED070000	MEDICAL / Perinatology & Neonatology
MED071000	MEDICAL / Pharmacology
MED072000	MEDICAL / Pharmacy
MED073000	MEDICAL / Physical Medicine & Rehabilitation
MED074000	MEDICAL / Physician & Patient
MED104000	MEDICAL / Physicians
MED075000	MEDICAL / Physiology
	MEDICAL / Plastic Surgery see Surgery / Plastic & Cosmetic
MED100000	MEDICAL / Podiatry
MED095000	MEDICAL / Practice Management & Reimbursement
MED076000	MEDICAL / Preventive Medicine
MED077000	MEDICAL / Prosthesis
MED105000	MEDICAL / Psychiatry / General
MED105010	MEDICAL / Psychiatry / Child & Adolescent
MED105020	MEDICAL / Psychiatry / Psychopharmacology
MED078000	MEDICAL / Public Health
MED079000	MEDICAL / Pulmonary & Thoracic Medicine
MED080000	MEDICAL / Radiology, Radiotherapy & Nuclear Medicine
MED081000	MEDICAL / Reference
	MEDICAL / Reimbursement see Practice Management & Reimbursement
MED082000	MEDICAL / Reproductive Medicine & Technology
MED106000	MEDICAL / Research

MED083000 MEDICAL / Rheumatology
MEDICAL / Speech Pathology see Audiology & Speech Pathology
MED084000 MEDICAL / Sports Medicine
MEDICAL / Supplies see Instruments & Supplies
MED085000 MEDICAL / Surgery / General
MED085060 MEDICAL / Surgery / Colon & Rectal
MED085080 MEDICAL / Surgery / Laparoscopic & Robotic
MED085010 MEDICAL / Surgery / Neurosurgery
MED085020 MEDICAL / Surgery / Oral & Maxillofacial
MED085030 MEDICAL / Surgery / Plastic & Cosmetic
MED085040 MEDICAL / Surgery / Thoracic
MED085070 MEDICAL / Surgery / Transplant
MED085050 MEDICAL / Surgery / Vascular
MED042000 MEDICAL / Terminal Care
MED086000 MEDICAL / Test Preparation & Review
MEDICAL / Thoracic Medicine see Pulmonary & Thoracic Medicine
MED096000 MEDICAL / Toxicology
MED087000 MEDICAL / Transportation
MED097000 MEDICAL / Tropical Medicine
MED088000 MEDICAL / Urology
MED089000 MEDICAL / Veterinary Medicine / General
MED089010 MEDICAL / Veterinary Medicine / Equine
MED089020 MEDICAL / Veterinary Medicine / Food Animal
MED089030 MEDICAL / Veterinary Medicine / Small Animal

MUSIC
MUS000000 MUSIC / General
MUS004000 MUSIC / Business Aspects
MUSIC / Buyer's Guides see Discography & Buyer's Guides
MUSIC / Christian see headings under Religious
MUS012000 MUSIC / Discography & Buyer's Guides
MUS014000 MUSIC / Ethnic
MUS015000 MUSIC / Ethnomusicology
MUS049000 MUSIC / Genres & Styles / General
MUS002000 MUSIC / Genres & Styles / Ballet
MUS053000 MUSIC / Genres & Styles / Big Band & Swing
MUSIC / Genres & Styles / Bluegrass see Genres & Styles / Country & Bluegrass
MUS003000 MUSIC / Genres & Styles / Blues
MUS005000 MUSIC / Genres & Styles / Chamber
MUS026000 MUSIC / Genres & Styles / Children's
MUS051000 MUSIC / Genres & Styles / Choral
MUS006000 MUSIC / Genres & Styles / Classical
MUSIC / Genres & Styles / Computer see Genres & Styles / Electronic
MUS010000 MUSIC / Genres & Styles / Country & Bluegrass
MUS011000 MUSIC / Genres & Styles / Dance
MUS013000 MUSIC / Genres & Styles / Electronic
MUS017000 MUSIC / Genres & Styles / Folk & Traditional
MUS019000 MUSIC / Genres & Styles / Heavy Metal
MUS024000 MUSIC / Genres & Styles / International
MUS025000 MUSIC / Genres & Styles / Jazz
MUS036000 MUSIC / Genres & Styles / Latin
MUSIC / Genres & Styles / Lullabies see Genres & Styles / Children's
MUS045000 MUSIC / Genres & Styles / Military & Marches
MUS046000 MUSIC / Genres & Styles / Musicals
MUS027000 MUSIC / Genres & Styles / New Age
MUS028000 MUSIC / Genres & Styles / Opera
MUS029000 MUSIC / Genres & Styles / Pop Vocal
MUS030000 MUSIC / Genres & Styles / Punk
MUS031000 MUSIC / Genres & Styles / Rap & Hip Hop

MUS047000	MUSIC / Genres & Styles / Reggae
	MUSIC / Genres & Styles / Religious see headings under Religious
	MUSIC / Genres & Styles / Rhythm & Blues see Genres & Styles / Soul & R 'n B
MUS035000	MUSIC / Genres & Styles / Rock
	MUSIC / Genres & Styles / Salsa see Genres & Styles / Latin
MUS039000	MUSIC / Genres & Styles / Soul & R 'n B
	MUSIC / Genres & Styles / World Beat see Genres & Styles / International
MUS020000	MUSIC / History & Criticism
MUS050000	MUSIC / Individual Composer & Musician
MUS022000	MUSIC / Instruction & Study / General
MUS001000	MUSIC / Instruction & Study / Appreciation
MUS007000	MUSIC / Instruction & Study / Composition
MUS008000	MUSIC / Instruction & Study / Conducting
MUS016000	MUSIC / Instruction & Study / Exercises
MUS038000	MUSIC / Instruction & Study / Songwriting
MUS040000	MUSIC / Instruction & Study / Techniques
MUS041000	MUSIC / Instruction & Study / Theory
MUS042000	MUSIC / Instruction & Study / Voice
	MUSIC / Instruments see headings under Musical Instruments
MUS052000	MUSIC / Lyrics
MUS023000	MUSIC / Musical Instruments / General
MUS023010	MUSIC / Musical Instruments / Brass
MUS023060	MUSIC / Musical Instruments / Guitar
MUS023020	MUSIC / Musical Instruments / Percussion
MUS023030	MUSIC / Musical Instruments / Piano & Keyboard
MUS023040	MUSIC / Musical Instruments / Strings
MUS023050	MUSIC / Musical Instruments / Woodwinds
MUS037000	MUSIC / Printed Music / General
MUS037010	MUSIC / Printed Music / Artist Specific
MUS037020	MUSIC / Printed Music / Band & Orchestra
MUS037120	MUSIC / Printed Music / Brass
MUS037030	MUSIC / Printed Music / Choral
MUS037040	MUSIC / Printed Music / Guitar & Fretted Instruments
MUS037050	MUSIC / Printed Music / Mixed Collections
MUS037060	MUSIC / Printed Music / Musicals, Film & TV
MUS037070	MUSIC / Printed Music / Opera & Classical Scores
MUS037080	MUSIC / Printed Music / Percussion
MUS037090	MUSIC / Printed Music / Piano & Keyboard Repertoire
MUS037100	MUSIC / Printed Music / Piano-Vocal-Guitar
MUS037130	MUSIC / Printed Music / Strings
MUS037110	MUSIC / Printed Music / Vocal
MUS037140	MUSIC / Printed Music / Woodwinds
MUS032000	MUSIC / Recording & Reproduction
MUS033000	MUSIC / Reference
MUS048000	MUSIC / Religious / General
MUS048010	MUSIC / Religious / Christian
MUS009000	MUSIC / Religious / Contemporary Christian
MUS018000	MUSIC / Religious / Gospel
MUS021000	MUSIC / Religious / Hymns
MUS048020	MUSIC / Religious / Jewish
MUS048030	MUSIC / Religious / Muslim
	MUSIC / Sacred see headings under Religious

NATURE

NAT000000	NATURE / General
NAT039000	NATURE / Animal Rights
NAT001000	NATURE / Animals / General
NAT003000	NATURE / Animals / Bears
NAT042000	NATURE / Animals / Big Cats

Bo Bryant & Thax Turner

NAT043000   NATURE / Animals / Birds
NAT005000   NATURE / Animals / Butterflies & Moths
NAT007000   NATURE / Animals / Dinosaurs & Prehistoric Creatures
NAT012000   NATURE / Animals / Fish
NAT016000   NATURE / Animals / Horses
NAT017000   NATURE / Animals / Insects & Spiders
NAT019000   NATURE / Animals / Mammals
NAT020000   NATURE / Animals / Marine Life
NAT002000   NATURE / Animals / Primates
NAT028000   NATURE / Animals / Reptiles & Amphibians
NAT037000   NATURE / Animals / Wildlife
NAT044000   NATURE / Animals / Wolves
NAT004000   NATURE / Birdwatching Guides
NAT009000   NATURE / Earthquakes & Volcanoes
NAT010000   NATURE / Ecology
NAT045000   NATURE / Ecosystems & Habitats / General
NAT045050   NATURE / Ecosystems & Habitats / Coastal Regions & Shorelines
NAT045010   NATURE / Ecosystems & Habitats / Deserts
NAT014000   NATURE / Ecosystems & Habitats / Forests & Rainforests
NAT018000   NATURE / Ecosystems & Habitats / Lakes, Ponds & Swamps
NAT041000   NATURE / Ecosystems & Habitats / Mountains
NAT025000   NATURE / Ecosystems & Habitats / Oceans & Seas
NAT045020   NATURE / Ecosystems & Habitats / Plains & Prairies
NAT045030   NATURE / Ecosystems & Habitats / Polar Regions
NAT029000   NATURE / Ecosystems & Habitats / Rivers
NAT045040   NATURE / Ecosystems & Habitats / Wilderness
NAT046000   NATURE / Endangered Species
NAT011000   NATURE / Environmental Conservation & Protection
NAT024000   NATURE / Essays
NAT015000   NATURE / Fossils
             NATURE / Minerals see Rocks & Minerals
NAT023000   NATURE / Natural Disasters
NAT038000   NATURE / Natural Resources
NAT026000   NATURE / Plants / General
NAT047000   NATURE / Plants / Aquatic
NAT048000   NATURE / Plants / Cacti & Succulents
NAT013000   NATURE / Plants / Flowers
NAT022000   NATURE / Plants / Mushrooms
NAT034000   NATURE / Plants / Trees
NAT027000   NATURE / Reference
NAT049000   NATURE / Regional
NAT030000   NATURE / Rocks & Minerals
NAT031000   NATURE / Seashells
NAT032000   NATURE / Seasons
NAT033000   NATURE / Sky Observation
             NATURE / Volcanoes see Earthquakes & Volcanoes or SCIENCE / Earth Sciences / Seismology & Volcanism
NAT036000   NATURE / Weather

PERFORMING ARTS
PER000000   PERFORMING ARTS / General
PER001000   PERFORMING ARTS / Acting & Auditioning
PER017000   PERFORMING ARTS / Animation
             PERFORMING ARTS / Broadway & Musical Revue see Theater / Broadway & Musical Revue
PER014000   PERFORMING ARTS / Business Aspects
PER002000   PERFORMING ARTS / Circus
PER015000   PERFORMING ARTS / Comedy
PER003000   PERFORMING ARTS / Dance / General

158

PER003050	PERFORMING ARTS / Dance / Choreography & Dance Notation
PER003010	PERFORMING ARTS / Dance / Classical & Ballet
PER003090	PERFORMING ARTS / Dance / Ballroom
PER003020	PERFORMING ARTS / Dance / Folk
PER003100	PERFORMING ARTS / Dance / History & Criticism
PER003030	PERFORMING ARTS / Dance / Jazz
PER003040	PERFORMING ARTS / Dance / Modern
PER003060	PERFORMING ARTS / Dance / Popular
PER003070	PERFORMING ARTS / Dance / Reference
PER003080	PERFORMING ARTS / Dance / Tap
PER004000	PERFORMING ARTS / Film & Video / General
PER004010	PERFORMING ARTS / Film & Video / Direction & Production
PER004020	PERFORMING ARTS / Film & Video / Guides & Reviews
PER004030	PERFORMING ARTS / Film & Video / History & Criticism
PER004040	PERFORMING ARTS / Film & Video / Reference
PER004050	PERFORMING ARTS / Film & Video / Screenwriting
PER018000	PERFORMING ARTS / Individual Director (see also BIOGRAPHY &

AUTOBIOGRAPHY / Entertainment & Performing Arts)

PERFORMING ARTS / Mass Media see SOCIAL SCIENCE / Media Studies

PERFORMING ARTS / Miming see Theater / Miming

PER020000	PERFORMING ARTS / Monologues & Scenes
PER007000	PERFORMING ARTS / Puppets & Puppetry
PER008000	PERFORMING ARTS / Radio / General
PER008010	PERFORMING ARTS / Radio / History & Criticism
PER008020	PERFORMING ARTS / Radio / Reference
PER009000	PERFORMING ARTS / Reference
PER016000	PERFORMING ARTS / Screenplays
PER019000	PERFORMING ARTS / Storytelling
PER010000	PERFORMING ARTS / Television / General
PER010010	PERFORMING ARTS / Television / Direction & Production
PER010020	PERFORMING ARTS / Television / Guides & Reviews
PER010030	PERFORMING ARTS / Television / History & Criticism
PER010040	PERFORMING ARTS / Television / Reference
PER010050	PERFORMING ARTS / Television / Screenwriting
PER011000	PERFORMING ARTS / Theater / General
PER013000	PERFORMING ARTS / Theater / Broadway & Musical Revue
PER011010	PERFORMING ARTS / Theater / Direction & Production
PER011020	PERFORMING ARTS / Theater / History & Criticism
PER006000	PERFORMING ARTS / Theater / Miming
PER011030	PERFORMING ARTS / Theater / Playwriting
PER011040	PERFORMING ARTS / Theater / Stagecraft

PERFORMING ARTS / Video see headings under Film & Video

PETS

PET000000	PETS / General

PETS / Amphibians see Reptiles, Amphibians & Terrariums

PETS / Aquarium see Fish & Aquariums

PET002000	PETS / Birds
PET003000	PETS / Cats / General
PET003010	PETS / Cats / Breeds

PETS / Cooking for Pets see COOKING / Pet Food

PET004000	PETS / Dogs / General
PET004010	PETS / Dogs / Breeds
PET004020	PETS / Dogs / Training
PET010000	PETS / Essays & Narratives
PET005000	PETS / Fish & Aquariums
PET012000	PETS / Food & Nutrition
PET006000	PETS / Horses
PET011000	PETS / Rabbits, Mice, Hamsters, Guinea Pigs, etc.

PET008000   PETS / Reference
PET009000   PETS / Reptiles, Amphibians & Terrariums
      PETS / Travel see TRAVEL / Special Interest / Pets

PHILOSOPHY
PHI000000   PHILOSOPHY / General
PHI001000   PHILOSOPHY / Aesthetics
PHI028000   PHILOSOPHY / Buddhist
PHI026000   PHILOSOPHY / Criticism
PHI003000   PHILOSOPHY / Eastern
PHI004000   PHILOSOPHY / Epistemology
PHI035000   PHILOSOPHY / Essays
PHI005000   PHILOSOPHY / Ethics & Moral Philosophy
      PHILOSOPHY / Ethnophilosophy see headings under SOCIAL SCIENCE / Ethnic Studies
      PHILOSOPHY / Feminism see SOCIAL SCIENCE / Feminism & Feminist Theory
PHI007000   PHILOSOPHY / Free Will & Determinism
PHI008000   PHILOSOPHY / Good & Evil
PHI036000   PHILOSOPHY / Hermeneutics
PHI033000   PHILOSOPHY / Hindu
PHI009000   PHILOSOPHY / History & Surveys / General
PHI002000   PHILOSOPHY / History & Surveys / Ancient & Classical
PHI012000   PHILOSOPHY / History & Surveys / Medieval
PHI037000   PHILOSOPHY / History & Surveys / Renaissance
PHI016000   PHILOSOPHY / History & Surveys / Modern
PHI038000   PHILOSOPHY / Language
PHI011000   PHILOSOPHY / Logic
PHI013000   PHILOSOPHY / Metaphysics
PHI014000   PHILOSOPHY / Methodology
PHI015000   PHILOSOPHY / Mind & Body
      PHILOSOPHY / Moral Philosophy see Ethics & Moral Philosophy
PHI031000   PHILOSOPHY / Movements / General
PHI039000   PHILOSOPHY / Movements / Analytic
PHI040000   PHILOSOPHY / Movements / Critical Theory
PHI027000   PHILOSOPHY / Movements / Deconstruction
PHI041000   PHILOSOPHY / Movements / Empiricism
PHI006000   PHILOSOPHY / Movements / Existentialism
PHI010000   PHILOSOPHY / Movements / Humanism
PHI042000   PHILOSOPHY / Movements / Idealism
PHI018000   PHILOSOPHY / Movements / Phenomenology
PHI043000   PHILOSOPHY / Movements / Post-Structuralism
PHI020000   PHILOSOPHY / Movements / Pragmatism
PHI032000   PHILOSOPHY / Movements / Rationalism
PHI044000   PHILOSOPHY / Movements / Realism
PHI029000   PHILOSOPHY / Movements / Structuralism
PHI045000   PHILOSOPHY / Movements / Transcendentalism *
PHI030000   PHILOSOPHY / Movements / Utilitarianism
      PHILOSOPHY / Mysticism see BODY, MIND & SPIRIT / Mysticism or RELIGION / Mysticism
      PHILOSOPHY / Philosophy of Education see EDUCATION / Philosophy & Social Aspects
      PHILOSOPHY / Philosophy of Language see Language
      PHILOSOPHY / Philosophy of Religion see RELIGION / Philosophy
      PHILOSOPHY / Philosophy of Science see SCIENCE / Philosophy & Social Aspects
PHI019000   PHILOSOPHY / Political
PHI021000   PHILOSOPHY / Reference
PHI022000   PHILOSOPHY / Religious
PHI034000   PHILOSOPHY / Social
PHI023000   PHILOSOPHY / Taoist

PHILOSOPHY / Utopian see POLITICAL SCIENCE / Utopias
PHILOSOPHY / Western see specific headings in this section
PHILOSOPHY / Yoga see Hindu or HEALTH & FITNESS / Yoga
PHI025000   PHILOSOPHY / Zen

PHOTOGRAPHY
PHO000000   PHOTOGRAPHY / General
PHO025000   PHOTOGRAPHY / Annuals
PHOTOGRAPHY / Basic Techniques see headings under Techniques
PHO003000   PHOTOGRAPHY / Business Aspects
PHOTOGRAPHY / Camera Specific see Techniques / Equipment
PHO004000   PHOTOGRAPHY / Collections, Catalogs, Exhibitions / General
PHO004010   PHOTOGRAPHY / Collections, Catalogs, Exhibitions / Group Shows
PHO004020   PHOTOGRAPHY / Collections, Catalogs, Exhibitions / Permanent
Collections
PHO021000   PHOTOGRAPHY / Commercial
PHO005000   PHOTOGRAPHY / Criticism
PHO010000   PHOTOGRAPHY / History
PHO011000   PHOTOGRAPHY / Individual Photographers / General
PHO011010   PHOTOGRAPHY / Individual Photographers / Artists' Books
PHO011020   PHOTOGRAPHY / Individual Photographers / Essays
PHO011030   PHOTOGRAPHY / Individual Photographers / Monographs
PHOTOGRAPHY / Nature & Wildlife see Subjects & Themes / Plants & Animals
PHO014000   PHOTOGRAPHY / Photoessays & Documentaries
PHO015000   PHOTOGRAPHY / Photojournalism
PHO017000   PHOTOGRAPHY / Reference
PHO023000   PHOTOGRAPHY / Subjects & Themes / General
PHO023010   PHOTOGRAPHY / Subjects & Themes / Aerial
PHO001000   PHOTOGRAPHY / Subjects & Themes / Architectural & Industrial
PHO023070   PHOTOGRAPHY / Subjects & Themes / Celebrations & Events
PHO023080   PHOTOGRAPHY / Subjects & Themes / Celebrity
PHO023020   PHOTOGRAPHY / Subjects & Themes / Children
PHO023030   PHOTOGRAPHY / Subjects & Themes / Erotica
PHO009000   PHOTOGRAPHY / Subjects & Themes / Fashion
PHO023100   PHOTOGRAPHY / Subjects & Themes / Historical
PHO023040   PHOTOGRAPHY / Subjects & Themes / Landscapes
PHO023090   PHOTOGRAPHY / Subjects & Themes / Lifestyles
PHO023050   PHOTOGRAPHY / Subjects & Themes / Nudes
PHO013000   PHOTOGRAPHY / Subjects & Themes / Plants & Animals
PHO016000   PHOTOGRAPHY / Subjects & Themes / Portraits
PHO019000   PHOTOGRAPHY / Subjects & Themes / Regional (see also TRAVEL /
Pictorials)
PHO023060   PHOTOGRAPHY / Subjects & Themes / Sports
PHO018000   PHOTOGRAPHY / Techniques / General
PHO022000   PHOTOGRAPHY / Techniques / Cinematography & Videography
PHO020000   PHOTOGRAPHY / Techniques / Color
PHO006000   PHOTOGRAPHY / Techniques / Darkroom
PHO024000   PHOTOGRAPHY / Techniques / Digital (see also COMPUTERS /
Digital Media / Photography)
PHO007000   PHOTOGRAPHY / Techniques / Equipment
PHO012000   PHOTOGRAPHY / Techniques / Lighting
PHOTOGRAPHY / Travel see Subjects & Themes / Regional
PHOTOGRAPHY / Videography see Techniques / Cinematography & Videography

POETRY
POE000000   POETRY / General
POE007000   POETRY / African
POE005010   POETRY / American / General
POE005050   POETRY / American / African American

Bo Bryant & Thax Turner

POE005060   POETRY / American / Asian American
POE005070   POETRY / American / Hispanic American
POE008000   POETRY / Ancient & Classical
POE001000   POETRY / Anthologies (multiple authors)
POE009000   POETRY / Asian / General
POE009010   POETRY / Asian / Chinese
POE009020   POETRY / Asian / Japanese
POE010000   POETRY / Australian & Oceanian
POE011000   POETRY / Canadian
POE012000   POETRY / Caribbean & Latin American
POE014000   POETRY / Epic
POE005030   POETRY / European / General
POE005020   POETRY / European / English, Irish, Scottish, Welsh
POE017000   POETRY / European / French
POE018000   POETRY / European / German
POE019000   POETRY / European / Italian
POE020000   POETRY / European / Spanish & Portuguese
             POETRY / History & Criticism see LITERARY CRITICISM / Poetry
POE021000   POETRY / LGBT
POE022000   POETRY / Medieval
POE013000   POETRY / Middle Eastern
POE015000   POETRY / Native American
             POETRY / Nursery Rhymes see JUVENILE FICTION / Nursery Rhymes
POE016000   POETRY / Russian & Former Soviet Union
POE023000   POETRY / Subjects & Themes / General
POE023010   POETRY / Subjects & Themes / Death, Grief, Loss
POE023050   POETRY / Subjects & Themes / Family
POE003000   POETRY / Subjects & Themes / Inspirational & Religious
POE023020   POETRY / Subjects & Themes / Love & Erotica
POE023030   POETRY / Subjects & Themes / Nature
POE023040   POETRY / Subjects & Themes / Places
             POETRY / Turkic see Middle Eastern
POE024000   POETRY / Women Authors

POLITICAL SCIENCE
POL000000   POLITICAL SCIENCE / General
POL040000   POLITICAL SCIENCE / American Government / General
POL040010   POLITICAL SCIENCE / American Government / Executive Branch
POL040030   POLITICAL SCIENCE / American Government / Judicial Branch
POL006000   POLITICAL SCIENCE / American Government / Legislative Branch
POL040040   POLITICAL SCIENCE / American Government / Local
POL030000   POLITICAL SCIENCE / American Government / National
POL020000   POLITICAL SCIENCE / American Government / State & Provincial
POL039000   POLITICAL SCIENCE / Censorship
POL003000   POLITICAL SCIENCE / Civics & Citizenship
POL004000   POLITICAL SCIENCE / Civil Rights
POL045000   POLITICAL SCIENCE / Colonialism & Post-Colonialism
POL046000   POLITICAL SCIENCE / Commentary & Opinion
POL009000   POLITICAL SCIENCE / Comparative Politics
             POLITICAL SCIENCE / Congress see American Government / Legislative Branch
POL022000   POLITICAL SCIENCE / Constitutions
POL064000   POLITICAL SCIENCE / Corruption & Misconduct *
POL032000   POLITICAL SCIENCE / Essays
             POLITICAL SCIENCE / Federal Government see American Government / National or
headings under World
POL061000   POLITICAL SCIENCE / Genocide & War Crimes
POL062000   POLITICAL SCIENCE / Geopolitics
POL033000   POLITICAL SCIENCE / Globalization
POL010000   POLITICAL SCIENCE / History & Theory

162

POL035010   POLITICAL SCIENCE / Human Rights
POL047000   POLITICAL SCIENCE / Imperialism
POL036000   POLITICAL SCIENCE / Intelligence & Espionage
POL048000   POLITICAL SCIENCE / Intergovernmental Organizations
POL011000   POLITICAL SCIENCE / International Relations / General
POL001000   POLITICAL SCIENCE / International Relations / Arms Control
POL011010   POLITICAL SCIENCE / International Relations / Diplomacy
POL011020   POLITICAL SCIENCE / International Relations / Trade & Tariffs
POL021000   POLITICAL SCIENCE / International Relations / Treaties
POL013000   POLITICAL SCIENCE / Labor & Industrial Relations
POL014000   POLITICAL SCIENCE / Law Enforcement
POL041000   POLITICAL SCIENCE / NGOs (Non-Governmental Organizations)
POL034000   POLITICAL SCIENCE / Peace
POL023000   POLITICAL SCIENCE / Political Economy
POL035000   POLITICAL SCIENCE / Political Freedom
POL042000   POLITICAL SCIENCE / Political Ideologies / General
POL042010   POLITICAL SCIENCE / Political Ideologies / Anarchism
POL005000   POLITICAL SCIENCE / Political Ideologies / Communism, Post-Communism & Socialism
POL042020   POLITICAL SCIENCE / Political Ideologies / Conservatism & Liberalism
POL007000   POLITICAL SCIENCE / Political Ideologies / Democracy
POL042030   POLITICAL SCIENCE / Political Ideologies / Fascism & Totalitarianism
POL042050   POLITICAL SCIENCE / Political Ideologies / Libertarianism *
POL031000   POLITICAL SCIENCE / Political Ideologies / Nationalism & Patriotism
              POLITICAL SCIENCE / Political Ideologies / Racism see SOCIAL SCIENCE / Discrimination & Race Relations
POL042040   POLITICAL SCIENCE / Political Ideologies / Radicalism
POL016000   POLITICAL SCIENCE / Political Process / General
POL008000   POLITICAL SCIENCE / Political Process / Campaigns & Elections
POL025000   POLITICAL SCIENCE / Political Process / Leadership
POL065000   POLITICAL SCIENCE / Political Process / Media & Internet *
POL043000   POLITICAL SCIENCE / Political Process / Political Advocacy
POL015000   POLITICAL SCIENCE / Political Process / Political Parties
              POLITICAL SCIENCE / Practical Politics see headings under Political Process
POL066000   POLITICAL SCIENCE / Privacy & Surveillance (see also SOCIAL SCIENCE / Privacy & Surveillance) *
POL049000   POLITICAL SCIENCE / Propaganda
POL017000   POLITICAL SCIENCE / Public Affairs & Administration
POL028000   POLITICAL SCIENCE / Public Policy / General
POL067000   POLITICAL SCIENCE / Public Policy / Agriculture & Food Policy (see also SOCIAL SCIENCE / Agriculture & Food) *
POL002000   POLITICAL SCIENCE / Public Policy / City Planning & Urban Development
              POLITICAL SCIENCE / Public Policy / Commercial Policy see BUSINESS & ECONOMICS / Commercial Policy
POL038000   POLITICAL SCIENCE / Public Policy / Cultural Policy
POL050000   POLITICAL SCIENCE / Public Policy / Communication Policy
POL024000   POLITICAL SCIENCE / Public Policy / Economic Policy
              POLITICAL SCIENCE / Public Policy / Education see headings under EDUCATION / Educational Policy & Reform
POL044000   POLITICAL SCIENCE / Public Policy / Environmental Policy
              POLITICAL SCIENCE / Public Policy / Health & Medicine see MEDICAL / Health Policy
POL026000   POLITICAL SCIENCE / Public Policy / Regional Planning
POL063000   POLITICAL SCIENCE / Public Policy / Science & Technology Policy
POL029000   POLITICAL SCIENCE / Public Policy / Social Policy
POL027000   POLITICAL SCIENCE / Public Policy / Social Security
POL019000   POLITICAL SCIENCE / Public Policy / Social Services & Welfare

POL018000 POLITICAL SCIENCE / Reference
POL012000 POLITICAL SCIENCE / Security (National & International)
 POLITICAL SCIENCE / State & Local Government see American Government / Local or American Government / State
POL037000 POLITICAL SCIENCE / Terrorism
POL051000 POLITICAL SCIENCE / Utopias
POL052000 POLITICAL SCIENCE / Women in Politics
POL040020 POLITICAL SCIENCE / World / General
POL053000 POLITICAL SCIENCE / World / African
POL054000 POLITICAL SCIENCE / World / Asian
POL055000 POLITICAL SCIENCE / World / Australian & Oceanian
POL056000 POLITICAL SCIENCE / World / Canadian
POL057000 POLITICAL SCIENCE / World / Caribbean & Latin American
POL058000 POLITICAL SCIENCE / World / European
POL059000 POLITICAL SCIENCE / World / Middle Eastern
POL060000 POLITICAL SCIENCE / World / Russian & Former Soviet Union

PSYCHOLOGY
PSY000000 PSYCHOLOGY / General
 PSYCHOLOGY / Abnormal Psychology see headings under Psychopathology
PSY003000 PSYCHOLOGY / Applied Psychology
PSY042000 PSYCHOLOGY / Assessment, Testing & Measurement
PSY007000 PSYCHOLOGY / Clinical Psychology
PSY051000 PSYCHOLOGY / Cognitive Neuroscience & Cognitive Neuropsychology
PSY008000 PSYCHOLOGY / Cognitive Psychology & Cognition
PSY034000 PSYCHOLOGY / Creative Ability
PSY039000 PSYCHOLOGY / Developmental / General
PSY002000 PSYCHOLOGY / Developmental / Adolescent
PSY043000 PSYCHOLOGY / Developmental / Adulthood & Aging
PSY004000 PSYCHOLOGY / Developmental / Child
PSY044000 PSYCHOLOGY / Developmental / Lifespan Development
PSY012000 PSYCHOLOGY / Education & Training
PSY013000 PSYCHOLOGY / Emotions
PSY050000 PSYCHOLOGY / Ethnopsychology
PSY040000 PSYCHOLOGY / Experimental Psychology
PSY014000 PSYCHOLOGY / Forensic Psychology
PSY052000 PSYCHOLOGY / Grief & Loss
 PSYCHOLOGY / Group Psychology see Social Psychology
PSY015000 PSYCHOLOGY / History
PSY016000 PSYCHOLOGY / Human Sexuality
PSY035000 PSYCHOLOGY / Hypnotism
PSY021000 PSYCHOLOGY / Industrial & Organizational Psychology
PSY017000 PSYCHOLOGY / Interpersonal Relations
PSY036000 PSYCHOLOGY / Mental Health
 PSYCHOLOGY / Mental Illness see headings under Psychopathology
 PSYCHOLOGY / Methodology see Research & Methodology
PSY045000 PSYCHOLOGY / Movements / General
PSY045010 PSYCHOLOGY / Movements / Behaviorism
PSY045070 PSYCHOLOGY / Movements / Cognitive Behavioral Therapy (CBT)
PSY045040 PSYCHOLOGY / Movements / Existential
PSY045050 PSYCHOLOGY / Movements / Gestalt
PSY045020 PSYCHOLOGY / Movements / Humanistic
PSY045060 PSYCHOLOGY / Movements / Jungian
PSY026000 PSYCHOLOGY / Movements / Psychoanalysis
PSY045030 PSYCHOLOGY / Movements / Transpersonal
PSY020000 PSYCHOLOGY / Neuropsychology
 PSYCHOLOGY / Occupational Psychology see Industrial & Organizational Psychology
 PSYCHOLOGY / Pathological Psychology see headings under Psychopathology
PSY023000 PSYCHOLOGY / Personality

PSY024000	PSYCHOLOGY / Physiological Psychology
PSY046000	PSYCHOLOGY / Practice Management
	PSYCHOLOGY / Psychiatry see headings under MEDICAL / Psychiatry
	PSYCHOLOGY / Psychoanalysis see Movements / Psychoanalysis
PSY022000	PSYCHOLOGY / Psychopathology / General
PSY038000	PSYCHOLOGY / Psychopathology / Addiction
PSY022060	PSYCHOLOGY / Psychopathology / Anxieties & Phobias
PSY022010	PSYCHOLOGY / Psychopathology / Attention-Deficit Disorder (ADD-ADHD)
PSY022020	PSYCHOLOGY / Psychopathology / Autism Spectrum Disorders
PSY022030	PSYCHOLOGY / Psychopathology / Bipolar Disorder
PSY009000	PSYCHOLOGY / Psychopathology / Compulsive Behavior
PSY049000	PSYCHOLOGY / Psychopathology / Depression
PSY022070	PSYCHOLOGY / Psychopathology / Dissociative Identity Disorder
PSY011000	PSYCHOLOGY / Psychopathology / Eating Disorders
PSY022080	PSYCHOLOGY / Psychopathology / Personality Disorders
PSY022040	PSYCHOLOGY / Psychopathology / Post-Traumatic Stress Disorder (PTSD)
PSY022050	PSYCHOLOGY / Psychopathology / Schizophrenia
	PSYCHOLOGY / Psychopharmacology see MEDICAL / Psychiatry / Psychopharmacology
PSY028000	PSYCHOLOGY / Psychotherapy / General
PSY006000	PSYCHOLOGY / Psychotherapy / Child & Adolescent
PSY010000	PSYCHOLOGY / Psychotherapy / Counseling
PSY041000	PSYCHOLOGY / Psychotherapy / Couples & Family
PSY048000	PSYCHOLOGY / Psychotherapy / Group
PSY029000	PSYCHOLOGY / Reference
PSY030000	PSYCHOLOGY / Research & Methodology
	PSYCHOLOGY / Sexuality see Human Sexuality
PSY031000	PSYCHOLOGY / Social Psychology
PSY032000	PSYCHOLOGY / Statistics
	PSYCHOLOGY / Substance Abuse see Psychopathology / Addiction
PSY037000	PSYCHOLOGY / Suicide
	PSYCHOLOGY / Testing & Measurement see Assessment, Testing & Measurement

REFERENCE

REF000000	REFERENCE / General
REF001000	REFERENCE / Almanacs
	REFERENCE / Annuals see Yearbooks & Annuals
REF002000	REFERENCE / Atlases, Gazetteers & Maps (see also TRAVEL / Maps & Road Atlases)
	REFERENCE / Basic Skills see Personal & Practical Guides
REF004000	REFERENCE / Bibliographies & Indexes
	REFERENCE / Biographical Dictionaries see BIOGRAPHY & AUTOBIOGRAPHY / Reference
	REFERENCE / Business Skills see BUSINESS & ECONOMICS / Skills
REF006000	REFERENCE / Catalogs
REF030000	REFERENCE / Consumer Guides
REF007000	REFERENCE / Curiosities & Wonders
REF008000	REFERENCE / Dictionaries
REF009000	REFERENCE / Directories
REF010000	REFERENCE / Encyclopedias
REF011000	REFERENCE / Etiquette
	REFERENCE / Etymology see LANGUAGE ARTS & DISCIPLINES / Linguistics / Etymology
REF013000	REFERENCE / Genealogy & Heraldry
REF028000	REFERENCE / Handbooks & Manuals
	REFERENCE / Indexes see Bibliographies & Indexes
REF015000	REFERENCE / Personal & Practical Guides

REFERENCE / Public Speaking see LANGUAGE ARTS & DISCIPLINES / Public Speaking

REFERENCE / Publishing see LANGUAGE ARTS & DISCIPLINES / Publishing

REF018000   REFERENCE / Questions & Answers

REF019000   REFERENCE / Quotations

REF020000   REFERENCE / Research

REFERENCE / Secretarial Aids & Training see BUSINESS & ECONOMICS / Secretarial Aids & Training

REF031000   REFERENCE / Survival & Emergency Preparedness

REFERENCE / Synonyms & Antonyms see Thesauri

REF022000   REFERENCE / Thesauri

REF023000   REFERENCE / Trivia

REF024000   REFERENCE / Weddings

REF025000   REFERENCE / Word Lists

REF026000   REFERENCE / Writing Skills

REF027000   REFERENCE / Yearbooks & Annuals

RELIGION

REL000000   RELIGION / General

REL001000   RELIGION / Agnosticism

REL114000   RELIGION / Ancient

REL072000   RELIGION / Antiquities & Archaeology

RELIGION / Archaeology see Antiquities & Archaeology

REL004000   RELIGION / Atheism

REL005000   RELIGION / Baha'i

REL006020   RELIGION / Biblical Biography / General

REL006030   RELIGION / Biblical Biography / Old Testament

REL006040   RELIGION / Biblical Biography / New Testament

REL006050   RELIGION / Biblical Commentary / General

REL006060   RELIGION / Biblical Commentary / Old Testament

REL006070   RELIGION / Biblical Commentary / New Testament

REL006080   RELIGION / Biblical Criticism & Interpretation / General

REL006090   RELIGION / Biblical Criticism & Interpretation / Old Testament

REL006100   RELIGION / Biblical Criticism & Interpretation / New Testament

REL006110   RELIGION / Biblical Meditations / General

REL006120   RELIGION / Biblical Meditations / Old Testament

REL006130   RELIGION / Biblical Meditations / New Testament

REL006160   RELIGION / Biblical Reference / General

REL006650   RELIGION / Biblical Reference / Atlases

REL006660   RELIGION / Biblical Reference / Concordances

REL006670   RELIGION / Biblical Reference / Dictionaries & Encyclopedias

REL006680   RELIGION / Biblical Reference / Handbooks

REL006410   RELIGION / Biblical Reference / Language Study

REL006150   RELIGION / Biblical Reference / Quotations

REL006000   RELIGION / Biblical Studies / General

REL006700   RELIGION / Biblical Studies / Bible Study Guides

REL006400   RELIGION / Biblical Studies / Exegesis & Hermeneutics

REL006630   RELIGION / Biblical Studies / History & Culture

REL006710   RELIGION / Biblical Studies / Jesus, the Gospels & Acts

REL006210   RELIGION / Biblical Studies / Old Testament

REL006220   RELIGION / Biblical Studies / New Testament

REL006720   RELIGION / Biblical Studies / Paul's Letters

REL006140   RELIGION / Biblical Studies / Prophecy

REL006730   RELIGION / Biblical Studies / Prophets

REL006740   RELIGION / Biblical Studies / Wisdom Literature

REL115000   RELIGION / Blasphemy, Heresy & Apostasy

REL007000   RELIGION / Buddhism / General (see also PHILOSOPHY / Buddhist)

REL007010   RELIGION / Buddhism / History

REL007020   RELIGION / Buddhism / Rituals & Practice

The 48 Hour Author

REL007030	RELIGION / Buddhism / Sacred Writings
REL007040	RELIGION / Buddhism / Theravada
REL007050	RELIGION / Buddhism / Tibetan
REL092000	RELIGION / Buddhism / Zen (see also PHILOSOPHY / Zen)
	RELIGION / Canon & Ecclesiastical Law see Christian Church / Canon & Ecclesiastical

Law

	RELIGION / Catechisms see Christianity / Catechisms or specific non-Christian religions
REL108000	RELIGION / Christian Church / General
REL014000	RELIGION / Christian Church / Administration
REL008000	RELIGION / Christian Church / Canon & Ecclesiastical Law
REL108010	RELIGION / Christian Church / Growth
REL108020	RELIGION / Christian Church / History
REL108030	RELIGION / Christian Church / Leadership
REL011000	RELIGION / Christian Education / General
REL095000	RELIGION / Christian Education / Adult
REL091000	RELIGION / Christian Education / Children & Youth
REL012000	RELIGION / Christian Life / General
REL012010	RELIGION / Christian Life / Death, Grief, Bereavement
REL012020	RELIGION / Christian Life / Devotional
REL012030	RELIGION / Christian Life / Family
REL012040	RELIGION / Christian Life / Inspirational
REL012050	RELIGION / Christian Life / Love & Marriage
REL012060	RELIGION / Christian Life / Men's Issues
REL012070	RELIGION / Christian Life / Personal Growth
REL012080	RELIGION / Christian Life / Prayer
REL012090	RELIGION / Christian Life / Professional Growth
REL012100	RELIGION / Christian Life / Relationships
REL012110	RELIGION / Christian Life / Social Issues
REL012120	RELIGION / Christian Life / Spiritual Growth
REL099000	RELIGION / Christian Life / Spiritual Warfare
REL063000	RELIGION / Christian Life / Stewardship & Giving
REL012130	RELIGION / Christian Life / Women's Issues
	RELIGION / Christian Literature see Christianity / Literature & the Arts
REL109000	RELIGION / Christian Ministry / General
REL109010	RELIGION / Christian Ministry / Adult
REL109020	RELIGION / Christian Ministry / Children
REL050000	RELIGION / Christian Ministry / Counseling & Recovery
REL023000	RELIGION / Christian Ministry / Discipleship
REL030000	RELIGION / Christian Ministry / Evangelism
REL045000	RELIGION / Christian Ministry / Missions
REL074000	RELIGION / Christian Ministry / Pastoral Resources
REL080000	RELIGION / Christian Ministry / Preaching
REL109030	RELIGION / Christian Ministry / Youth
REL055000	RELIGION / Christian Rituals & Practice / General
REL055010	RELIGION / Christian Rituals & Practice / Sacraments
REL055020	RELIGION / Christian Rituals & Practice / Worship & Liturgy
REL067000	RELIGION / Christian Theology / General
REL067010	RELIGION / Christian Theology / Angelology & Demonology
REL067020	RELIGION / Christian Theology / Anthropology
REL067030	RELIGION / Christian Theology / Apologetics
REL067040	RELIGION / Christian Theology / Christology
	RELIGION / Christian Theology / Doctrinal see Christian Theology / Systematic
REL067050	RELIGION / Christian Theology / Ecclesiology
REL067060	RELIGION / Christian Theology / Eschatology
REL067070	RELIGION / Christian Theology / Ethics
REL067080	RELIGION / Christian Theology / History
REL067120	RELIGION / Christian Theology / Liberation
REL104000	RELIGION / Christian Theology / Mariology
REL067090	RELIGION / Christian Theology / Pneumatology

167

REL067130	RELIGION / Christian Theology / Process
REL067100	RELIGION / Christian Theology / Soteriology
REL067110	RELIGION / Christian Theology / Systematic
REL070000	RELIGION / Christianity / General
REL002000	RELIGION / Christianity / Amish
REL003000	RELIGION / Christianity / Anglican
REL073000	RELIGION / Christianity / Baptist
REL093000	RELIGION / Christianity / Calvinist
REL009000	RELIGION / Christianity / Catechisms
REL010000	RELIGION / Christianity / Catholic
REL083000	RELIGION / Christianity / Christian Science
REL046000	RELIGION / Christianity / Church of Jesus Christ of Latter-day Saints (Mormon)
	RELIGION / Christianity / Congregational see Christianity / United Church of Christ
REL094000	RELIGION / Christianity / Denominations
REL027000	RELIGION / Christianity / Episcopalian
	RELIGION / Christianity / Friends see Christianity / Quaker
REL015000	RELIGION / Christianity / History
	RELIGION / Christianity / Holidays see headings under Holidays
	RELIGION / Christianity / Holy Spirit see Christian Theology / Pneumatology
REL096000	RELIGION / Christianity / Jehovah's Witnesses
REL013000	RELIGION / Christianity / Literature & the Arts
REL082000	RELIGION / Christianity / Lutheran
REL043000	RELIGION / Christianity / Mennonite
REL044000	RELIGION / Christianity / Methodist
	RELIGION / Christianity / Mormon see Christianity / Church of Jesus Christ of Latter-day Saints (Mormon)
REL049000	RELIGION / Christianity / Orthodox
REL079000	RELIGION / Christianity / Pentecostal & Charismatic
	RELIGION / Christianity / Prayerbooks see Prayerbooks / Christian
REL097000	RELIGION / Christianity / Presbyterian
REL053000	RELIGION / Christianity / Protestant
REL088000	RELIGION / Christianity / Quaker
	RELIGION / Christianity / Roman Catholic see Christianity / Catholic
REL110000	RELIGION / Christianity / Saints & Sainthood
	RELIGION / Christianity / Sermons see Sermons / Christian
REL098000	RELIGION / Christianity / Seventh-Day Adventist
REL059000	RELIGION / Christianity / Shaker
	RELIGION / Christianity / Society of Friends see Christianity / Quaker
	RELIGION / Christianity / Unitarian Universalism see Unitarian Universalism
REL111000	RELIGION / Christianity / United Church of Christ
	RELIGION / Church Administration see Christian Church / Administration
	RELIGION / Church & State see Religion, Politics & State
	RELIGION / Church Institutions & Organizations see Institutions & Organizations
REL081000	RELIGION / Clergy
REL017000	RELIGION / Comparative Religion
REL018000	RELIGION / Confucianism
REL019000	RELIGION / Counseling
REL020000	RELIGION / Cults
REL021000	RELIGION / Deism
REL100000	RELIGION / Demonology & Satanism
REL022000	RELIGION / Devotional
	RELIGION / Discipleship see Christian Ministry / Discipleship
REL024000	RELIGION / Eastern
	RELIGION / Ecclesiastical Law see Christian Church / Canon & Ecclesiastical Law
REL107000	RELIGION / Eckankar
REL025000	RELIGION / Ecumenism & Interfaith
REL026000	RELIGION / Education
REL085000	RELIGION / Eschatology

REL113000   RELIGION / Essays
REL028000   RELIGION / Ethics
REL029000   RELIGION / Ethnic & Tribal
　　　　　　RELIGION / Evangelism see Christian Ministry / Evangelism
REL077000   RELIGION / Faith
　　　　　　RELIGION / Freemasonry see SOCIAL SCIENCE / Freemasonry & Secret Societies
REL078000   RELIGION / Fundamentalism
REL112000   RELIGION / Gnosticism
REL032000   RELIGION / Hinduism / General
REL032010   RELIGION / Hinduism / History
REL032020   RELIGION / Hinduism / Rituals & Practice
REL032030   RELIGION / Hinduism / Sacred Writings
REL032040   RELIGION / Hinduism / Theology
REL033000   RELIGION / History
REL034000   RELIGION / Holidays / General
REL034010   RELIGION / Holidays / Christian
REL034020   RELIGION / Holidays / Christmas & Advent
REL034030   RELIGION / Holidays / Easter & Lent
REL034040   RELIGION / Holidays / Jewish
REL034050   RELIGION / Holidays / Other
　　　　　　RELIGION / I Ching see BODY, MIND & SPIRIT / I Ching
REL036000   RELIGION / Inspirational
REL016000   RELIGION / Institutions & Organizations
REL037000   RELIGION / Islam / General
REL037010   RELIGION / Islam / History
REL041000   RELIGION / Islam / Koran & Sacred Writings
REL037020   RELIGION / Islam / Law
REL037030   RELIGION / Islam / Rituals & Practice
REL037040   RELIGION / Islam / Shi'a
REL090000   RELIGION / Islam / Sufi
REL037050   RELIGION / Islam / Sunni
REL037060   RELIGION / Islam / Theology
REL038000   RELIGION / Jainism
　　　　　　RELIGION / Jewish Life see Judaism / Rituals & Practice
REL040000   RELIGION / Judaism / General
REL040050   RELIGION / Judaism / Conservative
REL040030   RELIGION / Judaism / History
　　　　　　RELIGION / Judaism / Holocaust see HISTORY / Holocaust
REL040060   RELIGION / Judaism / Kabbalah & Mysticism
REL040070   RELIGION / Judaism / Orthodox
　　　　　　RELIGION / Judaism / Prayerbooks, Prayers, Liturgy see Prayerbooks / Jewish
REL040080   RELIGION / Judaism / Reform
REL040010   RELIGION / Judaism / Rituals & Practice
REL040040   RELIGION / Judaism / Sacred Writings
REL064000   RELIGION / Judaism / Talmud
REL040090   RELIGION / Judaism / Theology
　　　　　　RELIGION / Koran see Islam / Koran & Sacred Writings
REL071000   RELIGION / Leadership
REL042000   RELIGION / Meditations
REL101000   RELIGION / Messianic Judaism
REL086000   RELIGION / Monasticism
　　　　　　RELIGION / Muslim see headings under Islam
REL047000   RELIGION / Mysticism
　　　　　　RELIGION / Mythology see SOCIAL SCIENCE / Folklore & Mythology
REL117000   RELIGION / Paganism & Neo-Paganism
　　　　　　RELIGION / Pastoral Counseling see Christian Ministry / Counseling & Recovery
　　　　　　RELIGION / Pastoral Ministry see Christian Ministry / Pastoral Resources
REL051000   RELIGION / Philosophy
REL087000   RELIGION / Prayer

REL052000   RELIGION / Prayerbooks / General
REL052010   RELIGION / Prayerbooks / Christian
REL052030   RELIGION / Prayerbooks / Islamic
REL052020   RELIGION / Prayerbooks / Jewish
REL075000   RELIGION / Psychology of Religion
REL054000   RELIGION / Reference
REL106000   RELIGION / Religion & Science
REL084000   RELIGION / Religion, Politics & State
REL116000   RELIGION / Religious Intolerance, Persecution & Conflict
       RELIGION / Rituals & Practice see specific religions
       RELIGION / Rosicrucianism see BODY, MIND & SPIRIT / Hermetism & Rosicrucianism
       RELIGION / Satanism see Demonology & Satanism
REL089000   RELIGION / Scientology
REL058000   RELIGION / Sermons / General
REL058010   RELIGION / Sermons / Christian
REL058020   RELIGION / Sermons / Jewish
REL105000   RELIGION / Sexuality & Gender Studies
REL060000   RELIGION / Shintoism
REL061000   RELIGION / Sikhism
       RELIGION / Sociology of Religion see SOCIAL SCIENCE / Sociology of Religion
REL062000   RELIGION / Spirituality
       RELIGION / Stewardship see Christian Life / Stewardship & Giving
       RELIGION / Sufi see Islam / Sufi
       RELIGION / Talmud see Judaism / Talmud
REL065000   RELIGION / Taoism (see also PHILOSOPHY / Taoist)
REL066000   RELIGION / Theism
REL102000   RELIGION / Theology
REL068000   RELIGION / Theosophy
REL103000   RELIGION / Unitarian Universalism
REL118000   RELIGION / Wicca (see also BODY, MIND & SPIRIT / Witchcraft)
       RELIGION / Youth Ministries see Christian Education / Children & Youth
       RELIGION / Zen Buddhism see Buddhism / Zen
REL069000   RELIGION / Zoroastrianism

SCIENCE

SCI000000   SCIENCE / General
SCI001000   SCIENCE / Acoustics & Sound
SCI003000   SCIENCE / Applied Sciences
SCI004000   SCIENCE / Astronomy
SCI010000   SCIENCE / Biotechnology
SCI012000   SCIENCE / Chaotic Behavior in Systems
SCI013000   SCIENCE / Chemistry / General
SCI013010   SCIENCE / Chemistry / Analytic
       SCIENCE / Chemistry / Biochemistry see Life Sciences / Biochemistry
SCI013020   SCIENCE / Chemistry / Clinical
SCI013070   SCIENCE / Chemistry / Computational & Molecular Modeling
SCI013080   SCIENCE / Chemistry / Environmental (see also Environmental Science)
SCI013060   SCIENCE / Chemistry / Industrial & Technical
SCI013030   SCIENCE / Chemistry / Inorganic
SCI013040   SCIENCE / Chemistry / Organic
SCI013050   SCIENCE / Chemistry / Physical & Theoretical
SCI013090   SCIENCE / Chemistry / Toxicology
SCI090000   SCIENCE / Cognitive Science
SCI015000   SCIENCE / Cosmology
SCI019000   SCIENCE / Earth Sciences / General
SCI030000   SCIENCE / Earth Sciences / Geography
SCI031000   SCIENCE / Earth Sciences / Geology
       SCIENCE / Earth Sciences / Geophysics see Physics / Geophysics

SCI081000	SCIENCE / Earth Sciences / Hydrology
SCI083000	SCIENCE / Earth Sciences / Limnology
SCI042000	SCIENCE / Earth Sciences / Meteorology & Climatology
SCI048000	SCIENCE / Earth Sciences / Mineralogy
SCI052000	SCIENCE / Earth Sciences / Oceanography
SCI091000	SCIENCE / Earth Sciences / Sedimentology & Stratigraphy
SCI082000	SCIENCE / Earth Sciences / Seismology & Volcanism
SCI023000	SCIENCE / Electron Microscopes & Microscopy
SCI024000	SCIENCE / Energy
SCI026000	SCIENCE / Environmental Science (see also Chemistry / Environmental)
SCI080000	SCIENCE / Essays
SCI028000	SCIENCE / Experiments & Projects
SCI092000	SCIENCE / Global Warming & Climate Change
SCI033000	SCIENCE / Gravity
SCI034000	SCIENCE / History
SCI093000	SCIENCE / Laboratory Techniques
SCI086000	SCIENCE / Life Sciences / General
SCI056000	SCIENCE / Life Sciences / Anatomy & Physiology (see also Life Sciences / Human Anatomy & Physiology)
SCI006000	SCIENCE / Life Sciences / Bacteriology
SCI007000	SCIENCE / Life Sciences / Biochemistry
SCI088000	SCIENCE / Life Sciences / Biological Diversity
SCI008000	SCIENCE / Life Sciences / Biology
SCI009000	SCIENCE / Life Sciences / Biophysics
SCI011000	SCIENCE / Life Sciences / Botany
SCI017000	SCIENCE / Life Sciences / Cell Biology
	SCIENCE / Life Sciences / Cytology see Life Sciences / Cell Biology
SCI072000	SCIENCE / Life Sciences / Developmental Biology
SCI020000	SCIENCE / Life Sciences / Ecology
SCI027000	SCIENCE / Life Sciences / Evolution
SCI029000	SCIENCE / Life Sciences / Genetics & Genomics
SCI073000	SCIENCE / Life Sciences / Horticulture
SCI036000	SCIENCE / Life Sciences / Human Anatomy & Physiology
SCI039000	SCIENCE / Life Sciences / Marine Biology
SCI045000	SCIENCE / Life Sciences / Microbiology
SCI049000	SCIENCE / Life Sciences / Molecular Biology
SCI094000	SCIENCE / Life Sciences / Mycology
SCI089000	SCIENCE / Life Sciences / Neuroscience
	SCIENCE / Life Sciences / Physiology see Life Sciences / Anatomy & Physiology
SCI087000	SCIENCE / Life Sciences / Taxonomy
SCI099000	SCIENCE / Life Sciences / Virology
SCI070000	SCIENCE / Life Sciences / Zoology / General
SCI025000	SCIENCE / Life Sciences / Zoology / Entomology
SCI070010	SCIENCE / Life Sciences / Zoology / Ichthyology & Herpetology
SCI070020	SCIENCE / Life Sciences / Zoology / Invertebrates
SCI070030	SCIENCE / Life Sciences / Zoology / Mammals
SCI070040	SCIENCE / Life Sciences / Zoology / Ornithology
SCI070050	SCIENCE / Life Sciences / Zoology / Primatology
	SCIENCE / Light see Physics / Optics & Light
SCI041000	SCIENCE / Mechanics / General
SCI084000	SCIENCE / Mechanics / Aerodynamics
SCI018000	SCIENCE / Mechanics / Dynamics
SCI085000	SCIENCE / Mechanics / Fluids
SCI095000	SCIENCE / Mechanics / Hydrodynamics
	SCIENCE / Mechanics / Materials Science see TECHNOLOGY & ENGINEERING / Materials Science
SCI096000	SCIENCE / Mechanics / Solids
SCI079000	SCIENCE / Mechanics / Statics
SCI065000	SCIENCE / Mechanics / Thermodynamics

SCIENCE / Methodology see Research & Methodology
SCI047000   SCIENCE / Microscopes & Microscopy
SCI050000   SCIENCE / Nanoscience
SCI100000   SCIENCE / Natural History
SCI054000   SCIENCE / Paleontology
SCI075000   SCIENCE / Philosophy & Social Aspects
SCI055000   SCIENCE / Physics / General
SCI005000   SCIENCE / Physics / Astrophysics
SCI074000   SCIENCE / Physics / Atomic & Molecular
SCIENCE / Physics / Biophysics see Life Sciences / Biophysics
SCI077000   SCIENCE / Physics / Condensed Matter
SCI016000   SCIENCE / Physics / Crystallography
SCI021000   SCIENCE / Physics / Electricity
SCI022000   SCIENCE / Physics / Electromagnetism
SCI032000   SCIENCE / Physics / Geophysics
SCI038000   SCIENCE / Physics / Magnetism
SCI040000   SCIENCE / Physics / Mathematical & Computational
SCI051000   SCIENCE / Physics / Nuclear
SCI053000   SCIENCE / Physics / Optics & Light
SCI097000   SCIENCE / Physics / Polymer
SCI057000   SCIENCE / Physics / Quantum Theory
SCI061000   SCIENCE / Physics / Relativity
SCIENCE / Projects see Experiments & Projects
SCI058000   SCIENCE / Radiation
SCI059000   SCIENCE / Radiography
SCI060000   SCIENCE / Reference
SCI043000   SCIENCE / Research & Methodology
SCI076000   SCIENCE / Scientific Instruments
SCIENCE / Social Aspects see Philosophy & Social Aspects
SCIENCE / Sound see Acoustics & Sound
SCI098000   SCIENCE / Space Science
SCI078000   SCIENCE / Spectroscopy & Spectrum Analysis
SCI063000   SCIENCE / Study & Teaching
SCI064000   SCIENCE / System Theory
SCI066000   SCIENCE / Time
SCI067000   SCIENCE / Waves & Wave Mechanics
SCI068000   SCIENCE / Weights & Measures

SELF-HELP
SEL000000   SELF-HELP / General
SEL001000   SELF-HELP / Abuse
SELF-HELP / Addiction see headings under Substance Abuse & Addictions
SEL003000   SELF-HELP / Adult Children of Substance Abusers
SEL004000   SELF-HELP / Affirmations
SEL005000   SELF-HELP / Aging
SEL036000   SELF-HELP / Anxieties & Phobias
SELF-HELP / Bereavement see Death, Grief, Bereavement
SELF-HELP / Chemical Dependence see headings under Substance Abuse & Addictions
SEL008000   SELF-HELP / Codependency
SEL040000   SELF-HELP / Communication & Social Skills
SEL041000   SELF-HELP / Compulsive Behavior / General
SEL041010   SELF-HELP / Compulsive Behavior / Gambling
SEL041020   SELF-HELP / Compulsive Behavior / Hoarding
SEL041030   SELF-HELP / Compulsive Behavior / Obsessive Compulsive Disorder (OCD)
SEL041040   SELF-HELP / Compulsive Behavior / Sex & Pornography Addiction
SEL009000   SELF-HELP / Creativity
SEL010000   SELF-HELP / Death, Grief, Bereavement
SEL012000   SELF-HELP / Dreams

SEL014000	SELF-HELP / Eating Disorders & Body Image
SEL042000	SELF-HELP / Emotions
SEL038000	SELF-HELP / Fashion & Style
SEL039000	SELF-HELP / Green Lifestyle
	SELF-HELP / Grief see Death, Grief, Bereavement
SEL015000	SELF-HELP / Handwriting Analysis
	SELF-HELP / Hypnotism see Self-Hypnosis
SEL045000	SELF-HELP / Journaling *
SEL019000	SELF-HELP / Meditations
	SELF-HELP / Memory Improvement see Personal Growth / Memory Improvement
SEL020000	SELF-HELP / Mood Disorders/ General
SEL020010	SELF-HELP / Mood Disorders/ Bipolar Disorder
SEL011000	SELF-HELP / Mood Disorders/ Depression
SEL021000	SELF-HELP / Motivational & Inspirational
SEL037000	SELF-HELP / Neuro-Linguistic Programming (NLP)
SEL031000	SELF-HELP / Personal Growth / General
SEL016000	SELF-HELP / Personal Growth / Happiness
SEL030000	SELF-HELP / Personal Growth / Memory Improvement
SEL023000	SELF-HELP / Personal Growth / Self-Esteem
SEL027000	SELF-HELP / Personal Growth / Success
SEL043000	SELF-HELP / Post-Traumatic Stress Disorder (PTSD)
	SELF-HELP / Recovery see specific headings in this section
	SELF-HELP / Relaxation see Self-Management / Stress Management
SEL017000	SELF-HELP / Self-Hypnosis
SEL034000	SELF-HELP / Sexual Instruction
SEL032000	SELF-HELP / Spiritual
SEL044000	SELF-HELP / Self-Management / General
SEL033000	SELF-HELP / Self-Management / Anger Management (see also FAMILY & RELATIONSHIPS / Anger)
SEL024000	SELF-HELP / Self-Management / Stress Management
SEL035000	SELF-HELP / Self-Management / Time Management
SEL026000	SELF-HELP / Substance Abuse & Addictions / General
SEL006000	SELF-HELP / Substance Abuse & Addictions / Alcohol
SEL013000	SELF-HELP / Substance Abuse & Addictions / Drugs
SEL026010	SELF-HELP / Substance Abuse & Addictions / Tobacco
SEL029000	SELF-HELP / Twelve-Step Programs

SOCIAL SCIENCE

SOC000000	SOCIAL SCIENCE / General
SOC046000	SOCIAL SCIENCE / Abortion & Birth Control
	SOCIAL SCIENCE / African American Studies see Ethnic Studies / African American Studies
SOC055000	SOCIAL SCIENCE / Agriculture & Food (see also POLITICAL SCIENCE / Public Policy / Agriculture & Food Policy)
SOC002000	SOCIAL SCIENCE / Anthropology / General
SOC002010	SOCIAL SCIENCE / Anthropology / Cultural
SOC002020	SOCIAL SCIENCE / Anthropology / Physical
SOC003000	SOCIAL SCIENCE / Archaeology
SOC056000	SOCIAL SCIENCE / Black Studies (Global)
SOC061000	SOCIAL SCIENCE / Body Language & Nonverbal Communication
	SOCIAL SCIENCE / Charity see Philanthropy & Charity
SOC047000	SOCIAL SCIENCE / Children's Studies
SOC058000	SOCIAL SCIENCE / Conspiracy Theories
SOC004000	SOCIAL SCIENCE / Criminology
SOC005000	SOCIAL SCIENCE / Customs & Traditions
SOC036000	SOCIAL SCIENCE / Death & Dying
SOC006000	SOCIAL SCIENCE / Demography
SOC042000	SOCIAL SCIENCE / Developing & Emerging Countries
	SOCIAL SCIENCE / Disabled see People with Disabilities

Bo Bryant & Thax Turner

SOC040000   SOCIAL SCIENCE / Disasters & Disaster Relief
SOC057000   SOCIAL SCIENCE / Disease & Health Issues
SOC031000   SOCIAL SCIENCE / Discrimination & Race Relations
SOC007000   SOCIAL SCIENCE / Emigration & Immigration
SOC041000   SOCIAL SCIENCE / Essays
SOC008000   SOCIAL SCIENCE / Ethnic Studies / General
SOC001000   SOCIAL SCIENCE / Ethnic Studies / African American Studies
SOC043000   SOCIAL SCIENCE / Ethnic Studies / Asian American Studies
SOC044000   SOCIAL SCIENCE / Ethnic Studies / Hispanic American Studies
SOC021000   SOCIAL SCIENCE / Ethnic Studies / Native American Studies
        SOCIAL SCIENCE / Ethnology see Anthropology / Cultural
SOC010000   SOCIAL SCIENCE / Feminism & Feminist Theory
SOC011000   SOCIAL SCIENCE / Folklore & Mythology
SOC038000   SOCIAL SCIENCE / Freemasonry & Secret Societies
SOC037000   SOCIAL SCIENCE / Future Studies
SOC012000   SOCIAL SCIENCE / Gay Studies
SOC032000   SOCIAL SCIENCE / Gender Studies
SOC013000   SOCIAL SCIENCE / Gerontology
        SOCIAL SCIENCE / Handicapped see People with Disabilities
SOC014000   SOCIAL SCIENCE / Holidays (non-religious)
        SOCIAL SCIENCE / Homosexuality see Gay Studies
SOC015000   SOCIAL SCIENCE / Human Geography
SOC016000   SOCIAL SCIENCE / Human Services
        SOCIAL SCIENCE / Immigration see Emigration & Immigration
SOC062000   SOCIAL SCIENCE / Indigenous Studies
SOC048000   SOCIAL SCIENCE / Islamic Studies
SOC049000   SOCIAL SCIENCE / Jewish Studies
SOC017000   SOCIAL SCIENCE / Lesbian Studies
SOC052000   SOCIAL SCIENCE / Media Studies
SOC018000   SOCIAL SCIENCE / Men's Studies
SOC019000   SOCIAL SCIENCE / Methodology
SOC020000   SOCIAL SCIENCE / Minority Studies
        SOCIAL SCIENCE / Native American Studies see Ethnic Studies / Native American
Studies
SOC030000   SOCIAL SCIENCE / Penology
SOC029000   SOCIAL SCIENCE / People with Disabilities
SOC033000   SOCIAL SCIENCE / Philanthropy & Charity
SOC022000   SOCIAL SCIENCE / Popular Culture
SOC034000   SOCIAL SCIENCE / Pornography
SOC045000   SOCIAL SCIENCE / Poverty & Homelessness
SOC063000   SOCIAL SCIENCE / Privacy & Surveillance (see also POLITICAL
SCIENCE / Privacy & Surveillance) *
SOC059000   SOCIAL SCIENCE / Prostitution & Sex Trade
        SOCIAL SCIENCE / Race Relations see Discrimination & Race Relations
SOC023000   SOCIAL SCIENCE / Reference
SOC053000   SOCIAL SCIENCE / Regional Studies
SOC024000   SOCIAL SCIENCE / Research
SOC060000   SOCIAL SCIENCE / Sexual Abuse & Harassment
SOC054000   SOCIAL SCIENCE / Slavery
SOC050000   SOCIAL SCIENCE / Social Classes
        SOCIAL SCIENCE / Social History see HISTORY / Social History
SOC025000   SOCIAL SCIENCE / Social Work
SOC026000   SOCIAL SCIENCE / Sociology / General
SOC026010   SOCIAL SCIENCE / Sociology / Marriage & Family
SOC026020   SOCIAL SCIENCE / Sociology / Rural
SOC026030   SOCIAL SCIENCE / Sociology / Urban
SOC039000   SOCIAL SCIENCE / Sociology of Religion
        SOCIAL SCIENCE / Sociology of Sports see SPORTS & RECREATION / Sociology of
Sports

174

SPO027000	SPORTS & RECREATION / Martial Arts & Self-Defense
SPO028000	SPORTS & RECREATION / Motor Sports
SPO029000	SPORTS & RECREATION / Mountaineering
SPO058000	SPORTS & RECREATION / Olympics & Paralympics
SPO030000	SPORTS & RECREATION / Outdoor Skills
SPO055000	SPORTS & RECREATION / Polo
SPO060000	SPORTS & RECREATION / Pool, Billiards, Snooker
SPO031000	SPORTS & RECREATION / Racket Sports
SPO032000	SPORTS & RECREATION / Racquetball
SPO033000	SPORTS & RECREATION / Reference
SPO065000	SPORTS & RECREATION / Rodeos
SPO034000	SPORTS & RECREATION / Roller & In-Line Skating
SPO056000	SPORTS & RECREATION / Rugby
SPO035000	SPORTS & RECREATION / Running & Jogging
SPO036000	SPORTS & RECREATION / Sailing
SPO059000	SPORTS & RECREATION / Scuba & Snorkeling
	SPORTS & RECREATION / Self-Defense see Martial Arts & Self-Defense
SPO037000	SPORTS & RECREATION / Shooting
SPO038000	SPORTS & RECREATION / Skateboarding
SPO039000	SPORTS & RECREATION / Skiing
	SPORTS & RECREATION / Snorkeling see Scuba & Snorkeling
SPO072000	SPORTS & RECREATION / Snowboarding
SPO040000	SPORTS & RECREATION / Soccer
SPO066000	SPORTS & RECREATION / Sociology of Sports
SPO067000	SPORTS & RECREATION / Softball
SPO041000	SPORTS & RECREATION / Sports Psychology
SPO042000	SPORTS & RECREATION / Squash
SPO069000	SPORTS & RECREATION / Surfing
SPO043000	SPORTS & RECREATION / Swimming & Diving
SPO044000	SPORTS & RECREATION / Table Tennis
SPO045000	SPORTS & RECREATION / Tennis
SPO046000	SPORTS & RECREATION / Track & Field
SPO047000	SPORTS & RECREATION / Training
SPO048000	SPORTS & RECREATION / Triathlon
SPO049000	SPORTS & RECREATION / Volleyball
SPO050000	SPORTS & RECREATION / Walking
SPO051000	SPORTS & RECREATION / Water Sports
	SPORTS & RECREATION / Weight Training see Bodybuilding & Weight Training
SPO052000	SPORTS & RECREATION / Winter Sports
SPO053000	SPORTS & RECREATION / Wrestling

STUDY AIDS

STU000000	STUDY AIDS / General
STU001000	STUDY AIDS / ACT
STU002000	STUDY AIDS / Advanced Placement
STU003000	STUDY AIDS / Armed Forces
STU034000	STUDY AIDS / Bar Exam
STU004000	STUDY AIDS / Book Notes (see also JUVENILE NONFICTION / Study Aids / Book Notes)
STU006000	STUDY AIDS / Citizenship
STU007000	STUDY AIDS / Civil Service
STU008000	STUDY AIDS / CLEP (College-Level Examination Program)
STU009000	STUDY AIDS / College Entrance
STU010000	STUDY AIDS / College Guides
STU011000	STUDY AIDS / CPA (Certified Public Accountant)
STU031000	STUDY AIDS / Financial Aid
STU012000	STUDY AIDS / GED (General Educational Development Tests)
STU013000	STUDY AIDS / GMAT (Graduate Management Admission Test)
STU015000	STUDY AIDS / Graduate School Guides

STU016000   STUDY AIDS / GRE (Graduate Record Examination)
STU025000   STUDY AIDS / High School Entrance
STU017000   STUDY AIDS / LSAT (Law School Admission Test)
STU018000   STUDY AIDS / MAT (Miller Analogies Test)
STU032000   STUDY AIDS / MCAT (Medical College Admission Test)
    STUDY AIDS / Medical Certification & Licensing see MEDICAL / Test Preparation &
Review
    STUDY AIDS / NCLEX see MEDICAL / Nursing / Test Preparation & Review
STU019000   STUDY AIDS / NTE (National Teacher Examinations)
STU021000   STUDY AIDS / Professional
STU033000   STUDY AIDS / PSAT & NMSQT (National Merit Scholarship Qualifying
Test)
STU022000   STUDY AIDS / Regents
STU024000   STUDY AIDS / SAT
    STUDY AIDS / Scholarships & Loans see Financial Aid
STU026000   STUDY AIDS / Study Guides
STU027000   STUDY AIDS / Tests
STU028000   STUDY AIDS / TOEFL (Test of English as a Foreign Language)
STU029000   STUDY AIDS / Vocational

TECHNOLOGY & ENGINEERING

TEC000000   TECHNOLOGY & ENGINEERING / General
TEC001000   TECHNOLOGY & ENGINEERING / Acoustics & Sound
TEC002000   TECHNOLOGY & ENGINEERING / Aeronautics & Astronautics
TEC003000   TECHNOLOGY & ENGINEERING / Agriculture / General
TEC003080   TECHNOLOGY & ENGINEERING / Agriculture / Agronomy /
General
TEC003030   TECHNOLOGY & ENGINEERING / Agriculture / Agronomy / Crop
Science
TEC003060   TECHNOLOGY & ENGINEERING / Agriculture / Agronomy / Soil
Science
TEC003020   TECHNOLOGY & ENGINEERING / Agriculture / Animal Husbandry
TEC003100   TECHNOLOGY & ENGINEERING / Agriculture / Beekeeping
    TECHNOLOGY & ENGINEERING / Agriculture / Business Aspects see BUSINESS
& ECONOMICS / Industries / Agribusiness
TEC003110   TECHNOLOGY & ENGINEERING / Agriculture / Enology &
Viticulture
TEC003040   TECHNOLOGY & ENGINEERING / Agriculture / Forestry
TEC003050   TECHNOLOGY & ENGINEERING / Agriculture / Irrigation
TEC003090   TECHNOLOGY & ENGINEERING / Agriculture / Organic
    TECHNOLOGY & ENGINEERING / Agriculture / Pest Control see Pest Control
TEC003070   TECHNOLOGY & ENGINEERING / Agriculture / Sustainable
Agriculture
TEC003010   TECHNOLOGY & ENGINEERING / Agriculture / Tropical
Agriculture
    TECHNOLOGY & ENGINEERING / Aquaculture see Fisheries & Aquaculture
    TECHNOLOGY & ENGINEERING / Astronautics see Aeronautics & Astronautics
TEC004000   TECHNOLOGY & ENGINEERING / Automation
TEC009090   TECHNOLOGY & ENGINEERING / Automotive
TEC059000   TECHNOLOGY & ENGINEERING / Biomedical
TEC048000   TECHNOLOGY & ENGINEERING / Cartography
TEC009010   TECHNOLOGY & ENGINEERING / Chemical & Biochemical
TEC009020   TECHNOLOGY & ENGINEERING / Civil / General
TEC009100   TECHNOLOGY & ENGINEERING / Civil / Bridges
TEC009110   TECHNOLOGY & ENGINEERING / Civil / Dams & Reservoirs
TEC009120   TECHNOLOGY & ENGINEERING / Civil / Earthquake
TEC009130   TECHNOLOGY & ENGINEERING / Civil / Flood Control
TEC009140   TECHNOLOGY & ENGINEERING / Civil / Highway & Traffic

TEC009150   TECHNOLOGY & ENGINEERING / Civil / Soil & Rock
TEC009160   TECHNOLOGY & ENGINEERING / Civil / Transport
TEC005000   TECHNOLOGY & ENGINEERING / Construction / General
TEC005010   TECHNOLOGY & ENGINEERING / Construction / Carpentry
TEC005020   TECHNOLOGY & ENGINEERING / Construction / Contracting
TEC005030   TECHNOLOGY & ENGINEERING / Construction / Electrical
TEC005040   TECHNOLOGY & ENGINEERING / Construction / Estimating
TEC005050   TECHNOLOGY & ENGINEERING / Construction / Heating, Ventilation & Air Conditioning
TEC005060   TECHNOLOGY & ENGINEERING / Construction / Masonry
TEC005070   TECHNOLOGY & ENGINEERING / Construction / Plumbing
TEC005080   TECHNOLOGY & ENGINEERING / Construction / Roofing
TEC006000   TECHNOLOGY & ENGINEERING / Drafting & Mechanical Drawing
TEC007000   TECHNOLOGY & ENGINEERING / Electrical
TEC008000   TECHNOLOGY & ENGINEERING / Electronics / General
TEC008010   TECHNOLOGY & ENGINEERING / Electronics / Circuits / General
TEC008020   TECHNOLOGY & ENGINEERING / Electronics / Circuits / Integrated
TEC008030   TECHNOLOGY & ENGINEERING / Electronics / Circuits / Logic
TEC008050   TECHNOLOGY & ENGINEERING / Electronics / Circuits / VLSI & ULSI
TEC008060   TECHNOLOGY & ENGINEERING / Electronics / Digital
TEC008070   TECHNOLOGY & ENGINEERING / Electronics / Microelectronics
TEC008080   TECHNOLOGY & ENGINEERING / Electronics / Optoelectronics
TEC008090   TECHNOLOGY & ENGINEERING / Electronics / Semiconductors
TEC008100   TECHNOLOGY & ENGINEERING / Electronics / Solid State
TEC008110   TECHNOLOGY & ENGINEERING / Electronics / Transistors
TEC065000   TECHNOLOGY & ENGINEERING / Emergency Management
            TECHNOLOGY & ENGINEERING / Energy Resources see headings under Power Resources
TEC009000   TECHNOLOGY & ENGINEERING / Engineering (General)
TEC010000   TECHNOLOGY & ENGINEERING / Environmental / General
TEC010010   TECHNOLOGY & ENGINEERING / Environmental / Pollution Control
TEC010020   TECHNOLOGY & ENGINEERING / Environmental / Waste Management
TEC010030   TECHNOLOGY & ENGINEERING / Environmental / Water Supply
TEC011000   TECHNOLOGY & ENGINEERING / Fiber Optics
TEC045000   TECHNOLOGY & ENGINEERING / Fire Science
TEC049000   TECHNOLOGY & ENGINEERING / Fisheries & Aquaculture
TEC012000   TECHNOLOGY & ENGINEERING / Food Science
TEC013000   TECHNOLOGY & ENGINEERING / Fracture Mechanics
            TECHNOLOGY & ENGINEERING / Geographic Information Systems see Remote Sensing & Geographic Information Systems
TEC056000   TECHNOLOGY & ENGINEERING / History
TEC050000   TECHNOLOGY & ENGINEERING / Holography
TEC014000   TECHNOLOGY & ENGINEERING / Hydraulics
            TECHNOLOGY & ENGINEERING / Hydrology see SCIENCE / Earth Sciences / Hydrology
TEC015000   TECHNOLOGY & ENGINEERING / Imaging Systems
TEC016000   TECHNOLOGY & ENGINEERING / Industrial Design / General
TEC016010   TECHNOLOGY & ENGINEERING / Industrial Design / Packaging
TEC016020   TECHNOLOGY & ENGINEERING / Industrial Design / Product
TEC009060   TECHNOLOGY & ENGINEERING / Industrial Engineering
TEC017000   TECHNOLOGY & ENGINEERING / Industrial Health & Safety
TEC018000   TECHNOLOGY & ENGINEERING / Industrial Technology
TEC057000   TECHNOLOGY & ENGINEERING / Inventions
TEC019000   TECHNOLOGY & ENGINEERING / Lasers & Photonics
TEC046000   TECHNOLOGY & ENGINEERING / Machinery

TEC020000	TECHNOLOGY & ENGINEERING / Manufacturing
TEC060000	TECHNOLOGY & ENGINEERING / Marine & Naval
TEC021000	TECHNOLOGY & ENGINEERING / Materials Science
TEC022000	TECHNOLOGY & ENGINEERING / Measurement
TEC009070	TECHNOLOGY & ENGINEERING / Mechanical
	TECHNOLOGY & ENGINEERING / Mechanical Drawing see Drafting & Mechanical Drawing
TEC023000	TECHNOLOGY & ENGINEERING / Metallurgy
TEC024000	TECHNOLOGY & ENGINEERING / Microwaves
TEC025000	TECHNOLOGY & ENGINEERING / Military Science
TEC026000	TECHNOLOGY & ENGINEERING / Mining
TEC061000	TECHNOLOGY & ENGINEERING / Mobile & Wireless Communications
TEC027000	TECHNOLOGY & ENGINEERING / Nanotechnology & MEMS
TEC029000	TECHNOLOGY & ENGINEERING / Operations Research
TEC030000	TECHNOLOGY & ENGINEERING / Optics
TEC058000	TECHNOLOGY & ENGINEERING / Pest Control
TEC047000	TECHNOLOGY & ENGINEERING / Petroleum
	TECHNOLOGY & ENGINEERING / Polymers see Textiles & Polymers
TEC031000	TECHNOLOGY & ENGINEERING / Power Resources / General
TEC031010	TECHNOLOGY & ENGINEERING / Power Resources / Alternative & Renewable
TEC031020	TECHNOLOGY & ENGINEERING / Power Resources / Electrical
TEC031030	TECHNOLOGY & ENGINEERING / Power Resources / Fossil Fuels
TEC028000	TECHNOLOGY & ENGINEERING / Power Resources / Nuclear
TEC062000	TECHNOLOGY & ENGINEERING / Project Management
TEC032000	TECHNOLOGY & ENGINEERING / Quality Control
TEC033000	TECHNOLOGY & ENGINEERING / Radar
TEC034000	TECHNOLOGY & ENGINEERING / Radio
TEC035000	TECHNOLOGY & ENGINEERING / Reference
TEC036000	TECHNOLOGY & ENGINEERING / Remote Sensing & Geographic Information Systems
TEC066000	TECHNOLOGY & ENGINEERING / Research
TEC037000	TECHNOLOGY & ENGINEERING / Robotics
TEC064000	TECHNOLOGY & ENGINEERING / Sensors
TEC067000	TECHNOLOGY & ENGINEERING / Signals & Signal Processing
TEC052000	TECHNOLOGY & ENGINEERING / Social Aspects
	TECHNOLOGY & ENGINEERING / Sound see Acoustics & Sound
	TECHNOLOGY & ENGINEERING / Spectroscopy see SCIENCE / Spectroscopy & Spectrum Analysis
TEC063000	TECHNOLOGY & ENGINEERING / Structural
TEC039000	TECHNOLOGY & ENGINEERING / Superconductors & Superconductivity
TEC054000	TECHNOLOGY & ENGINEERING / Surveying
TEC040000	TECHNOLOGY & ENGINEERING / Technical & Manufacturing Industries & Trades
TEC044000	TECHNOLOGY & ENGINEERING / Technical Writing
TEC041000	TECHNOLOGY & ENGINEERING / Telecommunications
TEC043000	TECHNOLOGY & ENGINEERING / Television & Video
TEC055000	TECHNOLOGY & ENGINEERING / Textiles & Polymers
TEC068000	TECHNOLOGY & ENGINEERING / Tribology

TRANSPORTATION

TRA000000	TRANSPORTATION / General
TRA001000	TRANSPORTATION / Automotive / General
TRA001010	TRANSPORTATION / Automotive / Antique & Classic
TRA001020	TRANSPORTATION / Automotive / Buyer's Guides
TRA001030	TRANSPORTATION / Automotive / Customizing
TRA001080	TRANSPORTATION / Automotive / Driver Education

TRANSPORTATION / Automotive / High Performance & Engine Rebuilding see Automotive / Customizing
TRA001050   TRANSPORTATION / Automotive / History
TRA001060   TRANSPORTATION / Automotive / Pictorial
TRA001140   TRANSPORTATION / Automotive / Repair & Maintenance
TRA001150   TRANSPORTATION / Automotive / Trucks
TRA002000   TRANSPORTATION / Aviation / General
TRA002040   TRANSPORTATION / Aviation / Commercial
TRA002010   TRANSPORTATION / Aviation / History
TRA002050   TRANSPORTATION / Aviation / Piloting & Flight Instruction
TRA002030   TRANSPORTATION / Aviation / Repair & Maintenance
TRA010000   TRANSPORTATION / Bicycles
TRANSPORTATION / Commercial see BUSINESS & ECONOMICS / Industries / Transportation
TRA003000   TRANSPORTATION / Motorcycles / General
TRA003010   TRANSPORTATION / Motorcycles / History
TRA003020   TRANSPORTATION / Motorcycles / Pictorial
TRA003030   TRANSPORTATION / Motorcycles / Repair & Maintenance
TRA008000   TRANSPORTATION / Navigation
TRA009000   TRANSPORTATION / Public Transportation
TRA004000   TRANSPORTATION / Railroads / General
TRA004010   TRANSPORTATION / Railroads / History
TRA004020   TRANSPORTATION / Railroads / Pictorial
TRA006000   TRANSPORTATION / Ships & Shipbuilding / General
TRA006010   TRANSPORTATION / Ships & Shipbuilding / History
TRA006020   TRANSPORTATION / Ships & Shipbuilding / Pictorial
TRA006030   TRANSPORTATION / Ships & Shipbuilding / Repair & Maintenance

TRAVEL
TRV000000   TRAVEL / General
TRAVEL / Adventure see Special Interest / Adventure
TRV002000   TRAVEL / Africa / General
TRV002010   TRAVEL / Africa / Central
TRV002020   TRAVEL / Africa / East
TRV002030   TRAVEL / Africa / Kenya
TRV002040   TRAVEL / Africa / Morocco
TRV002050   TRAVEL / Africa / North
TRV002060   TRAVEL / Africa / Republic of South Africa
TRV002070   TRAVEL / Africa / South
TRV002080   TRAVEL / Africa / West
TRAVEL / Antarctica see Polar Regions
TRV003000   TRAVEL / Asia / General
TRV003010   TRAVEL / Asia / Central
TRV003020   TRAVEL / Asia / China
TRV003030   TRAVEL / Asia / Far East
TRV003040   TRAVEL / Asia / India & South Asia
TRV003050   TRAVEL / Asia / Japan
TRV003060   TRAVEL / Asia / Southeast
TRV003070   TRAVEL / Asia / Southwest
TRV004000   TRAVEL / Australia & Oceania
TRAVEL / Campgrounds see Parks & Campgrounds
TRV006000   TRAVEL / Canada / General
TRV006010   TRAVEL / Canada / Atlantic Provinces (NB, NL, NS, PE)
TRV006020   TRAVEL / Canada / Ontario (ON)
TRV006030   TRAVEL / Canada / Prairie Provinces (MB, SK)
TRV006060   TRAVEL / Canada / Quebec (QC)
TRV006040   TRAVEL / Canada / Territories & Nunavut (NT, NU, YT)
TRV006050   TRAVEL / Canada / Western Provinces (AB, BC)
TRV007000   TRAVEL / Caribbean & West Indies

TRV008000	TRAVEL / Central America
TRV010000	TRAVEL / Essays & Travelogues
TRV009000	TRAVEL / Europe / General
TRV009010	TRAVEL / Europe / Austria
TRV009020	TRAVEL / Europe / Benelux Countries (Belgium, Netherlands, Luxembourg)
TRV009160	TRAVEL / Europe / Cyprus
TRV009030	TRAVEL / Europe / Denmark
TRV009040	TRAVEL / Europe / Eastern
TRV009050	TRAVEL / Europe / France
TRV009060	TRAVEL / Europe / Germany
TRV009070	TRAVEL / Europe / Great Britain
TRV009080	TRAVEL / Europe / Greece
TRV009090	TRAVEL / Europe / Iceland & Greenland
TRV009100	TRAVEL / Europe / Ireland
TRV009110	TRAVEL / Europe / Italy
TRV009120	TRAVEL / Europe / Scandinavia (Finland, Norway, Sweden)
TRV009130	TRAVEL / Europe / Spain & Portugal
TRV009140	TRAVEL / Europe / Switzerland
TRV009150	TRAVEL / Europe / Western
	TRAVEL / Family Travel see Special Interest / Family
TRV036000	TRAVEL / Food, Lodging & Transportation / General *
TRV005000	TRAVEL / Food, Lodging & Transportation / Bed & Breakfast
TRV028000	TRAVEL / Food, Lodging & Transportation / Cruises
TRV013000	TRAVEL / Food, Lodging & Transportation / Hotels, Inns & Hostels
TRV035000	TRAVEL / Food, Lodging & Transportation / Rail Travel
TRV030000	TRAVEL / Food, Lodging & Transportation / Resorts & Spas
TRV022000	TRAVEL / Food, Lodging & Transportation / Restaurants
TRV031000	TRAVEL / Food, Lodging & Transportation / Road Travel
TRV012000	TRAVEL / Former Soviet Republics
TRV027000	TRAVEL / Maps & Road Atlases (see also REFERENCE / Atlases, Gazetteers & Maps)
TRV014000	TRAVEL / Mexico
TRV015000	TRAVEL / Middle East / General
TRV015010	TRAVEL / Middle East / Egypt
TRV015020	TRAVEL / Middle East / Israel
TRV015030	TRAVEL / Middle East / Turkey
TRV016000	TRAVEL / Museums, Tours, Points of Interest
	TRAVEL / National Parks see Parks & Campgrounds
	TRAVEL / Oceania see Australia & Oceania
TRV018000	TRAVEL / Parks & Campgrounds
TRV019000	TRAVEL / Pictorials (see also PHOTOGRAPHY / Subjects & Themes / Regional)
TRV020000	TRAVEL / Polar Regions
TRV021000	TRAVEL / Reference
TRV023000	TRAVEL / Russia
TRV024000	TRAVEL / South America / General
TRV024010	TRAVEL / South America / Argentina
TRV024020	TRAVEL / South America / Brazil
TRV024030	TRAVEL / South America / Chile & Easter Island
TRV024040	TRAVEL / South America / Ecuador & Galapagos Islands
TRV024050	TRAVEL / South America / Peru
TRV026000	TRAVEL / Special Interest / General
TRV001000	TRAVEL / Special Interest / Adventure
TRV029000	TRAVEL / Special Interest / Amusement & Theme Parks
TRV026100	TRAVEL / Special Interest / Bicycling *
TRV033000	TRAVEL / Special Interest / Budget
TRV026010	TRAVEL / Special Interest / Business
TRV026030	TRAVEL / Special Interest / Disabilities & Special Needs

TRV026020	TRAVEL / Special Interest / Ecotourism
TRV011000	TRAVEL / Special Interest / Family
TRV034000	TRAVEL / Special Interest / Hikes & Walks
TRV026070	TRAVEL / Special Interest / LGBT
TRV026090	TRAVEL / Special Interest / Literary
TRV026110	TRAVEL / Special Interest / Military *
TRV026040	TRAVEL / Special Interest / Pets
TRV026060	TRAVEL / Special Interest / Religious
TRV026050	TRAVEL / Special Interest / Senior
TRV032000	TRAVEL / Special Interest / Shopping
TRV026080	TRAVEL / Special Interest / Sports
TRV025000	TRAVEL / United States / General
TRV025010	TRAVEL / United States / Midwest / General
TRV025020	TRAVEL / United States / Midwest / East North Central (IL, IN, MI, OH, WI)
TRV025030	TRAVEL / United States / Midwest / West North Central (IA, KS, MN, MO, ND, NE, SD)
TRV025040	TRAVEL / United States / Northeast / General
TRV025050	TRAVEL / United States / Northeast / Middle Atlantic (NJ, NY, PA)
TRV025060	TRAVEL / United States / Northeast / New England (CT, MA, ME, NH, RI, VT)
TRV025070	TRAVEL / United States / South / General
TRV025080	TRAVEL / United States / South / East South Central (AL, KY, MS, TN)
TRV025090	TRAVEL / United States / South / South Atlantic (DC, DE, FL, GA, MD, NC, SC, VA, WV)
TRV025100	TRAVEL / United States / South / West South Central (AR, LA, OK, TX)
TRV025110	TRAVEL / United States / West / General
TRV025120	TRAVEL / United States / West / Mountain (AZ, CO, ID, MT, NM, NV, UT, WY)
TRV025130	TRAVEL / United States / West / Pacific (AK, CA, HI, OR, WA)
	TRAVEL / West Indies see Caribbean & West Indies

TRUE CRIME

TRU000000	TRUE CRIME / General
TRU001000	TRUE CRIME / Espionage
TRU004000	TRUE CRIME / Hoaxes & Deceptions
TRU002000	TRUE CRIME / Murder / General
TRU002010	TRUE CRIME / Murder / Serial Killers
TRU003000	TRUE CRIME / Organized Crime
TRU005000	TRUE CRIME / White Collar Crime

www.ingramcontent.com/pod-product-compliance
Lightning Source LLC
Chambersburg PA
CBHW051910170526
45168CB00001B/316

* 9 7 8 1 5 1 5 1 6 1 3 2 5 *